The Queen of Spades

and Other Stories

The Queen of Spades

and Other Stories

Alexander Pushkin

Translated by Paul Debreczeny

Verse Passages Translated
by Roger Clarke

Series Editor: Roger Clarke

ONEWORLD
CLASSICS

ONEWORLD CLASSICS LTD
London House
243-253 Lower Mortlake Road
Richmond
Surrey TW9 2LL
United Kingdom
www.oneworldclassics.com

This edition first published by Oneworld Classics Ltd in 2011

Printed in Great Britain by CPI Antony Rowe

ISBN: 978-1-84749 -181-7

Contents

Publisher's Foreword

This is one of a series of volumes, to be published by Oneworld Classics during the coming years, that will present the complete works of Alexander Pushkin in English. The series will be a successor to the fifteen-volume Complete Works of Alexander Pushkin published by Milner and Company between 1999 and 2003, the rights to which have been acquired by Oneworld Classics. Some of the translations contained in the new volumes will, as here, be reprints of those in the Milner edition (corrected as necessary); others will be reworkings of the earlier translations; others again will be entirely new. The aim of the series is to build on the Milner edition's work in giving readers in the English-speaking world access to the entire corpus of Pushkin's writings in readable modern versions that are faithful to Pushkin's meaning and spirit.

In publishing this series, Oneworld Classics wishes to pay a warm tribute to the initiative and drive of Iain Sproat, managing director and owner of Milner and Company and chairman of the original project's editorial board, in achieving the publication of Pushkin's complete works in English for the first time. Scholars, lovers of Pushkin and general readers wishing to gain knowledge of one of Europe's finest writers owe him the heartiest gratitude.

– Alessandro Gallenzi

OTHER WORKS OF ALEXANDER PUSHKIN ALREADY
AVAILABLE FROM ONEWORLD CLASSICS:

Ruslan and Lyudmila, a dual-language text
trans. Roger Clarke, 2009

Boris Godunov and *Little Tragedies*
trans. Roger Clarke, 2010

Eugene Onegin, a dual-language text
trans. Roger Clarke, 2011

Alexander Pushkin (1799–1837)

Abram Petrovich Gannibal,
Pushkin's great-grandfather

Sergei Lvovich Pushkin,
Pushkin's father

Nadezhda Osipovna Pushkina,
Pushkin's mother

Natalya Nikolayevna Pushkina,
Pushkin's wife

The Imperial Lyceum in Tsarskoye Selo,
which Pushkin entered in 1811

Pushkin's manuscript of the penultimate
stanza of his ode 'Liberty'

The Countess in G.D. Yepifanov's 1950s illustrations
to 'The Queen of Spades'

Hermann in G.D. Yepifanov's 1950s illustrations
to 'The Queen of Spades'

An inkstand from Pushkin's study

Note by Series Editor

This volume, which corresponds to Volume Nine of the Milner Edition of Pushkin's Works in English, contains all of Pushkin's prose fiction, finished and unfinished, with the exception of: *The Captain's Daughter* and *The Tales of Belkin* – which, as Pushkin's two most substantial completed works in the form, will be published separately – and those manuscript notes and brief fragments less than a page long that are of minimal literary interest. I have also excluded the story 'A Lonely Cottage on Vasilyev Island' as an inauthentic piece of Pushkin's writing.

The two works in this volume completed and published during Pushkin's lifetime – 'The Queen of Spades' and 'Kirdzhali' – come first; there follow in Part Two the unfinished works found among Pushkin's papers after his death, arranged in order (so far as can be ascertained) of composition, so as to give an impression of how Pushkin's projected use of this form developed over time. The unfinished works contain both those that are clearly interrupted or fragmentary and some more substantial and polished compositions – such as 'Roslavlev', 'Dubrovsky' and 'Egyptian Nights' – where arguably Pushkin had come to realize that he had achieved his main objectives and need say no more.

The late Paul Debreczeny's edition of these works was first published by Stanford University Press in 1983. For this edition I have made only sparing revisions and corrections to Professor Debreczeny's excellent translations; his notes I have revised and supplemented more extensively. His introduction is included in a slightly shortened form.

Professor Debreczeny incorporated translations of verse passages (notably in 'A Tale from Roman Life', 'We Were Spending the Evening at Princess D.'s Dacha...' and 'Egyptian Nights') by Walter Arndt. To my mind the somewhat antique and florid diction of these verse translations is alien to Pushkin, and the quest for English rhymes has dragged the sense too far from that of Pushkin's words, so I have substituted my own versions, which replicate Pushkin's metres but not, in the interests of clarity and accuracy, his rhyme schemes.

Dates of events in Russian and Eastern Europe are given in the Old Style.

I should like to record my own and Oneworld Classics' gratitude to Stanford University Press for their permission to reprint Professor Debreczeny's material; and to Professor Michel Basker of Bristol University for his contribution of the translation of 'The Last of the Lineage of Joan of Arc', which was not included in the Stanford University Press volume.

Asterisks in the text of the translation indicate endnotes on pp. 307*ff*.

– Roger Clarke, 2011

Foreword

"WITH PROSE – I HAVE TROUBLE," Pushkin remarked to a friend at the end of the 1820s, a time when he had no trouble with poetry at all. But it would be a mistake to think of Pushkin's creative journey as divided, both formally and chronologically, into his works in poetry and the separate and contrasting work in prose. At all periods of his creative life he was, as it were, trying his hand at all sorts of both kinds, and filling copybooks with sketches imaginary and autobiographical – many of which, written during his exile in southern Russia, he destroyed after the failure of the Decembrist uprising in 1825. He continued nonetheless to produce ideas for novels and stories, and to scribble them down.

But, as he confessed, prose caused him trouble. It required thought and theory and technique in a way that poetry did not. Poetry flowed from him; it was the natural speech of his genius, a fact he ironically acknowledges in 'Egyptian Nights' in his sketch of an Italian improviser who can become instantly inspired by any topic, provided he can treat it in verse. The contrast shows significantly in the difference between Pushkin's unfinished poems and his many unfinished or abortive fragments in prose. He seems to have broken off a poem – for example the wonderful uncompleted poetic drama *Rusalka*, or even, it could be said, his greatest masterpiece *Eugene Onegin* – because he knew that it had already done what was in its nature and genius to do as a work of art. Eugene's story was over: there was no point in conducting him on his aimless chance wanderings in the style of Byron's Don Juan.

The Prince in *Rusalka* has similarly made his choice, and paid for it. He has abandoned the miller's daughter who loved him and who drowns herself, and he finds too late that he cannot be contented with a cold and loveless marriage. He can only long hopelessly for the passion and fire that he has lost. There is no further need, as Pushkin once observed of his poetry, "to spell it out".

Pushkin might well have continued to add a few more lines to *Rusalka*, but the work of art was already there and totally visible, even though unfinished. The implicit and sophisticated irony wonderfully contradicts the folk melodrama of the theme. There is no need for the miller's daughter, transformed into a "cold Rusalka" to take revenge on her lover by dragging him down into the stream. The deeper retribution, which was certainly in Pushkin's first idea for the drama, is implicit in the news brought to his unfortunate and unloved Princess by whom he has no child. The huntsmen report that they have seen the Prince "alone in the forest on the Dnieper's bank" – a line of pure Pushkinian magic in the force of its internal meaning. There was no need for Pushkin's poetry to continue to spell it out.

Prose, however, was another matter. I have introduced the case of *Rusalka* because it shows very clearly how Pushkin's poetry could achieve the implied and unspoken effects which he may have been attempting, in his other persona and in quite a different way, to achieve in prose. But prose was a much more recalcitrant medium. In several of the fragments of story or novel which were begun, Pushkin seems to be attempting something analogous to the suggestiveness of his stories in verse, transposing them into the sophisticated metropolitan centre of the capital. This was the sort of theme, of fate and the will, desire and retribution, which Stendhal was to analyse in his masterpiece *Le Rouge et le noir*. But Stendhal was an unabashed analyst and demonstrator; and that does not seem to have been Pushkin's forte, or the manner he wanted to adopt in his tales of high society and urban life. The whole subject is necessarily a speculative one although highly fascinating; and the interested reader cannot do better than to investigate it in detail in Professor Paul Debreczeny's admirable study *The Other Pushkin*. In this introduction I must restrict myself to the prose pieces which Pushkin left mostly in an uncompleted state, an exception being one of his masterpieces as well as his best known tale: 'The Queen of Spades'.

Pushkin's first-published and most formalized prose stories were *The Tales of Belkin*, written in 1830 in one of those magical autumns at his Boldino estate which also produced the *Little Tragedies*, miniature plays in verse. *The Tales of Belkin* are not only formalized but deliberately impersonal, told through the medium of several different and contrasting voices. But when he wrote 'The Queen of Spades' three years later, Pushkin must have decided that an impersonal and omniscient technique of narration would best suit the melodrama of the story he proposed to tell.

At the same time the narrative takes for granted the reader's knowledge of the world about which it is written, the St Petersburg world of high society, balls and gambling. Because the narrative assumes that we know about faro or *shtos* (the gambling game which Hermann watches and in which he eventually participates), its assurance carries us along. The game as played here is indeed very simple, although in point of fact it could be much more complex, with many possible gambling permutations open to the punter. For our benefit, the procedure is simply the punter (Hermann) and the banker (Chekalinsky) each having a fresh pack of cards: Hermann puts his card – the three on the first night – face down on the table with his stake; the banker deals from his pack, facing a card alternatively left and right; if a card of the same points as the punter has selected comes up on his right the banker wins, and if on his left he loses. Hermann therefore wins on his first deal two nights running. Fate strikes on the third.

The social critics like Belinsky who were to be so influential in Russian literature a few years after Pushkin's death admired his work in general, but they disapproved of the frivolous society atmosphere in the stories like 'The Queen of Spades'. In fact, like many of Pushkin's tales, it has a complicated background, its main character Hermann inheriting characteristics from 'A Novel in Letters', the tale which Pushkin began and adapted a year or so earlier. This promising beginning, with its echoes of Richardson's sentiment in the enormously popular novel, *Clarissa Harlowe*, and of Benjamin Constant's penetrating psychology in *Adolphe*, would have satisfied the later critics by its degree of social seriousness. But Pushkin was no more able than Byron to be overtly serious for long, as he had demonstrated in such sparkling fashion in *Eugene Onegin*. His first stories, *The Tales of Belkin*, had been based on subtle but good-natured parody; and in 'The Queen of Spades' he barely suggests the idea of exploring modern romantic love before beginning to parody it.

He parodies not only *Clarissa* but his own earlier and abortive 'A Novel in Letters'. In 'The Queen of Spades' Hermann's object is not the passionate seduction of the heroine Lizaveta, but the secret for winning at cards that is rumoured to belong to the aged Countess. Hermann even thinks of making love to the old lady in order to obtain it. It is this object which is his only passion; but he is sincere in pursuing it, and Lizaveta is duly thrilled by the intensity of his feelings, expressed as they are in the tenderly respectful tones he has copied from books. When he sees her "fresh young face and dark eyes" at the window of the Countess's house, the moment "decided his fate". What Pushkin has done, in fact, as he did with the story of 'The Stationmaster's Daughter' in *The Tales of Belkin*, is to transpose the language of sentiment into an incongruous setting: a story of inexorable ambition and melodramatic intrigue.

Intrigue is based on the gossip and anecdote of contemporary society. Bartenev, an indefatigable collector of Pushkiniana and of the gossip current in the poet's time, records a note of Pushkin to a friend in which he says that the model for the old Countess was Natalya Petrovna Golitsyna, whose grandson had told him an anecdote of her life in Paris very similar to the one used in the tale. No text of 'The Queen of Spades' exists in Pushkin's autograph, but there are two manuscript fragments which clearly represent his first jottings: one describing the climactic game of cards, the other a more humorous variant of the love theme. Hermann lives in the house of a worthy German, and he and the daughter of the house "love each other as only Germans in our time can". From all these more or less flippant and incongruous beginnings Hermann emerges in 'The Queen of Spades' as a highly convincing and arresting psychological type: ruthless, ambitious, a Man of the Will in Napoleonic mode; his lack of their kind of humour amuses the well-born young Russians; yet they respect him too.

And so the tale grew up from other abandoned story projects, and their characters were given a colouring of modish *diablerie*, and grafted on to an anecdote from real life. At the same time, and contrary to what Belinsky said, there is its own kind of seriousness and weight in the story, the kind of seriousness Pushkin could obtain with the economy of his lightning psychological insight, as if almost offhand.

It is this kind of weight which we associate with the novel rather than with the story form; and this must be because Pushkin's ideas for novels – all, as one would expect, intriguing and psychologically challenging – lurk in the background of his completed tales and his prose works. Pushkin was perhaps hovering on the verge of a new form, which he might have called *Little Novels*, in succession to the *Little Tragedies*. Like the plays, the novels might have depended on psychological contrast and confrontation: for example, the Countess and Hermann might be said to parallel such contrasting pairs in the *Little Tragedies* as Mozart and Salieri, Don Juan and Don Carlos, Iñez and Doña Ana, the Covetous Knight and his son. This could well have proved a fertile new field for Pushkin's genius, but – "with prose – I have trouble". Pushkin could never have turned to prose with that effortless ease with which, like a swimmer or skater, he had glided onto the field of verse. Again we might recall his own ironical self-awareness in creating an Italian improviser to celebrate in glittering verse the theme of Cleopatra and her 'Egyptian Nights'. This could scarcely have been done in his sober prose.

While the *Little Tragedies* take place in a historical setting, the unwritten "little novels" would have depended on the contemporary social scene, and on Pushkin's own perceptions of it. In the one that begins "In the corner of a small square" we have the theme, presented in Benjamin Constant's *Adolphe*, of a mature woman about to be abandoned by her younger lover; and in the related piece, 'The Guests Were Arriving at the Dacha', we seem to be given the concept and portrait sketch of a woman, both exalted and unsophisticated, whose native passions are too strong to fit the close-knit and worldly society in which she has to live. Tolstoy, who even claimed that Pushkin's opening sentence – "The guests were arriving…" – had given him the impulse to begin writing *Anna Karenina*, remarked that Pushkin's stories were the best example he knew of the economy and simplicity with which a tale should ideally be composed.

As Tolstoy took a hint from Pushkin's story, so Dostoevsky, a great admirer of 'The Queen of Spades', and himself at one stage of his life an obsessive gambler, made use in his novel *Crime and Punishment* of the confrontation between Hermann and the old Countess. What in Pushkin is a bizarre, even uncanny, but thoroughly "society" situation – the modern young man of Napoleonic will, and the aged grande dame who exercised in her distant prime quite a different sort of power – becomes in *Crime and Punishment* a metaphysical problem. Should the worthless old moneylender stand between a talented young man and the fruits of his destiny? Hermann, unlike Raskolnikov, does not ask the question, because Pushkin's swiftness and simplicity implies the whole situation without proposing it in abstract or metaphysical form.

Pushkin's sense of "society", and the needs it imposes on the individual who lives in it and by it, is extraordinarily acute. Zinaida Volskaya, the heroine whom Pushkin sketched under various names in two or three of his openings, could well have become a prototype of Tolstoy's *Anna Karenina*. Pushkin sees her as trapped in society, and seeking to abandon its values and conventions even while she unconsciously needs them and lives by them. Separated from her husband and living alone in the outlying suburb of Kolomna, "in the corner of a small square", she has tried to give up the *monde* and feed on her lover Valerian, as Tolstoy's Anna was to be compelled to feed on Vronsky. For his part he misses the *monde*, and is irritated to discover that because of her he no longer holds the same accepted place in it: the dull balls he would once not have bothered to attend he is now not even asked to.

A pen sketch by Pushkin on the manuscript of 'In a Corner of a Small Square' presents a striking image of Volskaya – a face at the same time passionate and pathetic, a face that could light up "with the terrible glow of a conflagration on a dark night", as Tolstoy describes Anna Karenina's when she falls in love. Fate and the impulse to self-destruction were themes that fascinated Pushkin, as is revealed both by 'The Queen of Spades' and the fragment of the story 'Maria Schoning'. Tolstoy admired these suggestive character sketches of Pushkin's in novels barely begun. They were indeed rich mines for later writers to quarry, Tolstoy himself being the chief beneficiary.

Although the challenge of writing a novel about a subtly observed contemporary situation must have appealed to him, it seems possible that Pushkin, with his habitual clear-eyed modesty, felt he was not yet ready to take it on. Indeed he might never have written such a novel. We know he was generous with his ideas to younger writers, suggesting to Gogol the plot of *Dead Souls*. He himself continued to experiment, both in form and content. The success of 'The Queen of Spades', and its mingling of realism and melodrama, perhaps suggested to him the idea of making from the heroine of his society novel a parallel between ancient Alexandria and modern St Petersburg. In the fragment 'We Were Spending the Evening at Princess D.'s Dacha', the conversation turns on the topic of legendary women, and a gentleman quotes from a classical writer on Cleopatra: "Cleopatra offered her beauty for sale, and many bought a night with her at the price of their lives."

"How awful!" exclaim the ladies of the company, but later on the gentleman asks Volskaya, a heroine with the same name but a different persona, what she thinks about it, and she replies that there are women in modern St Petersburg who might exact the same sort of bargain. In response to his incredulity she gazes at him with her fiery eyes full of meaning, a *femme fatale* more in the style of Theda Bara than Anna Karenina.

Although the atmosphere of the contemporary *monde* is vividly conveyed in the opening of 'We Were Spending the Evening at Princess D.'s Dacha', any denouement of the story it suggests must surely have been more melodramatic than psychological. Perhaps Pushkin himself felt this, for he recast the Cleopatra motif into the hybrid form of 'Egyptian Nights', which adopts the same motif as that sketched in one of the brief fragments of 'A Tale of Roman Life', another of Pushkin's forays into the world of classical anecdote. The main interest of 'Egyptian Nights' is in fact concentrated on the ironic presentation of two types of poet: the young aristocrat Charsky, a sardonic self-portrait based on an earlier sketch; and the down-at-heel *improvvisatore*, attempting to make money by giving performances in fashionable society. After Pushkin's death, 'Egyptian Nights' appeared in his periodical *Sovremennik*, but it is unlikely he would have published it himself in its present form. Nonetheless, like the verse play *Rusalka*, 'Egyptian Nights', with its combination of verse and prose, has the air of a piece that breaks off at the right moment. Unlike the novel fragments it does not seem to have been put aside undeveloped, as well as unfinished.

All Pushkin's fiction with a historical subject and setting reflects the influence of Sir Walter Scott, an influence almost inescapable at the time when Pushkin was writing. Both European and Russian fiction abounded in examples that were almost straight copies of Scott in terms of plot and emotion. Pushkin was far too original a writer to follow the mode literally, but his prose fiction, like some of his early poetry, reveals nonetheless the difficulty of evading the emotional and romantic clichés popularized by Scott. In two of the novels that Pushkin put aside in a fragmentary or unfinished state – 'Roslavlev' and 'Dubrovsky' – Scott trouble, as one might call it for convenience, is especially marked. Only in *The Captain's Daughter* does the firmness and vitality with which the native historical characters are brought to life successfully bridge the awkward gap between history and conventional romance.

Pushkin no doubt discontinued 'Roslavlev' because of the difficulty of reconciling the heterogeneous elements in the story, a mixture fundamentally unsuited to the sobriety and simplicity of his style. 'Roslavlev' is partly a satire on a novel with the same name by M.N. Zagoskin. But it is also in part serious historical research, in which Pushkin became more and more absorbed during the 1830s following Tsar Nicholas I's agreement to take him back into government service with permission to use official government archives.

But both serious history and the dry humour of satire are confused by the incongruous eruption of a third element: that of sentiment and romance, which reminds us of Miss K.I.T.'s contribution to *The Tales of Belkin*.

There are some excellent scenes of a historical and social nature in 'Dubrovsky', notably the burning of the manor house with the bailiffs inside by Arkhip the blacksmith. He deliberately locks the doors so that the unfortunate officials cannot escape, but he insists on rescuing a cat which is mewing desperately on top of a burning roof beam. Pushkin's growing interest in Russian history and in the types in Russian society which that history has produced was to result in such varied masterpieces in different forms as *The Captain's Daughter*, *The Bronze Horseman*, and the histories of Peter the Great and the Pugachov rebellion. But in the abortive Scott-type romances, with their motifs from Scott's *The Bride of Lammermoor* and *St Ronan's Well*, he was more or less compelled to envisage a denouement in sentimental terms, either happy or tragic. 'Roslavlev' and 'Dubrovsky' do not succeed in being much more than stock romantic types out of previous romances, although all such heroes in Pushkin – most notably Grinyov in *The Captain's Daughter* – have nonetheless something fresh, candid and unexpected in their presentation, revealing them as forerunners of Tolstoy's Nikolai Rostov in *War and Peace*.

More significant is Pushkin's not entirely hidden amusement at, and sympathy for, his heroines. Tatyana in *Eugene Onegin* is both touching and psychologically convincing when she refuses Onegin in the last scene even though she still loves him. But, as Belinsky observed, Maria in 'Dubrovsky' is a typical girl of the age who has read too many romantic novels: she is thrilled by the notion of being abducted at the altar of marriage with Prince Vereysky by the robber bridegroom. But, when it seems expedient, she is just as prepared to step into another role in the contemporary romantic novel: that of the wife whom fate has married to the man she does not love, but to whom she will now remain faithful to death.

As this clearly shows us, a hidden, or not so hidden, element of parody underlines many, if not most of, Pushkin's prose writings and fragments, including even 'The Negro of Peter the Great' and 'Maria Schoning' – the exceptions being his histories. He was a serious historian, fascinated by the growth of modern power in

Russia and its progenitor, Peter the Great. His almost obsessive interest in Peter is most dramatically revealed in that magnificent poem *The Bronze Horseman*. But like the two poets in 'Egyptian Nights', who can both be seen as amusing self-portraits of their creator, he was also capable of being inspired, however momentarily, by any subject that occurred to him or was suggested. Like Charsky, he could also shut himself away when the fit of writing overcame his gentlemanly indifference to the class and profession of writer, and scribble or compose for twenty hours a day.

– John Bayley, 2001

Introduction

ALEXANDER SERGEYEVICH PUSHKIN, widely acknowledged the progenitor of modern Russian literature, was born in 1799 and died of a wound received in a duel in 1837. His greatest achievement was in poetry – lyrical, epic, dramatic – and he did not turn to prose in a serious way until the end of the 1820s, but the fiction he wrote in the last decade of his life was to have a tremendous impact on the subsequent development of Russian prose.

The art of prose-writing in Russia could not boast of great accomplishments at the time Pushkin entered on the scene. Its healthiest tradition – an earthy realism in the adventure story of the seventeenth century – had left only faint traces on later picaresque novels, such as V.T. Narezhny's *Russian Gil Blas* (1814). The age of neoclassicism produced some works of fiction – most notably *Ernest's Letters to Doravra* (1766) by F.A. Yemin and *The Fair Cook* (1770) by M.D. Chulkov – but on the whole treated fiction as an inferior genre. The prose narrative as a serious kind of literature did not come into its own until the advent of sentimentalism in the late eighteenth century. The most widely renowned cultivator of the new sensibility, N.M. Karamzin, was to be acknowledged by Pushkin in 1822 as the best Russian prose-writer up to that time. Indeed, some of Karamzin's stories – especially 'Poor Liza' and 'Natalya the Boyar's Daughter' (both dated 1792) – were to evoke echoes in Pushkin's own prose works.

The 1820s saw sentimentalism grow into romanticism. This trend was most clearly manifested in the stories of A.A. Bestuzhev-Marlinsky, among which 'An Evening on Bivouac' (1823) and 'An Evening at a Caucasian Watering Place in 1824' (1830) were to provoke the strongest reaction from Pushkin. E.T.A. Hoffmann's influence was reflected, above all, in the tales of Antony Pogorelsky (A.A. Perovsky), collected in the volume *The Double*

(1828). Walter Scott found his most ardent Russian follower in M.N. Zagoskin, whose *Yury Miloslavsky* (1829) and *Roslavlev* (1831) bore the distinction of being the first Russian historical novels. The picaresque tradition, on the other hand, spawned such satirical-didactic novels of manners as the most popular work of the late 1820s, *Ivan Vyzhigin* (1829) by F.V. Bulgarin.

With the appearance of new writers and trends and with the growth of readership in the 1820s and early 1830s, prose fiction became increasingly popular. The royalties Bulgarin received from *Vyzhigin* were impressive. But the quality of this fiction, in a style that ranged from the romantics' florid rhetoric to Bulgarin's trivial verbosity parading as wit, was generally low. At least some of Pushkin's work in prose was a response to the banal trends of the time.

The few fictional fragments and outlines Pushkin jotted down before 1827 represented only occasional spurts of inspiration. There is some evidence, however, that between 1821 and 1825 he filled several copybooks with nonfictional sketches of his life and times. Since these sketches contained politically incriminating details about him and his friends, he destroyed most of them after the December 1825 uprising. But the few that survived, salvaged either by friends or by Pushkin himself, are important to the historian because they demonstrate that Pushkin's fiction – as it eventually emerged in the last decade of his life – had developed primarily from nonfictional prose.

This circumstance had a bearing on Pushkin's understanding of prose in the 1820s. At that time prose appeared to him as an antithesis to poetry, a mode of writing shorn of embellishments and deprived of histrionic gestures. Whereas poetry was all ornament and pleasant form, he wrote, prose represented pure content, tolerating no decorative frills and demanding "thoughts and thoughts, without which magniloquent phrases serve no purpose" (from the sketch 'On Russian Prose'). Prose was "humble", compared with contentious, turbulent poetry, but there was also something flat-footed about it, something unimaginative, to which one "stooped", like Belkin of 'A History of the Village of Goryukhino', when poetic inspiration was lacking.

Most of Pushkin's statements characterizing prose in this way were made in the 1820s, either before he had seriously tried his hand at fiction-writing or when he was just beginning to. In these statements no clear line was drawn between the prose of fiction and expository prose. At the end of the decade, however, as he became a practitioner of the trade, he came to differentiate between fiction and other kinds of prose, and increasingly appreciated prose's potential for varied application. His realization of this rich potential was a gradual and painful one, achieved through several failures and false starts. And though he modified his original concept of prose over the years, the idea of a mode of writing that eschewed all poetic gestures remained attractive to him. His development as a fiction writer was largely the result of the tension between his original concept of prose and its later modifications.

Pushkin's first serious attempt at writing fiction – 'The Negro of Peter the Great' – reflects the view of prose he held in the 1820s. It is narrated in a detached, omniscient manner, most unusual for the period. Jane Austen had developed a similar authorial stance in the preceding decades, but Pushkin was probably not familiar with her works. Balzac and Stendhal had not yet published the novels that were to make their fame. In the fiction popular at the time – most notably in the works of Walter Scott and Washington Irving – authors played elaborate games in order to disguise or reveal their identity, and narrators emerged as distinct personalities. Given these conventions of the period, it was a bold undertaking on the part of Pushkin to begin his career as a prose-writer with an impersonal narrative – of a kind that anticipated the development of fiction writing in the second half of the nineteenth century.

What mattered most, as Pushkin sought a new manner of writing, was not just the question of whether the author was hidden from the reader or revealed to him, whether he spoke in the first person or the third, but the question of whether he would be courageous enough to write as an intelligent chronicler whose attitudes would be subtle and implicit, without clownish masks and false assumptions. In 'The Negro' he projects the image of an author who does not have to pretend – for the sake of a joke with the reader or for any other reason – that he possesses only half the truth about his characters. Unencumbered by a play-acting narrator's jocular or sentimental postures, he can reveal his characters' feelings in their full complexity. His narrator knows that human affairs are beset with both passion and compromise, and he does not feel obliged to apologize for this knowledge.

Such a mode of narration, however, presented enormous technical difficulties, with which Pushkin was as yet unable to cope. Several successful scenes notwithstanding, 'The Negro' demonstrates that Pushkin the prose-writer had not yet mastered dialogue (Ibrahim, the central hero, hardly speaks at all), or point of view (which shifts from one character to another in a kaleidoscopic fashion), or atmosphere (which at times changes too rapidly from pathetic to comic). These technical difficulties – arising precisely from the pioneering nature of Pushkin's venture – were probably the reason why he abandoned his project.

Still, far from being discouraged by his experience with 'The Negro', in the following years Pushkin endeavoured to apply an omniscient mode of narration to the psychological novel – an even more formidable task. The two fragments remaining of his efforts – 'The Guests Were Arriving at the Dacha' and 'In the Corner of a Small Square' – were promising indeed: so much so that they subsequently influenced Leo Tolstoy in writing his *Anna Karenina* (1877). Once more, however, the technical difficulties – especially the task of expanding rapid synopsis into vivid scene – were so enormous that the two fragments remained fragments.

Pushkin's difficulty in all these early unfinished works – including an experiment with the epistolary form entitled 'A Novel in Letters' – was that he insisted on treating complex material, though he had not found the right key, the right narrative point of view, the right technique for the new genres he was experimenting with. In order to find a solution, he had to lower his sights.

The *Tales of the Late Ivan Petrovich Belkin* signalled a retreat towards simpler subject matter, to be presented by simpler narrators, much more in keeping with the conventions of the time. Ascribing his stories to fictitious narrators, Pushkin was openly following the example of Walter Scott's *Tales of My Landlord*

(1816–19) and such collections by Washington Irving as *Tales of a Traveller* (1824).

A fictitious narrator is employed in 'Roslavlev' too, but this time with less success. Perhaps the reason Pushkin left this projected novel unfinished is that its narrator, who starts out as a "lady" author intent on defending the "shade" of her late friend, soon loses her identity and instead of whitewashing her friend's memory, provides a fascinating, but at the same time unflattering, portrait of a complex woman – a portrait that a detached omniscient narrator might just as well have drawn.

Having written several pieces in compliance with the conventions of his time – or in mockery of those conventions – Pushkin once more attempted to create a detached third-person narrator in 'Dubrovsky'. What initially drew him to the subject was an interest in the causes of social unrest – much pressed on his mind by the turbulent times in which he lived. The account of the two landowners' litigation and of the subsequent riot of Dubrovsky's peasants does indeed add up to a narrative of social significance. The characters of Troyekurov and Andrei Dubrovsky, as well as of their servants and hirelings, are skilfully drawn, with the aid of vivid scenes and dialogues. But Pushkin, evidently hoping to combine a serious study of social processes with popular appeal, added to his narrative a conventional love intrigue, using time-worn clichés and stereotypes. The incongruity between the original social theme and the traditional love plot might have contributed to his decision not to complete the work.

A triumph of detached narration, 'The Queen of Spades', stands at the peak of Pushkin's achievements as a prose-writer. Its three main characters – all negative – are surrounded by an intricate system of images, signifying winter and night, doom and madness, chaos and destruction. In this story Pushkin succeeds in drawing the kind of complex characters that eluded his firm grasp in the early fragments. 'The Queen of Spades' also demonstrates how far he had revised his earlier concept of prose writing: instead of presenting bare thoughts with no decorative frills, here he conveys the meaning through a system of symbols worthy of epic poetry.

Although the narrative mode used in 'The Queen of Spades' proved fully successful, Pushkin was not about to limit his range to it. For one thing, he remained attracted to the spare, unadorned quality of expository prose, even though he had changed his tactics in fiction. The result of this attraction, *A History of Pugachov*, fulfilled Pushkin's expectations of objective, unadorned prose writing, while *The Captain's Daughter* followed the tradition of *The Tales of Belkin*. But the tradition of the early fragments, continued in 'The Queen of Spades', was not abandoned either.

Several of the unfinished works of Pushkin's last years indicate that he was deeply involved in an attempt to create psychological fiction, narrated by an all-seeing, detached, intelligent observer. 'Egyptian Nights', considered along with 'We Were Spending the Evening at Princess D.'s Dacha', is the most promising of these late fragments. Not only does it pick up the theme of the psychological complexities of a certain social type contemporary to Pushkin begun in 'The Guests Were Arriving' and 'In the Corner'; it also introduces the question of the artist's relation to society. The Italian *improvvisatore*, humiliatingly dependent on his audience's whims, and the aristocratic poet Charsky, torn between his social position and his vocation as a poet, both seem to be equally close to Pushkin's heart. Exploring this dual theme, Pushkin goes beyond the kind of poetic representation he made full use of in 'The Queen of Spades' to introduce verse into the very texture of prose.

Although many of Pushkin's prose projects remained unfinished, the extant fragments displayed such depth and variety that few of his successors in Russian fiction were able to escape their influence. And his completed masterpieces rank among the best not only in Russian, but in world literature of the nineteenth century.

– Paul Debreczeny, 1983

The Queen of Spades

and Other Stories

Part One

Works Published during
Pushkin's Lifetime

THE QUEEN OF SPADES*

(1833)

> The queen of spades signifies secret malevolence.
> *– from a recent fortune-telling book*

I

But on days when it rained
they assembled for cards
often;
they would double their stakes
(God forgive them!) from fifty
to a hundred.
They recorded their gains
and they marked up their losses
in chalk.
Thus on days when it rained
they were fully engaged
on business.*

THERE WAS A CARD PARTY* at the house of Narumov, an officer of the Horse Guards. The long winter night passed imperceptibly; it was close to five in the morning when the company sat down to supper. Those who had won were eating with good appetite; the others sat lost in thought before their empty plates. But champagne appeared, and the conversation grew lively, with everyone joining in.

"How did you do, Surin?" asked the host.

"Lost, as usual. You must admit I have no luck: I play a *mirandole* game,* always keep cool, never let anything confuse me, and yet I lose all the time!"

"Have you never been tempted? Have you never risked *routé*? Your firmness amazes me."

"And what about Hermann?" said one of the guests, pointing at a young engineer. "He's never in his life had a card in his hand, never bent down a *paroli*, yet he will sit with us until five in the morning watching our game!"

"The game interests me very much," said Hermann, "but I am not in a position to sacrifice the necessary in the hope of gaining the superfluous."

7

"Hermann is a German: he's thrifty, that's all," remarked Tomsky. "But if there's anybody I don't understand, it's my grandmother, Countess Anna Fedotovna."

"Why? How is that?" cried the guests.

"I cannot fathom," continued Tomsky, "why my grandmother never punts."

"Well, what's so surprising about it," said Narumov, "that an old lady of eighty doesn't punt?"

"So you don't know anything about her?"

"No, not a thing."

"Well, in that case, listen. I should mention, to begin with, that about sixty years ago my grandmother went to Paris, where she created quite a sensation. People ran after her, just to catch a glimpse of *la Vénus moscovite*; Richelieu* paid court to her, and grandmother asserts that he almost shot himself because of her cruelty.

"Ladies used to play faro in those days. On one occasion at the Court my grandmother lost a very large sum, on word of honour, to the Duke of Orleans. After she arrived home, as she was peeling off her beauty spots and untying her hooped petticoat, she informed my grandfather of her loss and ordered him to pay.

"My late grandfather, as I remember, played the part of a butler to my grandmother. He feared her like fire; but when he heard about such a terrible loss, he flew into a rage, brought in the ledgers, demonstrated to her that in half a year they had spent half a million, pointed out that around Paris they did not possess the kind of estates they had around Moscow and Saratov, and absolutely refused to pay. Grandmother slapped him on the face and went to bed by herself as an indication of her displeasure.

"The next day she sent for her husband, hoping that the domestic punishment had had its effect on him, but she found him unshaken. For the first time in her life she went as far as to argue with him and offer him explanations; she thought she could awaken his conscience if she condescended to demonstrate to him that not all debts were alike, and that there was a difference between a duke and a cartwright. But all in vain! Grandfather had risen in rebellion. No, and no! Grandmother did not know what to do.

"She was on friendly terms with a very remarkable man. You have heard of Count Saint-Germain,* the hero of so many miraculous tales. You know he pretended to be the Wandering Jew,* the inventor of the elixir of life and of the philosopher's stone, et cetera. He was ridiculed as a charlatan, and Casanova called him a spy in his *Memoirs*;* be that as it may, despite his mysteriousness, Saint-Germain was a man of highly respectable appearance and had excellent manners. To this day Grandmother loves him with a passion and gets cross if she hears disrespectful talk about him. She knew that Saint-Germain had a large fortune at his disposal. She decided to turn to him for help and sent him a note asking him to call on her without delay.

"The old eccentric came at once and found her terribly upset. Depicting her husband's barbarity in the darkest colours, she concluded that she was placing all her hope in his friendship and kindness.

"Saint-Germain became thoughtful. 'I could accommodate you with the required sum,' he said, 'but I know you would not rest until you had repaid me, and I wouldn't want to inflict new worries upon you. There is another way out: you can win the money back.'

"'But my dear Count,' answered Grandmother, 'I'm telling you we've run out of money altogether.'

"'It requires no money,' rejoined Saint-Germain. 'Pray, hear me out.' And he revealed to her a secret for which any of us would be willing to pay a high price…"

The young gamblers listened with redoubled attention. Tomsky lit his pipe, took a puff, and continued.

"That same evening Grandmother presented herself at Versailles, *au jeu de la Reine*.* The Duke of Orleans was holding the bank; Grandmother casually excused herself, spinning some little yarn, for not bringing what she owed, and set down to punt against the Duke. She chose three cards and bet on them in sequence: all three won *sonica*,* and grandmother regained everything she had lost."

"Mere chance!" said one of the guests.

"A fairy tale!" remarked Hermann.

"Perhaps they were powdered cards,"* joined in a third.

"I don't think so," Tomsky replied in a serious tone.

"How now!" said Narumov. "You have a grandmother who can predict three winning cards in a row, and you have still not tried to extract her cabalistic power from her?"

"The Devil I haven't!" answered Tomsky. "She has four sons, including my father: all four are desperate gamblers, but she has not revealed her secret to any one of them, even though it would be handy for each – or for me, for that matter. But I'll tell you what my uncle, Count Ivan Ilyich, has told me, and what he swears on his honour is true. The late Chaplitsky – the one who died in poverty, having squandered millions – once in his youth lost 300,000 to Zorich* if I am not mistaken. He was in despair. Grandmother, though she usually viewed young people's pranks with severity, somehow took pity on Chaplitsky. She named him three cards with the instruction to play them one after the other, and she made him give his word of honour that he would never again play afterwards. Chaplitsky went back to his vanquisher; they sat down to play. Chaplitsky staked 50,000 on the first card and won *sonica*; he bent down a *paroli*, then a *paroli-paix*;* he won back what he had lost, and even went away a winner…

"But it's time to go to bed: it is already quarter to six."

Indeed it was already getting light: the young men emptied their glasses and left.

II

"Il paraît que monsieur est décidément pour les suivantes."
"Que voulez-vouz, madame? Elles sont plus fraîches."

– conversation at a social gathering

THE OLD COUNTESS N. sat in front of the mirror in her boudoir. Three maids surrounded her. One was holding a jar of rouge, the second a box of pins, and the third a tall bonnet with flame-coloured ribbons. The Countess did not have the slightest pretensions to beauty, which had long since faded from her face, but she adhered to all the habits of her youth, strictly following the fashions of the 1770s, spending just as much time and trouble on her *toilette* as she had sixty years before. A young lady, her ward, was seated over an embroidery frame by the window.

"Good morning, *grand-maman*," said a young officer, entering. "*Bonjour, mademoiselle Lise. Grand-maman*, I have a favour to ask of you."

"What is it, Paul?"

"Let me introduce one of my friends to you and bring him to your ball on Friday."

"Bring him straight to the ball, and you can introduce him to me there. Were you at X's last night?"

"How could I have missed it! It was very jolly – dancing till five o'clock in the morning. Wasn't Yeletskaya lovely!"

"Oh my dear! What do you see in her? She couldn't hold a candle to her grandmother, Princess Darya Petrovna… By the way, she must be getting on, Princess Darya Petrovna?"

"What do you mean, getting on?" Tomsky answered absent-mindedly. "She's been dead these seven years."

The young lady raised her head and signalled to him. He remembered that the old Countess was never informed of the death of any of her contemporaries, and he bit his lip.

But the Countess took the tidings, new to her, with perfect equanimity.

"Dead!" she said. "And I didn't even know! We were appointed maids of honour together, and as we were being presented, the Empress…"

For the hundredth time, the Countess related the anecdote to her grandson.

"And now, Paul," she said afterwards, "help me to get up. Lizanka, where is my snuffbox?"

She proceeded behind the screen with her chambermaids in order to complete her *toilette*. Tomsky remained alone with the young lady.

"Who is it you want to introduce?" asked Lizaveta Ivanovna softly.

"Narumov. Do you know him?"

"No, I don't. Is he an officer or a civilian?"

"An officer."

"An engineer?"

"No, a cavalryman. What made you think he was an engineer?"

The young lady laughed and did not answer a word.

"Paul!" called the Countess from behind the screen. "Send me a new novel, will you, but please not the kind they write nowadays."

"What do you mean, *grand-maman*?"

"I mean a novel in which the hero does not strangle either his mother or his father, and which describes no drowned bodies. I am terribly scared of drowned bodies."

"There are no such novels these days. Would you perhaps like some Russian ones?"

"You don't mean to say there are Russian novels?… Send some to me, my dear, send some by all means!"

"I'm sorry, I must go now, *grand-maman*: I'm in a hurry… Goodbye, Lizaveta Ivanovna! I still want to know why you thought Narumov was an engineer."

And Tomsky left the boudoir.

Lizaveta Ivanovna remained by herself; she laid aside her work and looked out of the window. Soon a young officer appeared from behind a corner on the other side of the street. A blush spread over her cheeks; she took up her work again and bent her head right over the canvas. At that moment the Countess entered, fully dressed.

"Lizanka," she said, "would you give orders to have the horses harnessed; we'll go out for a ride."

Lizanka rose from behind the embroidery frame and began putting her work away.

"What's the matter with you, child? Are you deaf?" the Countess shouted. "Tell them to harness the horses at once."

"Yes, ma'am," the young lady answered softly and ran into the ante-room.

A servant came in and handed the Countess some books from Prince Pavel Alexandrovich.

"Very well. Give him my thanks," said the Countess. "Lizanka! Lizanka! Where are you running now?"

"To get dressed."

"You'll have plenty of time for that. Sit down here. Open the first volume and read to me…"

The young lady took the book and read a few lines.

"Louder!" said the Countess. "What's up with you, madam? Have you lost your voice or something?… Wait a minute: pull up that footstool for me, closer… Well now!"

Lizaveta Ivanovna read two pages. The Countess yawned.

"Put that book down," she said. "What nonsense! Send it back to Prince Pavel with my thanks… But what's happened to the carriage?"

"The carriage is ready," said Lizaveta Ivanovna, looking out on the street.

"And why aren't you dressed?" said the Countess. "One always has to wait for you! This, little madam, is unbearable."

Liza ran to her room. Two minutes had not gone by when the Countess started ringing with all her might. Three maids ran in through one door, and a footman through the other.

"It's totally impossible to get anyone's attention around her," the Countess said to them. "Go and tell Lizaveta Ivanovna that I am waiting for her."

Lizaveta Ivanovna came in, wearing a cape and bonnet.

"At long last, madam!" said the Countess. "But what finery! What's all this for? Whose head do you want to turn?… And what's the weather like? – There is a wind, it seems to me."

"No there isn't, so please your ladyship. It's entirely calm," said the footman.

"You always say what comes into your head first! Open the little window. Just as I thought: there is a wind! Chilling to the bones! Have the horses unharnessed! Lizanka, we're not going; you needn't have decked yourself out so."

"This is my life," thought Lizaveta Ivanovna.

In truth, Lizaveta Ivanovna was the unluckiest of creatures. "Bitter is the bread of others," says Dante, "and wearisome are the steps of another's staircase."* Who indeed would be more familiar with the bitter taste of dependence than the poor ward of an aristocratic old lady? The Countess N. was, of course, not an evil soul, but as the spoiled pet of society, she was capricious; she had grown mean and had sunk into a cold egoism, like all old people whose fondest memories lay in the past and to whom the present was alien. She participated in all the trivial events of high-society life, dragging herself to balls, where she would sit in a corner, all painted up and dressed according to an ancient fashion, like a misshapen but obligatory ornament of the ballroom; the guests, as they arrived, would go up to her bowing low, as if performing an established rite, but afterwards would pay no attention to her. She was scrupulous in receiving the whole city as etiquette decreed, but hardly recognized any of her guests. Her numerous domestics, grown fat and gray in her entrance hall and maids' quarters, did what they pleased, robbing the moribund old woman left, right and centre. Lizaveta Ivanovna was the martyr of the household. She poured the tea and was scolded for using too much sugar, read novels aloud and was blamed for all the faults of the authors, accompanied the Countess on her outings and was held responsible for both the weather and the condition of the streets. She had a fixed salary, but it was never paid in full; at the same time she was expected to be dressed like everyone else, that is, like the very few. In society she played the most pitiable role. Everybody knew her,

14

but nobody took any notice of her; at the balls she danced only when an extra partner was needed for a *vis-à-vis*; and ladies took her by the arm every time they needed to go to the dressing room in order to adjust something in their costume. She was proud; she felt her position keenly, and looked around impatiently waiting for a deliverer; but the young men, calculating in their whimsical vanity, did not honour Lizaveta Ivanovna with their attention, though she was a hundred times more appealing than the brazen and cold-hearted debutantes on whom they danced attendance. How many times did she steal out of the tedious but sumptuous salon in order to weep in her own poor room, furnished with a paper screen, a chest of drawers, a small mirror, a painted bedstead and a tallow candle faintly burning in its brass holder!

On one occasion – this was two days after the party described at the beginning of our story and a week before the scene that we have just detailed – on one occasion Lizaveta Ivanovna, sitting over her embroidery frame by the window, happened to glance at the street and caught sight of a young engineering officer who was standing there motionless with his eyes fixed on her window. She lowered her head and resumed her work; five minutes later she looked again – the young officer was standing in the same place. Since it had never been her way to flirt with unknown officers, she stopped looking at the street and embroidered for about two hours without raising her head. Dinner was announced. She stood up, started putting away her embroidery frame and, inadvertently glancing at the street, caught sight of the officer once more. This seemed rather strange to her. After dinner she went to the window with a certain feeling of apprehension, but the officer was no longer there, and she soon forgot about him...

About two days later, as she and the Countess came out of the house to get into the carriage, she saw him again. He was standing right by the entrance, his face hidden in his beaver collar, his dark eyes sparkling from under his cap. Lizaveta Ivanovna was frightened, though she did not know why, and got into the carriage, shaking inexplicably.

After she returned home she ran up to the window: the officer was standing in his former place, gazing at her; she turned away, tormented by curiosity and agitated by a feeling that was entirely new to her.

From that time on, not one day passed without the young man arriving, at a certain hour, under the windows of the house. A tacit relationship was established between him and her. Sitting in her place over her work, she could sense his approach; she raised her head and looked at him longer with each day. The young man seemed to be grateful for it: she could see with her keen young eyes that a sudden blush spread over his pale cheeks each time their glances met. By the end of the week she gave him a smile...

When Tomsky asked for the Countess's permission to introduce a friend, the poor girl's heart gave a thump. Having learnt, however, that Narumov was not an engineer but a cavalryman, she regretted the indiscreet question that had betrayed her secret to the flighty Tomsky.

Hermann was the son of a Russified German who had left him a little capital. Firmly resolved to ensure his independence, Hermann did not touch even the interest earned by these funds; he lived on his salary alone, denying himself even the slightest extravagance. Since he was also reserved and proud, his comrades rarely had occasion to laugh at his excessive thriftiness. He was fiercely passionate and had a fiery imagination, but his resoluteness saved him from the usual lapses of youth. He was, for example, a gambler at heart but never touched a card, reckoning that his circumstances did not allow him (as he was fond of saying) *to sacrifice the necessary in the hope of gaining the superfluous*. Yet at the same time he would sit by the card table nights on end and follow with feverish trembling the different turns of the game.

The anecdote about the three cards fired his imagination; he could not get it out of his head all night. "What if," he thought as he wandered about Petersburg the following evening, "what if the old Countess revealed her secret to me? If she named the three reliable cards for me? Why not try my luck?... I could be introduced to her, get into her good graces, become her lover if need be; but all this requires time, and she is eighty-seven: she may die in a week – in a couple of days!... And what about the anecdote itself? Can one put any faith in it? No! Calculation, moderation, and industry; these are my three faithful cards. They will treble my capital, increase it sevenfold, and bring me ease and independence!"

Lost thus in thought, he found himself on one of the main streets of Petersburg, in front of an old-style house. The street was crowded with carriages; one equipage after another rolled up to the lighted entrance. Now a young beauty's shapely leg, now a clinking riding boot, now a striped stocking and a diplomat's shoe emerged from the carriages. Fur coats and cloaks flitted by the stately doorman. Hermann stopped.

"Whose house is this?" he asked the watchman on the corner.

"The Countess N.'s," answered the watchman.

A shiver ran down Hermann's spine. The amazing anecdote arose in his imagination once more. He began to pace up and down by the house, thinking about its owner and her miraculous talent. It was late when he returned to his humble lodging; he could not get to sleep for a long time, and when he finally dropped off, he dreamt of cards, a green table, heaps of bank notes and piles of gold coins. He played one card after another, bent the corners resolutely, and kept winning, raking in the gold and stuffing the bank notes into his pockets. Waking up late, he sighed over the loss of his illusory riches; once more he went wandering about the city and once more found himself in front of Countess N.'s house. A mysterious force, it seemed, had drawn him there. He stopped and began to look at the windows. Behind one of them he noticed a dark-haired young head, bent, evidently, over a book or some work. The head was raised. Hermann beheld a fresh young face and dark eyes. That moment decided his fate.

III

*Vous m'écrivez, mon ange, des lettres de quatres pages plus vite que je ne puis les lire.**

– from a letter

N O SOONER HAD LIZAVETA IVANOVNA taken off her cape and bonnet than the Countess sent for her and once more ordered the carriage. They went downstairs to get in. Two servants had just lifted up the old lady and pushed her through the door of the carriage when Lizaveta Ivanovna beheld her engineer right by the wheel. He seized her hand; before she had time to recover from her fright, the young man had put a letter in her palm and was gone. She slipped it inside her glove, and was unable to hear or see anything during the whole ride. The Countess had a habit of constantly asking questions as she rode along: "Who was it we just passed?" "What's the name of this bridge?" "What's written on that sign?" This time Lizaveta Ivanovna answered at random and wide of the mark, making the Countess angry.

"What's the matter with you, child? Are you in a trance or something? Don't you hear me or understand what I am saying?... Thank God I don't slur my words and I'm not yet a dotard!"

Lizaveta Ivanovna paid no attention to her. As soon as they returned home she ran to her room and drew the letter out of her glove: it was not sealed. She read it. It contained a confession of love: it was tender, respectful – and translated word for word from a German novel. But Lizaveta Ivanovna did not know German and found it very satisfactory.

For all that, the letter, delightful as it was, worried her in the extreme. For the first time in her life she was entering into a close and clandestine relationship with a young man. His boldness terrified her. She reproached herself for her imprudent conduct and did not know what to do: should she leave off sitting by the

18

window and try, by her lack of attention, to discourage the young officer from further advances? Should she return his letter to him? Or should she answer him, coldly and resolutely? She had no one to turn to for advice; she had neither a friend nor a counsellor. In the end she decided to reply.

She sat down at her small desk, took out pen and paper – and fell to thinking. She began her letter several times but each time tore it up: her phrases seemed to her either too encouraging or too forbidding. At last she succeeded in penning a few lines that left her satisfied. She wrote:

> *I am convinced that you have honourable intentions and did not wish to offend me with a thoughtless act; but this is not the way to begin an acquaintance. I return your letter and hope to have no cause in the future to complain of an unwarranted disrespect."*

The next day, as soon as she saw Hermann walking below, she rose from her embroidery frame, went out to the reception hall, opened the transom, and threw her letter into the street, trusting in the young officer's agility. Hermann dashed for it, picked it up, and went to a confectionery shop. Tearing off the seal, he found his own letter as well as Lizaveta Ivanovna's answer. That was just what he had expected, and he returned home very much absorbed in his intrigue.

Three days later a pert young *mam'selle* from a ladies' dress shop brought a note to Lizaveta Ivanovna. She opened it with anxiety, anticipating a demand for payment, but suddenly recognized Hermann's hand.

"You've made a mistake, dearie," she said, "this note is not for me."

"No, it's definitely for you," answered the bold little girl, not concealing a sly smile. "Please read it!"

Lizaveta Ivanovna read through the note quickly. Hermann was demanding a rendezvous.

"Impossible!" said Lizaveta Ivanovna, frightened by both the rashness of Hermann's demand and the means he had chosen to convey it. "This is surely not written to me!" And she tore the letter into small pieces.

"If the letter was not for you, why did you tear it up?" said the little *mam'selle*. "I could have returned it to the sender."

"Please, dearie," said Lizaveta Ivanovna to the girl, whose remark made her blush, "in future do not bring notes to me. And tell the one who sent you that he should be ashamed of himself…"

But there was no stopping Hermann. Lizaveta Ivanovna received letters from him every day by one means or another. They were no longer translations from German. Inspired by passion, Hermann wrote them in a style that was characteristic of him, expressing both the uncompromising nature of his desires and the confusion of his unbridled imagination. It no longer occurred to Lizaveta Ivanovna to send them back: she revelled in them and began to answer them, her notes growing longer and tenderer by the day. In the end she threw the following letter to him from the window:

Tonight the Ambassador of Y. is giving a ball. The Countess is planning to attend. We shall stay there until about two in the morning. Here is an opportunity for you to see me alone. As soon as the Countess goes out, her servants will probably scatter in all directions; the doorman will remain by the entrance, but even he is likely to retreat, as is his habit, into his cubicle. Come at half-past eleven. Walk straight up the staircase. If you find anybody in the ante-room, enquire whether the Countess is at home. You will be told that she is not – and that will be the end of that. You will have to turn back. But it is likely that you will meet no one. The maids sit in their room, all of them together. From the ante-room turn left and walk straight through, all the way to the Countess's bedroom. In her bedroom, behind a screen, you will see two small doors: the one on the right leads to a study, which the Countess never enters; the one on the left opens into a corridor, where you will find a narrow winding staircase: this leads to my room.

Hermann waited for the appointed time, trembling like a tiger. At ten o'clock in the evening he was already in front of the Countess's house. The weather was terrible: the wind howled, wet snow fell in large flakes; the lights shone dimly; the streets were deserted. Only occasionally did a cab-driver shamble by with his scrawny nag, on the lookout for a late passenger. Hermann stood wearing only a jacket, yet feeling neither wind nor snow. At last the Countess's carriage drew up. Hermann watched as servants, grasping her by the arms, carried out the hunched-up old lady, wrapped in a sable coat. Right behind her, her ward flitted by, dressed in a light cloak, her head adorned with fresh flowers. The doors of the carriage were slammed to. The carriage rolled off heavily in the soft snow. The doorman shut the front door. The lights in the windows went out. Hermann started pacing up and down before the lifeless house. He went up to a street lamp and looked at his watch: it was twenty-past eleven. He stayed under the lamp with his eyes fixed on the hands of his watch, waiting for the remaining minutes to pass. At exactly half-past eleven he stepped onto the Countess's porch and went up to the brightly lit entrance hall. The doorman was not there. Hermann ran up the stairs, opened the door of the ante-room, and saw a servant asleep in an ancient soiled armchair under a lamp. Hermann walked past him with a light but firm step. The reception hall and the drawing room were dark, with only a feeble light falling on them from the lamp in the ante-room. Hermann entered the bedroom. A gold sanctuary lamp burned in front of an icon case filled with ancient icons. Armchairs with faded damask upholstery and down-cushioned sofas, their gilt coating worn, stood in melancholy symmetry along the walls, which were covered with Chinese silk. Two portraits, painted in Paris by Mme Lebrun,* hung on the wall. One of them showed a man about forty years old, red-faced and portly, wearing a light-green coat with a star; the other a beautiful young woman with an aquiline nose, her hair combed back from her temples and a rose in her powdered locks. Every nook and corner was crowded with china shepherdesses, table clocks made by the famous Leroy,* little boxes, strings of beads, fans, and diverse other ladies' toys invented at the end of the last century along with the Montgolfiers' balloon and Mesmer's magnetism.* Hermann went behind the screen. A small iron bedstead stood behind it; on the right was the door leading to the study; on the left the other one, leading to the corridor. Hermann opened the latter and saw the narrow winding staircase that led to the poor ward's room... But he drew back and went into the dark study.

Time went slowly. Everything was quiet. A clock struck twelve in the drawing room and, following it, all the clocks in all the rooms announced the hour; then everything grew quiet again. Hermann stood leaning against the cold stove. He was calm: his heart beat evenly, like that of a man embarked on a dangerous but unavoidable mission. The clocks struck one, then two in the morning; at last he heard the distant rumble of a carriage. An involuntary agitation seized him. The carriage drove up to the house and stopped. He heard the thump of the carriage's steps being lowered. The house began stirring. Servants were running, voices resounded, and lights came on. Three old chambermaids ran into the bedroom and the Countess, barely alive, came in and sank into a Voltaire-style armchair.* Hermann watched through a crack in the door: Lizaveta Ivanovna passed by him. He could hear her hasty steps up her staircase. Something akin to a pang of conscience stirred in his heart, but was soon stilled. He stood petrified.

The Countess began to undress in front of the mirror. The maids unpinned her bonnet bedecked with roses and removed the powdered wig from her closely cropped grey head. Pins came showering off her. Her yellow dress, embroidered with silver, fell to her swollen feet; Hermann became privy to the repellent mysteries of her *toilette*. At last she put on her bed jacket and nightcap: in these clothes, more appropriate for her age, she seemed less frightening and hideous.

Like most old people, the Countess suffered from insomnia. Having undressed, she sat in the armchair by the window and dismissed her chambermaids. The candles were taken away and once more the room was lit only by the sanctuary lamp. The Countess sat, all yellow, mumbling with her flabby lips and swaying right and left. Her dim eyes were completely empty of thought; looking at her, one might assume that the swaying of this horrifying old woman was caused, not by her own will, but by a mysterious nervous reaction.

Suddenly an inexpressible change came over her lifeless face. Her lips stopped mumbling, and her eyes lit up: a strange man stood before her.

"Don't be frightened, for Heaven's sake, don't!" he said in a clear but low voice. "I have no intention of harming you: I've come to beg a favour of you."

The old lady looked at him in silence and did not seem to hear him. Hermann assumed she was deaf and repeated his phrases, bending down toward her ear. The old lady kept silent as before.

"It is in your power to make my life happy," continued Hermann, "and it will cost you nothing: I know you are able to predict three winning cards in a row..."

Hermann stopped. The Countess seemed to have understood what was demanded of her; she seemed to be searching for words to reply.

"That was a joke," she said at last. "I swear to you it was only a joke!"

"It is no joking mater," rejoined Hermann angrily. "Remember Chaplitsky, whom you helped to win back his loss."

The Countess grew visibly confused. Her features betrayed a violent inner agitation, but she soon relapsed into her former numbness.

"Can you," continued Hermann, "can you name those three infallible cards for me?"

The Countess kept silent; Hermann went on:

"For whom are you saving your secret? For your grandsons? They are rich as it is, and they don't even know the value of money. A spendthrift will not benefit by your three cards. He who cannot guard his patrimony will die in poverty, whatever demonic machinations he may resort to. I am not a spendthrift; I know the value of money. Your three cards will not be wasted on me. Well, then..."

He stopped, trembling in anticipation of her answer. The Countess was silent; Hermann knelt down before her.

"If your heart ever knew the feeling of love," he said, "if you remember its ecstasies, if you once in your life smiled, hearing the cry of a newborn son, if anything human has ever pulsated within your bosom, then I beseech you, appealing to the feelings of a wife, mistress, mother – to everything that is sacred in life – do not refuse my request! Reveal your secret to me! Of what use is it to you?… Maybe it is linked with a terrible sin, a forfeiture of eternal bliss, a covenant with the Devil… Consider: you are old, you will not live long – I am willing to take your sin on my soul. Only reveal your secret to me. Consider that the happiness of a man is in your hands; not only I, but my children, grandchildren, and great-grandchildren will bless your memory and hold it sacred…"

The old woman did not answer a word.

Hermann stood up.

"You old witch!" he said, clenching his teeth. "Then I will make you answer…"

With these words he drew a pistol from his pocket.

At the sight of the pistol the Countess was once more visibly perturbed. She jerked back her head and raised her hands as if to shield herself from the shot… Then she rolled over backwards… and stayed motionless.

"Stop this childish game," said Hermann, grasping her hand. "I am asking you for the last time: will you or will you not name your three cards for me? Yes or no?"

The Countess did not answer. Hermann realized that she was dead.

IV

7 mai 18—
*Homme sans mœurs et sans religion!**
— from a letter

L IZAVETA IVANOVNA sat in her room deep in thought, still wearing her evening gown. On her arrival home she had hurriedly dismissed the sleepy maid who grudgingly offered her services; she said she would undress by herself and went to her room trembling, both hoping to find Hermann there and wishing not to. One glance was enough to convince her of his absence, and she thanked her fate for the obstacle that had prevented their meeting. She sat down without undressing and began to recollect all the circumstances that had led her so far in such a short time. Less than three weeks had passed since she had first caught sight of the young man through the window, and she was already corresponding with him, he had already made her consent to a nocturnal assignation! She knew his name only because some of his letters were signed, she had never spoken with him, never heard his voice, nor heard anything about him… until that evening. A strange thing! That very evening, at the ball, Tomsky was in a huff with the young Princess Polina, who had for the first time flirted with someone other than him; and wishing to take revenge on her by a show of indifference, he kept Lizaveta Ivanovna engaged in an endless mazurka. All through it he joked about her partiality for engineering officers, trying to convince her that he knew much more than she might suppose. Some of his jeers were so well aimed that several times Lizaveta Ivanovna thought her secret was known to him.

"Who told you all this?" she asked, laughing.

"A friend of a person you know," answered Tomsky, "a very remarkable man."

"And who is this remarkable man?"

"His name is Hermann."

Lizaveta Ivanovna did not say anything, but her hands and feet felt like ice...

"This Hermann," continued Tomsky, "is a truly romantic character: he has the profile of Napoleon and the soul of Mephistopheles. I think he has at least three crimes on his conscience. But how pale you've turned!..."

"I have a headache... What did this Hermann, or whatever his name is, tell you?..."

"Hermann is very dissatisfied with his friend: he says that in his friend's place he would have acted entirely differently... I even suspect that Hermann himself has an eye on you: at least he cannot remain calm listening to his friend's amorous exclamations."

"But where has he seen me?"

"At church, maybe, or when you went for a ride... Heaven only knows! Perhaps in your room while you were asleep: I wouldn't put it past him..."

The conversation, which was becoming painfully fascinating to Lizaveta Ivanovna, was interrupted by three ladies who approached to ask, "*oubli ou regret?*"*

The lady Tomsky chose turned out to be Princess Polina. She gave herself an opportunity to explain things to Tomsky by running an extra circle and spinning in front of her chair longer than usual. By the time Tomsky returned to his seat he had neither Hermann nor Lizaveta Ivanovna on his mind. The latter was still eager to resume the interrupted conversation, but the mazurka came to an end, and soon afterwards the old Countess was ready to leave.

Tomsky's words had been no more than a mazurka partner's chit-chat, but they had sunk deep into the young dreamer's soul. The portrait Tomsky had sketched in was rather like the image she herself had formed; and, thanks to the latest novels, her imagination was both daunted and enchanted by this already hackneyed type. She sat with her bare arms crossed and her head, still adorned with flowers, bent over the deep décolletage of her dress... Suddenly the door opened and Hermann came in. She shuddered...

"Where have you been?" she asked in an alarmed whisper.

"In the old Countess's bedroom," answered Hermann. "I have just left her. She is dead."

"My God!... What are you saying?..."

"And it seems to me," Hermann continued, "that I caused her death."

Lizaveta Ivanovna looked at him, and Tomsky's words echoed in her mind: *This man has at least three crimes on his conscience!* Hermann sat down on the window sill by her and told her the full story.

Lizaveta Ivanovna listened to him in horror. And so, those passionate letters, those ardent demands, that bold and dogged pursuit – all that was not love! Money was what his soul was craving! It was not in her power to quench his passion and make him happy. The poor ward had turned out to be no more than the blind accomplice of a burglar, of the murderer of her aged benefactress!... She shed bitter tears of agonizing, belated remorse. Hermann regarded her in silence: his heart was also crushed, but neither the poor girl's tears nor the wondrous charm of her sorrow could move his icy soul. He felt no pang of conscience over the old woman's death. The one thought appalling him was the irretrievable loss of the secret that he had expected to make him rich.

"You are a monster!" said Lizaveta Ivanovna at last.

"I did not wish her death," Hermann answered. "My pistol is not loaded."

They both grew silent.

It was getting toward morning. Lizaveta Ivanovna extinguished the burnt-down candles; a pale light spread across her room. She wiped her eyes, red from crying, and fixed them on Hermann: he was sitting on the window sill with arms folded and brows fiercely knitted. In this pose he bore an amazing resemblance to Napoleon's portrait. Even Lizaveta Ivanovna was struck by the likeness.

"How are you going to get out of the house?" she broke the silence. "I thought of leading you out by the secret staircase, but we would have to go past the bedroom, which scares me."

"Just tell me how to find this secret staircase, and I'll go out by myself."

Lizaveta Ivanovna got up, took a key from her chest of draw-ers, handed it to Hermann and gave him detailed instructions. Hermann pressed her cold, unresponsive hand, kissed her bowed head and went out.

He descended the winding staircase and once more entered the Countess's bedroom. The dead old woman sat petrified; profound tranquillity was reflected in her face. Hermann stopped before her, looked at her for a long time as if wishing to ascertain the terrible truth; at last he stepped into the study, felt for the door behind the wall hanging and began to descend the dark staircase, his mind agitated by strange feelings. "Perhaps," he thought, "up this very staircase, about sixty years ago, into this same bedroom, at this same hour, dressed in an embroidered coat, with his hair combed *à l'oiseau royal*,* pressing his three-cornered hat to his heart, there stole a lucky young man, now long since turned to dust in his grave; and the heart of his aged mistress has stopped beating today..."

At the bottom of the stairs Hermann opened another door with the same key, and found himself in a passageway leading to the street.

V

That night the late Baroness von W. appeared to me. She was dressed all in white, and said, "How do you do, Mr Councillor?"

— Swedenborg*

THREE DAYS AFTER the fatal night, at nine o'clock in the morning, Hermann set out for the Z. Monastery, where the funeral service for the deceased Countess was to be performed. Although he did not feel repentant, he could not completely silence the voice of his conscience, which kept telling him, "You are the old lady's murderer!" Deficient in true faith, he was nevertheless subject to many superstitions. He believed that the dead Countess could exercise an evil influence on his life, and he decided to go to her funeral in order to ask her pardon.

The church was full. Hermann had difficulty pushing his way through the crowd. The coffin lay on a sumptuous catafalque under a velvet canopy. The deceased lay in her coffin with her arms folded over her chest, in a lace cap and white satin dress. She was surrounded by her domestics and relations: her servants dressed in black caftans with the family's coat of arms on the shoulders and holding candles in their hands, and her family – children, grandchildren, great-grandchildren – dressed in full mourning. Nobody wept: tears would have been *une affectation*. The Countess was so very old that her death could not have come as a surprise to anyone; her relatives had considered her on the edge of the grave for quite some time. A young bishop gave the funeral sermon. He depicted in simple, moving words the peaceful ascent into heaven of the righteous woman, whose long years had been a serene and inspiring preparation for a Christian end. "The Angel of Death found her," said the orator, "waiting for the midnight bridegroom,* vigilant in godly meditation." The service was concluded in an atmosphere of sombre propriety. The relatives went first to pay their last respects to the deceased. Then came the numerous guests, filing by in order to take their last bow before the one who had so long participated in their frivolous amusements. Then all the domestics followed. Finally came the old housekeeper, a contemporary of the deceased. Two young girls led her by the arms. She was too weak to bow all the way to the ground; she alone shed a few tears as she kissed her mistress's cold hand. After her Hermann, too, decided to go up to the coffin. He prostrated himself on the ground and lay for several minutes on the cold floor strewn with fir branches. At last he rose to his feet, pale as the deceased herself, mounted the steps of the catafalque, and bent over… At that moment it seemed to him that the deceased cast a mocking glance at him, screwing up one of her eyes. He moved back hastily, missed his step and crashed to the ground flat on his back. As he was helped to his feet, Lizaveta Ivanovna had to be carried out onto the porch, unconscious. This episode disturbed for a few minutes the solemnity of the sombre rite. A muffled murmur arose among those in attendance, and a gaunt chamberlain – a close relative of the deceased – whispered into the ear of an Englishman standing by him that the young officer was the dead woman's illegitimate son, to which the Englishman responded with a cold "Oh?"

Hermann was extremely distressed that whole day. Dining at a secluded tavern, he drank too much, which was not his wont, in the hope of calming his inner agitation. But the wine only further inflamed his imagination. Returning home, he threw himself on his bed fully clothed and fell into a deep sleep.

It was night when he woke up; the moon was shining into his room. He glanced at his watch: it was quarter to three. Not feeling sleepy any more, he sat on his bed and thought about the old Countess's funeral.

Just then somebody looked in from the street through the window, and immediately went away. Hermann paid no attention. A minute later he could hear the door of the ante-room open. His orderly, thought Hermann, was returning from a nocturnal outing, drunk as usual. But he heard unfamiliar steps: somebody was softly shuffling along in slippers. The door opened, and a woman in a white dress came in. Hermann took her for his old nurse and wondered what could have brought her here at this time of night. But the woman in white glided across the room and suddenly appeared right before him: Hermann recognized the Countess!

"I have come to you against my will," she said to him in a firm voice. "I have been ordered to grant your request. The three, the seven, and the ace will win for you in succession, but only under the condition that you play no more than one card within one day, and that afterwards you never play again for the rest of your life. I will forgive you my death under the condition that you marry my ward, Lizaveta Ivanovna…"

After these words she quietly turned around, went to the door and left, shuffling her slippers. Hermann heard the front door slam and once more saw someone looking in through his window.

Hermann was unable to regain his senses for a long time. He went into the other room. His orderly was asleep on the floor; Hermann had great difficulty waking him up. The orderly was drunk as usual: it was impossible to get any sense out of him. The front door was locked. Hermann returned to his own room, lit a candle, and jotted down his vision.

VI

– *"Attendez!"*
– *"How dare you say 'attendez' to me?"*
– *"Your Excellency, I said, 'attendez, sir!'"*

T WO FIXED IDEAS can no more coexist in the moral sphere than can two bodies occupy the same space in the physical world. The three, the seven, and the ace soon eclipsed the image of the dead old woman in Hermann's mind. Three, seven, ace – the three-some haunted him and was perpetually on his lips. Seeing a young girl, he would say, "How shapely! Just like a three of hearts." If anybody asked him what time it was, he would answer, "Five to the seven." Every portly man reminded him of an ace. The three, the seven, and the ace hounded him even in his dreams, taking on every imaginable form: the three blossomed before him like a great luxu-riant flower; the seven appeared as a Gothic gate; and the ace as-sumed the shape of an enormous spider. All his thoughts converged on one idea – that of profiting from the secret for which he had paid so dearly. He began to consider retirement and travel. In the public gambling casinos of Paris he meant to wrest a fortune from a spell-bound Destiny. But chance saved him from any such effort.

In Moscow, wealthy gamblers had formed a group under the deanship of the famous Chekalinsky, who had spent all his life over the card table and had at one time made millions, even though he had been winning promissory notes while losing ready cash. His many years of experience had earned him the trust of his fellow gamblers; his open door, excellent cook, cordiality and cheerful-ness had won him universal admiration. He came to St Petersburg. Young men thronged to his house, forgetting balls for the sake of cards and preferring the seductions of faro to the enticements of gallantry. Narumov brought Hermann to him.

The two young men passed through a series of magnificently furnished rooms, well attended by polite waiters. Some generals and privy councillors were playing whist; there were young people eating ice cream or smoking their pipes, sprawled on damask-upholstered sofas. In the drawing room twenty or so players crowded around a long table, behind which sat the host, holding the bank. He was about sixty, of a highly respectable appearance. Silver hair covered his head; his fresh-complexioned round face reflected a good nature; his eyes sparkled, animated by a continual smile. Narumov introduced Hermann. Chekalinsky cordially shook the young man's hand, asked him not to stand on ceremony, and continued dealing.

The deal lasted a long time. There were more than thirty cards on the table. Chekalinsky stopped after each turn to give the players time to make their wishes known; he jotted down losses, courteously listened to requests, and even more courteously straightened out the odd corner that had been bent down incorrectly by a forgetful hand. At last the deal was completed. Chekalinsky shuffled the deck and was about to begin a new deal.

"Allow me to place a bet," said Hermann, reaching over from behind a corpulent gentleman who was punting at the table. Chekalinsky gave a smile and a silent bow in token of his humble compliance. Narumov laughingly congratulated Hermann on breaking his long-sustained fast and wished him beginner's luck.

"Ready," said Hermann, writing the amount above his card in chalk.*

"How much is that, sir?" the banker asked, screwing up his eyes. "Forgive me, I cannot make it out."

"Forty-seven thousand," said Hermann.

At these words all heads turned, and all eyes fastened on Hermann. "He has lost his mind," thought Narumov.

"Allow me to remark," said Chekalinsky, with his immutable smile, "that your game is bold. So far no one has placed more than two hundred and seventy-five on the first bet of a deal."

"What of it?" rejoined Hermann. "Will you make the play or not?"

Chekalinsky bowed with the same air of humble compliance. "All I wished to bring to your attention was," he said, "that, deemed worthy of my friends' confidence as I am, I can hold the bank only against ready cash. I am of course personally convinced that your word suffices, but for the sake of order in the game and the accounts, I ask you to place the money on the card."

Hermann took a banknote out of his pocket and gave it to Chekalinsky, who after a quick glance at it placed it on Hermann's card.

Chekalinsky proceeded to deal. A nine fell to his right, and a three to his left.

"It's a winner," said Hermann, showing his card.

A murmur arose among the players. Chekalinsky frowned for a moment, but the usual smile soon returned to his face.

"Do you wish to receive your winnings now?" he asked Hermann.

"If you please."

Chekalinsky took several bank notes out of his pocket and immediately settled his account. Hermann took the money and left the table. Narumov could hardly recover his senses. Hermann drank a glass of lemonade and went home.

The next evening he was at Chekalinsky's again. The host was dealing. The punters made room for Hermann as soon as he approached the table. Chekalinsky bowed to him affably.

Hermann waited until a new deal began; then he led a card, placing both his original forty-seven thousand and his win of the previous night on it.

Chekalinsky began dealing. A jack fell to his right and a seven to his left.

Hermann turned his seven face up.

Everybody gasped. Chekalinsky was visibly flustered. He counted out ninety-four thousand and handed it over to Hermann. The latter took it with equanimity and left at once.

The following evening Hermann once more presented himself at the table. Everybody had been expecting him. The generals and privy councillors abandoned their whist in order to watch such an extraordinary game. The young officers jumped up from their sofas and all the waiters gathered in the drawing room. Everyone crowded around Hermann. The other players made no wagers, impatiently waiting to see the outcome of his play. Hermann stood by the table, ready to punt against the pale, though still smiling,

Chekalinsky. Each unsealed a new pack of cards. Chekalinsky shuffled. Hermann picked a card and placed it on the table, covering it with a stack of bank notes. It was like a duel. A profound silence reigned over the gathering.

Chekalinsky started dealing with trembling hands. On his right showed a queen, on his left an ace.

"The ace has won!" said Hermann and turned his card face up.

"Your lady has been murdered," said Chekalinsky affably.

Hermann shuddered: indeed, instead of an ace, the queen of spades lay before him. He could not believe his eyes; he could not fathom how he could possibly have drawn the wrong card.

Suddenly, it seemed to him that the queen of spades screwed up her eyes and grinned. An extraordinary likeness struck him...

"The old woman!" he cried out in terror.

Chekalinsky gathered in the bank notes lost by Hermann. The young man stood by the table, motionless. When at last he left the table, the whole room burst into loud talk. "Bravely punted!" the players kept saying. Chekalinsky shuffled the cards anew: the game resumed it usual course.

* * *

CONCLUSION

Hermann has lost his mind. He is at the Obukhov Hospital,* Ward No. 17; he doesn't answer questions, just keeps muttering with uncommon rapidity, "Three, seven, ace! Three, seven, queen!"

Lizaveta Ivanovna has married a very pleasant young man; he holds a position somewhere in the civil service and is comfortably well off: he is the son of the old Countess's former steward. Lizaveta Ivanovna is bringing up the daughter of a poor relation.

Tomsky has been promoted to captain and is engaged to marry Princess Polina.

KIRDZHALI*

(1834)

KIRDZHALI WAS A BULGARIAN by birth. The word *kirdzhali* in Turkish means warrior, daredevil.* Kirdzhali terrorized the whole of Moldavia with his robberies. Let me recount one of his exploits, just to give an idea of them. One night he and the Albanian bandit, Mikhaylaki, just the two of them, attacked a Bulgarian village. They set it on fire from either end, and went from hut to hut. Kirdzhali murdered while Mikhaylaki carried the loot. They both shouted, "Kirdzhali! Kirdzhali!" The villagers scattered in all directions.

When Alexander Ypsilantis proclaimed his uprising* and began to recruit troops, Kirdzhali brought along several of his old comrades. They had no clear notion of what the *Hetaireia* was actually striving for, but they could plainly see that the war presented an opportunity to get rich at the expense of the Turks, and possibly of the Moldavians.

Alexander Ypsilantis was a courageous individual, but he did not possess the qualities required for the role he had so fervently and rashly undertaken. He could not cope with the men he was supposed to lead. They neither respected nor trusted him. After the ill-fated battle in which the flower of Greek youth perished, Iordaki Olimbioti advised him to step down and took his place.* Ypsilantis rode off to the borders of Austria and sent back a curse on his men, calling them insubordinate cowards and scoundrels. Most of these cowards and scoundrels had perished either within the walls of the Seku Monastery or on the banks of the Prut, desperately trying to fight off an enemy that outnumbered them ten to one.*

Kirdzhali served in the detachment of Georgy Kantakuzin,* about whom one could repeat what has already been said of Ypsilantis. On the eve of the battle near Skulyany, Kantakuzin asked the Russian authorities for permission to enter our border post. The detachment remained without a commander, but Kirdzhali,

Safyanos, Kantagoni and their comrades did not see any need for a commander.

No one, it seems, has described the battle near Skulyany in its full pathetic reality. Imagine seven hundred men – Albanian outlaws and regulars, Greeks, Bulgarians, and every other kind of rabble – who had no concept of military art and were retreating in the face of a Turkish cavalry of fifteen thousand. This detachment drew back to the bank of the Prut and set up two tiny cannon, brought along from the hospodar's courtyard at Jassy, where they had been used for firing salvos during dinner parties on the hospodar's name day. The Turks would have no doubt liked to fire grapeshot, but did not dare to without permission from the Russian authorities, for some would have inevitably hit our side of the river. The commander of the border station* (deceased by now), who had served in the military for forty years but had never heard a bullet whistle, at last had a God-given opportunity to hear some. Several whizzed by his ears. The old man lost his temper and gave the major of the Okhotsk Infantry Regiment, guarding the compound, a thorough dressing down. The major, not knowing what to do, ran down to the river, on the other side of which the Turkish cavalrymen were wheeling their horses, and shook his finger at them. Seeing his gesture, the Turkish cavalry turned around and galloped off, followed by the whole detachment. The major who shook his finger at them was called Khorchevsky. I do not know what became of him later.

Nevertheless, the next day the Turks attacked the Hetairists. Afraid to use either grapeshot or ball, as they normally would, they decided to use cold steel. The battle was ruthless. Both sides fought chiefly with yataghans. On the Turkish side, however, some spears could be seen as well, though the Turks had not been known to use that weapon. They turned out to be Russian spears: Nekrasa's descendants* were fighting in the Turks' ranks. The Hetairists had our Emperor's permission to cross the Prut and seek asylum in our compound. They began to move across. Kantagoni and Safyanos were the last ones to stay on the Turkish side. Kirdzhali, who had been wounded the evening before, was already abed in the border station. Safyanos was killed. Kantagoni, a very fat man, was stabbed in the stomach by a spear. He raised his sabre with one hand, grasped the enemy's spear with the other and thrust it deeper into himself; in this way he was able to reach his murderer with his sabre, and the two of them fell together.

It was all over. The Turks were the victors. Moldavia was cleared of the Hetairists. About six hundred Albanian irregulars were scattered throughout Bessarabia; although they had no livelihood, they were nevertheless grateful to Russia for her protection. They led an idle but by no means reprobate existence. One could always see them in the coffeehouses of semi-Turkish Bessarabia, with their long-stemmed pipes in their mouths, sipping thick coffee from tiny cups. Their embroidered jackets and red pointed slippers were beginning to look worn, but their tufted skullcaps still sat on their heads aslant, and their yataghans and pistols still protruded from their wide belts. Nobody had any complaints against them. It was impossible even to think that these poor, peaceful people had been the most notorious brigands of Moldavia, comrades of the ferocious Kirdzhali, and that he himself was among them.

The pasha serving as governor of Jassy learnt of this fact and, citing the provisions of the peace treaty, demanded the extradition of the brigand.

The police began an investigation. They learnt that Kirdzhali was indeed in Kishinyov, and captured him at the house of a runaway monk one evening when he was eating his supper, sitting in the dark with seven comrades.

He was put under arrest. Without the slightest attempt to conceal the truth, he admitted he was Kirdzhali.

"But," he added, "since the time I crossed the Prut I have not touched a shred of anyone else's property, have not harmed the lowliest gypsy. To the Turks, the Moldavians and the Wallachians I am, of course, a brigand, but among the Russians I am a guest. When Safyanos, having used up all his grapeshot, came into the compound to take the buttons, nails, chains and yataghan pommels from the wounded to be used for the last ammunition, I gave him twenty *beşliks** and was left without any money. God is my witness that I, Kirdzhali, have been living on alms! Why, then, are the Russians handing me over to my enemies?"

From then on Kirdzhali kept silent and calmly awaited the resolution of his fate.

He did not have to wait long. The authorities, not obliged to regard brigands in their romantic aspect and convinced that the demand for extradition was just, gave orders to transport Kirdzhali to Jassy.

A man of intelligence and sensitivity – at that time an unknown young civil servant, today an important official* – gave me a vivid description of Kirdzhali's departure.

A post-*căruţă* stood by the prison gate... (Perhaps you do not know what a *căruţă** is. It is a low wicker-covered cart, to which even recently six or eight nags were usually harnessed. A mustachioed Moldavian, wearing a sheepskin hat, would sit astride one of them, constantly shouting and cracking his whip, and the little nags would run at quite a lively trot. If one of them began to lag behind, he would unharness it with horrible oaths and abandon it on the road, not caring what became of it. On his way back he would be sure to find it calmly grazing in a green pasture near the same place. It happened quite frequently that a traveller who had left one post station with eight horses would arrive at another with only a pair. Nowadays, in Russified Bessarabia, Russian styles of harness and Russian carts have taken over.)

Such a *căruţă* stood by the prison gate one day towards the end of September 1821.* Jewesses, nonchalantly flopping their slippers, Albanian irregulars in their tattered, colourful costumes and shapely Moldavian women with black-eyed babies in their arms surrounded the *căruţă*. The men were silent, the women eagerly waited for something to happen.

The gate opened and several police officers came into the street; two soldiers followed them, bringing Kirdzhali out in fetters.

He seemed to be about thirty years old. The features of his swarthy face were regular and stern. He was tall and broad-shouldered, and in general appeared to possess uncommon physical strength. A colourful turban sat obliquely on his head; a wide belt hugged his narrow waist; a dolman* of thick blue cloth, a shirt with ample folds that hung almost to his knees, and handsome slippers made up the rest of his costume. The expression on his face was dignified and calm.

One of the officials, a red-faced little old man in a faded uniform with only three buttons dangling on it, clamped his nickel-framed glasses onto the purple lump that passed as his nose, unfolded a document and began reading it in Moldavian with a nasal twang. From time to time he cast a haughty glance at the fettered Kirdzhali, to whom the document evidently referred. Kirdzhali listened attentively. The official finished his reading, folded the document, bellowed menacingly at the crowd, commanding it to make way, and ordered the *căruţă* to be brought up. At that point Kirdzhali turned to him and said a few words in Moldavian; his voice trembled and the expression on his face changed; he burst into tears and, clanking his chains, threw himself at the police official's feet. The official, frightened, jumped back; the soldiers were about to lift Kirdzhali up, but he rose to his feet himself, gathered up his shackles, stepped into the *căruţă*, and cried out, "Go!" A gendarme got in next to him, the Moldavian cracked his whip, and the *căruţă* rolled off.

"What was it Kirdzhali said to you?" the young civil servant asked the police official.

"He asked me, my dear sir," replied the official laughing, "if I would protect his wife and child, who live not far from Kilia in a Bulgarian settlement: he is afraid that they will suffer *because of him*. Stupid people, my dear sir."

The young civil servant's account moved me profoundly. I felt sorry for poor Kirdzhali. For some time I knew nothing about his subsequent fate. It was several years later that I met the young civil servant again. We started talking about the past.

"And what about your friend Kirdzhali?" I asked. "Do you know what has become of him?"

"I do indeed," he answered, and told me the following.

Brought to Jassy, Kirdzhali was delivered over to the pasha, who sentenced him to be impaled. The execution was postponed until some holiday. For the time being he was locked up in prison.

The captive was guarded by seven Turks (simple people, and brigands at heart, just like Kirdzhali); they respected him and listened to his marvellous stories with the characteristic eagerness of people of the East.

A close bond developed between guards and captive. One day Kirdzhali said to them, "Brothers! My hour is drawing close. No one can escape his fate. I shall soon part with you. I would like to leave you something to remember me by."

The Turks pricked up their ears.

"Brothers," continued Kirdzhali, "three years ago, when I was marauding with the late Mikhaylaki, we buried in the steppe, not far from Jassy, a pot full of *galbens*.* It is evident that neither of us is destined to make use of that pot. Since that can't be helped, you take it for yourselves and divide it up amicably."

The Turks practically went out of their minds. They began a discussion of how they could find the hidden place. After lengthy deliberation they resolved that Kirdzhali himself should lead them there.

Night fell. The Turks took the fetters off the captive's feet, tied his hands with a rope and decamped with him, heading for the steppe.

Kirdzhali led them, keeping to the same direction, from one burial mound to the next.* They walked for a long time. At last Kirdzhali stopped by a wide rock, measured off twenty paces to the south, stamped his foot, and said, "Here."

The Turks set about the task. Four of them drew out their yataghans and began digging. Three of them kept guard. Kirdzhali sat on the rock and watched their work.

"Well, and how much longer?" he kept asking. "Haven't you reached it yet?"

"Not yet," answered the Turks, and laboured so hard that sweat came pouring off them.

Kirdzhali began to show impatience.

"What dumb people," he said. "They don't even know how to dig properly. I would have finished the whole business in two minutes. Look here, lads! Untie my hands and give me a yataghan."

The Turks pondered and debated the matter.

"Why not?" they decided. "Let us untie his hands and give him a yataghan. What harm could there be? He is just one man, and

44

there are seven of us." And they untied his hands and gave him a yataghan.

Kirdzhali was at last free, and armed. What a feeling it must have been! He began to dig briskly, with the guards helping... Suddenly he stuck his yataghan into one of them, left the blade in his chest, and grabbed the two pistols from the man's belt.

The other six, seeing Kirdzhali armed with two pistols, ran away.

Nowadays Kirdzhali preys upon the environs of Jassy. Not long ago he wrote to the hospodar, demanding five thousand *lei* and threatening, if the payment were not forthcoming, to burn Jassy and lay his hands on the hospodar himself. The five thousand *lei* were delivered to him.

Kirdzhali – what a man!

Part Two

Unfinished Works
Published Posthumously

THE NEGRO OF PETER THE GREAT*

(1827–28)

> Russia transformed by Peter's iron will.
> — *Yazykov**

1

...I am in Paris;
I have begun to live, not just to breathe.
— Dmitriev, *Diary of a Traveller**

A MONG THE YOUNG PEOPLE whom Peter the Great sent to foreign lands to acquire the knowledge needed in the transformed Russian state, there was a Negro called Ibrahim, a godson of the Emperor.* He received his training at the Military Academy of Paris, graduated with the rank of captain of artillery, distinguished himself in the Spanish War* and returned to Paris severely wounded. The Emperor, engrossed though he was in his vast undertakings, never neglected to inquire after his favourite, and always received laudatory reports about his progress and conduct. Highly satisfied with him, Peter urged him several times to return to Russia, but Ibrahim was in no hurry to do so. He kept excusing himself under various pretexts such as his wound, his desire to complete his education, and his lack of money. Peter, for his part, acceded to the young man's wishes with indulgence, told him to take care of his health, and expressed his apprecia-tion for his industry, and – though always extremely careful about his own expenses – he liberally provided for his godson from the Treasury, adding fatherly advice and cautionary exhortation to the gold coins.

All historical records show that the frivolity, folly and luxury of the French of that time were unprecedented. No trace was left by then of the last years of Louis XIV's reign, which had been characterized by fastidious piety at Court and by a grave tone and decorum. The Duke of Orleans,* whose brilliant qualities were combined with faults of all kinds, did not possess, unfortu-nately, one modicum of hypocrisy. The orgies at the Palais Royal were no secret in Paris, and the example was contagious. Just then Law made his appearance on the scene;* greed for money was united with thirst for amusement and dissipation; fortunes went to ruin; morality perished; and the French laughed and calculated, while the state was falling apart to the playful tunes of satirical vaudevilles.

Society provided an entertaining spectacle. Education and the demand for amusement drew the different estates together. Wealth, good manners, fame, talent, even eccentricity – all attributes that excited curiosity or promised enjoyment – were accepted with equal indulgence. Literature, scholarship and philosophy emerged from quiet study rooms to appear in the midst of high society, both bowing to fashion and governing it. Women ruled, but no longer demanded adoration. Superficial courtesy took the place of profound respect. The pranks of the Duc de Richelieu – the Alcibiades* of a latter-day Athens – are a matter of historical record, providing an insight into the mores of the period.

> *Temps fortuné, marqué par la licence,*
> *Où la folie, agitant son grelot,*
> *D'un pied léger parcourt toute la France,*
> *Où nul mortel ne daigne être dévot,*
> *Où l'on fait tout excepté pénitence.**

As soon as Ibrahim arrived in Paris, his outward appearance, his education and native intelligence caught everyone's attention. All the ladies, wishing to see *le Nègre du czar* in their drawing rooms, vied with each other in trying to captivate him; the Regent invited him to his merry soirées more than once; he was present at dinner parties enlivened by the youth of Arouet, by the old age of Chaulieu, and by the conversation of Montesquieu and Fontenelle;* he did not miss one ball, one festivity, one premiere; in general, he threw himself into the whirl of social life with all the ardour of his youth and race. What daunted Ibrahim, however, was not just the thought of exchanging this libertinage, all these splendid amusements, for the austere simplicity of the Petersburg Court. Other, more powerful, bonds tied him to Paris. The young African was in love.

The Countess D., though not in the first bloom of youth, was still renowned for her beauty. At the age of seventeen, right after leaving the convent school, she was married to a man to whom she had not had time to grow attached, a fact that had not particularly worried him, then or later. Rumour ascribed lovers to her, but thanks to the lenient code of high society, she enjoyed a good name simply because she could never be accused of any ridiculous or scandalous escapades. Her house was among the most fashionable, attracting the best Parisian society. Ibrahim was introduced to her by the youthful Merville, generally regarded as her latest lover – a rumour that the young man made every effort to make people believe.

The Countess greeted Ibrahim politely but without fanfare, which flattered him. As a rule, people looked at the young black man as if he were some strange phenomenon – they surrounded him and showered him with salutations and questions. Their curiosity, though disguised as courtesy, offended his pride. The sweet attention of women, almost the sole aim of our efforts, not only did not gladden his heart, but filled it with downright bitterness and indignation. He felt that in their eyes he was a kind of rare animal, a peculiar and alien creature, that had been accidentally brought into a world that had nothing in common with it. He even envied people who attracted no one's attention, regarding their insignificance as a happy state.

The thought that, by nature, he was destined not to have his affections reciprocated saved him from presumptuousness and vanity, and this lent a rare charm to his conduct with women. His conversation was simple and demure, and it attracted the Countess D., who had grown tired of the endless jests and subtle insinuations of French wit. He became a frequent guest at her house. Little by little she grew accustomed to the young black's appearance and even began finding something attractive in that curly head, standing out with its blackness among the powdered wigs in her drawing room. (Ibrahim had been wounded in the head and was wearing a bandage instead of a wig.) He was twenty-seven years old, tall and well built; and quite a few beautiful young women glanced at him with feelings more flattering than mere curiosity, though he in his prejudice either did not notice anything or fancied only flirtation. When, however, his eyes met those of the Countess, his distrustfulness vanished. Her glance conveyed such good nature, her conduct with him was so simple and unaffected, that it was impossible to suspect in her even a shade of coquetry or mockery.

The idea of love had not crossed his mind, but to see the Countess daily was becoming a necessity for him. He sought her out everywhere, and meeting her seemed to him an unexpected favour from heaven each time. The Countess recognized his feelings before he did himself. Whatever you say, love without aspirations and demands touches the feminine heart more surely than all the wiles of seduction. When she was with Ibrahim, the Countess followed every movement he made and listened carefully to every word he said; in his absence she grew thoughtful and sank into her habitual distractedness. Merville was the first to notice this mutual inclination, and he congratulated Ibrahim. Nothing inflames love so much as the encouraging remarks of an outsider. Love is blind; distrustful of itself, it eagerly grasps any support. Merville's words awakened Ibrahim. Until then the idea that he might possess the woman he loved had not even occurred to him; now hope suddenly lit up his soul; he fell madly in love. The Countess, frightened by the violence of his passion, tried to counter with friendly exhortations and prudent admonitions, but all in vain; she herself was weakening. Incautiously granted favours followed one another in quick succession. And at last, carried away by the force of the passion she had herself inspired, overpowered by its momentum, she gave herself to the ecstatic Ibrahim…

Nothing can be hidden from society's watchful eyes. The Countess's new liaison soon became common knowledge. Some ladies were surprised by her choice, but many found it perfectly natural. Some laughed; others thought she had committed an unforgivable indiscretion. In the first transports of passion, Ibrahim and the Countess did not notice anything, but the double entendres of the men and the caustic remarks of the women soon began to catch their attention. Ibrahim's demure, cold manner had previously protected him from all offensive behaviour; now he suffered the attacks with impatience and did not know how to ward them off. The Countess, accustomed to the respect of society, could not resign herself to being the butt of gossip and jests. She would now complain to Ibrahim in tears, now reproach him bitterly, now beg him not to take up her defence lest some useless row bring about her complete ruin.

A new circumstance confounded her situation even further. The consequences of her imprudent love had become apparent. All consolations, counsel, suggestions, were considered, and all rejected. The Countess saw that her ruin was inevitable and waited for it in despair.

As soon as the Countess's condition became known, common talk started up with renewed vigour. Ladies of sensibility moaned with horror; men took bets on whether the Countess would give birth to a white or black baby. Epigrams proliferated at the expense of her husband – the only person in Paris who knew nothing and suspected nothing.

The fateful moment was approaching. The Countess's situation was terrible. Ibrahim came to see her every day. He watched her spiritual and physical strength gradually wane. Her tears and horror burst forth every minute. At last she felt the first pains. Measures were taken quickly. A pretext was found for sending the Count away. The physician arrived. A couple of days before, a destitute woman had been persuaded to give up her newborn son; now a trusted agent was sent to fetch him. Ibrahim waited in a study right next door to the bedroom where the unfortunate Countess lay. Hardly daring to breathe, he heard her muted groans, the whisperings of the maid and the doctor's commands. She was in labour for a long time. Every groan rent his heart, every silent interval submerged him in horror... Suddenly he heard the feeble cry of a child; unable to contain his joy, he rushed into the Countess's room. A black baby lay on the bed at her feet. Ibrahim went up to it. His heart throbbed violently. He blessed his son with a shaking hand. The Countess gave a faint smile and stretched her weary hand towards him but the doctor, anxious to protect the invalid from too much excitement, drew Ibrahim away from her bed. The newborn was placed in a covered basket and taken out of the house by a secret staircase. The other child was brought in, and its cradle placed in the young mother's bedroom. Ibrahim left somewhat reassured. The Count was expected. He returned late, learnt about his wife's successful delivery and was satisfied. Thus the public, which had anticipated an uproarious scandal, was frustrated in its expectations and had to content itself with mere vilifications.

Everything returned to normal, but Ibrahim felt that the course of his life would have to change, since his love affair might sooner or later come to Count D.'s knowledge. In such a case, whatever the circumstances might be, the ruin of the Countess would be inevitable. Ibrahim was passionately in love, and was loved with an equal passion, but the Countess was capricious and careless. It was not the first time she had been in love. Revulsion and hatred might replace the most tender feelings in her heart. Ibrahim imagined the moment she would grow cold toward him. He had not experienced the feeling of jealousy before, but now he had a terrifying presentiment of it, and he fancied that the torments of separation would probably be less painful. He contemplated breaking up his ill-fated liaison, leaving Paris and returning to Russia, where he was being summoned both by Peter and by his own vague sense of duty.

2

No more does beauty bring delight,
No more does gladness overwhelm me,
My mind is no more fancy-free,
My heart feels no more satisfaction.
Ambition goads me to distraction;
Fame's voice – I hear it calling me!

– Derzhavin*

DAYS, MONTHS WENT BY, but the enamoured Ibrahim could not bring himself to leave the woman he had seduced. The Countess became each day more and more attached to him. Their son was being brought up in a remote province. The gossip began to abate and the lovers enjoyed greater peace, silently remembering the storm that had passed and trying not to think of the future.

One day Ibrahim attended the levee of the Duke of Orleans. Passing by him, the Duke stopped and gave Ibrahim a letter, telling him to read it at leisure. It was a letter from Peter I. The Emperor, guessing the real reason for Ibrahim's extended stay abroad, wrote to the Duke that he did not wish to coerce his foster son in any way, leaving it to him to decide whether he wanted to return to Russia or not, but that he, the Emperor, would in no case leave him without support. This letter touched the very heartstrings of Ibrahim. From that moment his fate was sealed. The next day he informed the Regent of his intention to leave for Russia immediately.

"Think what you're doing," the Duke said to him. "Russia is not your native land; I doubt whether you'll ever have an opportunity to see your own sultry fatherland again, but your long sojourn in France has made you unfit for both the climate and the way of life of semi-barbarous Russia. You were not born a subject of Peter's. Listen to me: take advantage of his generous permission.

Stay in France, for which you have already shed your blood, and you can rest assured that here, too, your services and talents will earn their just rewards."

Ibrahim sincerely thanked the Duke, but remained firm in his decision.

"I'm sorry to see you go," said the Duke, "but, actually, you are right." He promised to release Ibrahim from the service, and reported the whole matter to the Russian Tsar.

Ibrahim was soon ready to leave. He spent the eve of his departure, as he spent most evenings, at the house of the Countess D. She was not aware of anything: Ibrahim had not had the heart to reveal his plans to her. She was calm and cheerful. She called him to her side several times and teased him about his pensive mood. After supper all the guests left. Only the Countess, her husband and Ibrahim remained in the drawing room. The unfortunate Ibrahim would have given anything in the world to be left alone with her, but Count D. seemed to be so serenely settled by the fireplace that there was no hope of getting rid of him. All three were silent.

"*Bonne nuit,*" said the Countess at last.

Ibrahim's heart sank as he suddenly apprehended the full horror of parting. He stood motionless.

"*Bonne nuit, messieurs,*" repeated the Countess.

He still did not move... At last his vision became blurred, his head began swimming, and he could barely walk out of the room. Having reached home, he wrote the following letter in an almost unconscious state:

I am leaving, my dear Léonore, abandoning you forever. I am writing to you because I have not the strength to explain myself to you otherwise.

My happiness could not last. I have enjoyed it in defiance of fate and nature. You were bound to cease loving me: the enchantment was bound to vanish. This thought always haunted me, even at those moments when it seemed I was oblivious to everything, when I lay at your feet intoxicated with your fervent self-sacrifice, with your boundless tenderness... Society, with its fickle ways, ruthlessly persecutes in practice what it permits in theory: its cold mockery would have sooner or later overpowered you, it would have humbled your soaring spirit, and you would in the end have grown ashamed of your passion... What would then have become of me? No! I'd sooner die, I'd sooner leave you, than wait for that terrible moment...

Your tranquillity is dearest of all to me, and you could not enjoy it while the gaze of society was fixed on us. Remember everything you have endured, all the humiliations, all the torments of fear; remember the terrifying birth of our son. Just think: should I subject you to the same worries and dangers even longer? Why struggle to unite the fate of such a tender and graceful creature with the unlucky lot of a Negro, a pitiful being, scarcely granted the title of man?

Farewell, Léonore, farewell, my cherished, my only friend. Abandoning you, I abandon the first and last happy moments of my life. I have neither fatherland nor family. I am leaving for gloomy Russia, where my only comfort will be my complete isolation. Hard work, to which I am going to devote myself from now on, will, if not stifle, at least divert agonizing recollections of those days of rapture and bliss... Farewell Léonore – I am tearing myself away from this letter as if from your arms; farewell, be happy – and think sometimes of the poor Negro, of your faithful Ibrahim.

The same night he left for Russia.

The journey did not turn out to be quite as grim as he had expected. His imagination prevailed over reality. The further behind he left Paris, the more vividly, the more immediately, he could recall the things that he had abandoned forever.

He was on the Russian border before he knew it. Autumn was setting in, but the drivers, despite the bad roads, carried him on with the speed of the wind, and on the morning of the seventeenth day of his journey he arrived in Krasnoye Selo, through which the main highway led in those days.

Only twenty-eight versts* were left from here to Petersburg. While the horses were being harnessed Ibrahim went into the post station. In the corner a tall man, in a green caftan and with a clay pipe in his mouth, was leaning with his elbows on the table, reading the Hamburg newspapers. Hearing somebody enter, he raised his head.

"Ha! Ibrahim?" he exclaimed, getting up from the bench. "Welcome, godson."

Ibrahim, recognizing Peter, was about to rush up to him with joy, but stopped respectfully. The Emperor came up to him, embraced him, and kissed him on the head.

"I was informed you'd soon be arriving," said Peter, "and I came out to meet you. I've been here waiting for you since yesterday." Ibrahim could not find words to express his gratitude. "Let your carriage follow behind us," continued the Emperor, "while you sit with me. Let's set out for home."

The Emperor's carriage was driven up; he and Ibrahim got in and they galloped off. They arrived in Petersburg in an hour and a half. Ibrahim looked with curiosity at the newborn capital that had risen from the swamp at the bidding of autocracy. Open dykes, canals without embankments and wooden bridges testified everywhere to the recent victory of human will over the resistance of the elements. The houses, it seemed, had been erected hastily. There was nothing impressive in the whole city except for the Neva, not yet adorned by a granite frame but already strewn with warships and merchantmen. The Emperor's carriage stopped by the palace in the so-called Tsaritsa's Garden. A woman, aged about thirty-five, attractive and dressed according to the latest Parisian fashion, met Peter on the portico. He kissed her on the lips and, taking Ibrahim by the hand, said:

"Have you recognized my godson, Katenka? Please welcome him and be kind to him as in the old days."

Yekaterina turned her dark, penetrating eyes on Ibrahim and amiably gave him her hand. Two beautiful young girls,* tall, graceful and fresh as roses, stood behind her and respectfully approached Peter.

"Liza," he said to one of them, "do you remember the little black boy who used to steal apples for you from my garden in Oranienbaum? Here he is: I present him to you."

The Grand Duchess laughed and blushed. They entered the dining room. The table had been laid in anticipation of the Emperor's arrival. Peter sat down to dinner with his family, inviting Ibrahim to join them. Over dinner he talked with Ibrahim about various topics, questioning him about the Spanish War, the internal affairs of France, and the Regent, whom he loved though in many ways disapproved of. Ibrahim had a remarkably precise and perceptive mind; Peter was highly satisfied with his answers; on his part, he remembered some details of Ibrahim's childhood and related them with such warmth and gaiety that nobody would have suspected this cordial, gracious host of having been the hero of Poltava, the mighty, dreaded reformer of Russia.

After dinner the Emperor, in keeping with Russian custom, retired to rest. Ibrahim was left with the Empress and the Grand Duchesses. He did his best to satisfy their curiosity, describing the Parisian way of life, the festivities held in the French capital and its capricious fashions. In the meanwhile some persons of the Emperor's immediate circle were gathering at the palace. Ibrahim recognized the illustrious Prince Menshikov who, seeing the black man conversing with Yekaterina, cast a haughty glance at him; Prince Yakov Dolgoruky, Peter's stern counsellor; the learned Bruce, who had the reputation of a Russian Faust among the people; the young Raguzinsky,* Ibrahim's one-time friend; and others who were either bringing reports to the Emperor or awaiting his instructions.

The Emperor reappeared in about two hours.

"Let's see whether you still remember how to carry out your former duty," he said to Ibrahim. "Take a slate and follow me." Peter locked the door of the lathe shop on the two of them and busied himself with state affairs. One by one he called in Bruce, Prince Dolgoruky and the chief of police, de Vière; and he dictated several decrees and resolutions to Ibrahim. The latter was astounded by his quick and firm grasp of problems, the power and versatility of his concentration and the diversity of his activities. When the work was done, Peter pulled out a pocket notebook to check if everything planned for the day had been accomplished. Then, as he was leaving the workshop, he said to Ibrahim, "It's getting late; you're tired, I suppose. Spend the night here as you used to. I'll wake you up in the morning."

Ibrahim, left by himself, could scarcely collect his thoughts. He was in Petersburg, he had once again met the great man in whose company, not yet comprehending his worth, he had spent his child-hood. He had to confess to himself, almost with a sense of guilt, that for the first time since their separation, the Countess D. had not been the sole preoccupation of his day. He could see that the new way of life that was awaiting him – the work and constant activity – would be able to revive his soul, fatigued by passions, idleness and an unacknowledged despondency. The thought of being closely associated with a great man and of shaping, together with him, the destiny of a great nation awoke in his heart, for the first time in his life, a noble sentiment of ambition. It was in this state of mind that he lay down on the camp bed prepared for him. His wonted dreams soon carried him to faraway Paris, into the arms of the dear Countess.

3

Just like the clouds on high,
the thoughts we have are ever changing shape.
What pleases us today, we loathe tomorrow.

– V. Kyukhelbeker*

T HE NEXT DAY Peter woke Ibrahim up as he had promised and congratulated him on his appointment as first lieutenant in the Preobrazhensky Regiment's artillery platoon, of which he himself was the captain. The courtiers surrounded Ibrahim, each trying in his own way to show esteem for the new favourite. The haughty Prince Menshikov shook his hand cordially. Sheremetev enquired after his Parisian acquaintances, and Golovin invited Ibrahim to dinner.* Others followed Golovin's example, so much so that Ibrahim received enough invitations to last him at least a month.

Ibrahim's days were unvaried but busy; consequently, he felt no boredom. With every day he became more and more attached to the Emperor, more able to comprehend his lofty mind. To follow the thoughts of a great man is a most engrossing intellectual occupation. Ibrahim saw Peter in the Senate, where Buturlin and Dolgoruky were disputing with him and where he grappled with important legislative matters; watched him in the Admiralty, where he was building Russia's naval might; observed him in the company of Feofan, Gavriil Buzhinsky and Kopievich,* and in his hours of leisure as he examined translations of foreign political writers or visited merchants' warehouses, craftsmen's workshops, scholars' studies. Russia seemed to Ibrahim like an enormous manufacturing plant, where only machines were in motion and where each worker, subject to an established order, was busy with his assignment. He too felt obliged to work at his bench, trying to think of the amusements of Parisian life with as little regret as he possibly could. It was more difficult to dismiss from his mind another, dear recollection: he often thought of the Countess D., imagined her just indignation, tears and despair... At times a dreadful thought took his breath away: the distractions of high society, a new liaison, another lucky man – he shuddered. Jealousy began to seethe in his African blood, and burning tears were ready to course down his black face.

One morning he was sitting surrounded by official papers in his study when he heard a loud greeting in French; turning around in excitement, he found himself in the embrace, accompanied by joyous exclamations, of the young Korsakov,* whom he had left behind in Paris, in the whirl of society life.

"I've only just arrived," said Korsakov, "and came directly to see you. All our Parisian acquaintances are missing you and send their regards; the Countess D. enjoined me to summon you to return without fail. Here is a letter from her."

Ibrahim grabbed the letter with a trembling hand and looked at the familiar handwriting on the envelope, not daring to believe his eyes.

"I'm glad to see that you have not yet died of boredom in this barbarous Petersburg," Korsakov continued. "What do people do here, how do they pass their time? Who is your tailor? Has at least an opera house been established?"

Ibrahim, lost in thought, answered that the Emperor was probably at work in the shipyard. Korsakov burst out laughing.

"I can see that your mind is elsewhere at the moment," he said. "We'll have a good talk later; right now I'll go and present myself to the Emperor." Having said this, he spun around on one heel and ran out of the room.

Left by himself, Ibrahim hastened to open the letter. The Countess tenderly complained, reproaching him for his dissemblance and distrust. "You say," she wrote, "that my tranquillity is dearest of all to you. Ibrahim! If that were true, could you have subjected me to the predicament to which the unexpected news of your departure reduced me? You were afraid that I would hold you back, but I assure you that, though I love you, I could have sacrificed my love for your well-being and for what you consider your obligation." She concluded the letter with passionate assurances of love and implored him at least to write to her occasionally, even if there was no hope for them ever to meet again.

Ibrahim reread this letter twenty times, kissing the precious lines in ecstasy. He burned with impatience to hear more about the Countess, and was just about ready to go to the Admiralty in the hope of finding Korsakov still there when the door opened and Korsakov himself reappeared: he had already presented himself to the Emperor and, as usual, seemed very satisfied with himself.

"*Entre nous*," he said to Ibrahim, "the Emperor is a peculiar man: just imagine, when I found him he was wearing some sort of sackcloth vest and was perched on the mast of a new ship, where I had to clamber after him with my dispatches. Standing on a rope ladder, I did not have enough room even to bow properly and became all confused, which had never happened to me before. But the Emperor, having read the papers I had brought, looked me over from head to foot and was, to all appearances, pleasantly surprised by the taste and refinement of my attire: at least he smiled and invited me to tonight's assembly. But I am a total stranger in Petersburg: during my six-year absence I have completely forgotten the local customs, and I'd like to ask you to please be my mentor, come with me and introduce me."

Ibrahim agreed and hastened to steer the conversation to a topic more interesting to himself. "Well, how is Countess D.?"

"The Countess? As you might expect, she was at first very much upset by your departure; but then, as you might expect, she gradually regained her equanimity and took a new lover. Do you know whom? That lanky Marquis of R. But what are you staring at me for with those Negro eyeballs of yours? Or does all this seem strange to you? Don't you know that lasting grief is not in the nature of a human being, especially of a woman? Think this over thoroughly while I go to take a rest after my journey, and don't forget to come and fetch me."

What sensations filled Ibrahim's heart? Jealousy? Rage? Despair? No; rather a deep, benumbed feeling of depression. He kept repeating to himself: I foresaw this; this had to happen. Then he opened the Countess's letter, read it once more, hung his head and burst into bitter tears. He wept for a long time. The tears eased his sorrow. Then, looking at his watch, he realized it was time to go. He would have been glad to excuse himself, but the assembly was an official function, and the Emperor rigidly insisted on the attendance of members of his close circle. Ibrahim got dressed and set out to fetch Korsakov.

Korsakov was sitting in his dressing gown, reading a French book. "So early?" he asked seeing Ibrahim.

"Mercy!" the latter responded. "It's already half-past five. We'll be late – get dressed quickly and let's go."

This threw Korsakov into a flurry, and he started ringing with all his might; his servants rushed in; he began dressing hastily. His French valet fetched his red-heeled shoes, his blue velvet breeches and his pink caftan embroidered with spangles; his wig, quickly powdered in the ante-room, was brought in, and he thrust his close-cropped small head into it; he asked for his sword and gloves, turned around before the mirror about ten times, and declared himself ready. The footman helped him and Ibrahim into their bearskin coats, and the two young men set out for the Winter Palace.

Korsakov showered Ibrahim with questions. Who was the most beautiful woman in Petersburg? Who had the reputation of being the best dancer? What dance was currently in vogue? Ibrahim satisfied his friend's curiosity grudgingly. Meanwhile they had arrived at the palace. A large number of long sleds, old coaches and gilded barouches stood in the field already. By the portico there was a large crowd of liveried and mustachioed coachmen, of mace-bearing footmen resplendent in tawdry finery and plumes, of hussars, pages and awkward-looking attendants in exotic uniforms laden down with their masters' fur coats and muffs – an indispensable retinue in the opinion of the boyars of that time. Ibrahim's arrival provoked a general murmur among them: "The Negro, the Negro, the Tsar's Negro!" He led Korsakov through this motley crowd of servants as fast as he could. A palace servant opened the doors wide for them, and they entered the hall. Korsakov was dumbfounded... In the large room, lit by tallow candles that burnt dimly in the clouds of tobacco smoke, droves of dignitaries with blue sashes across their shoulders, ambassadors, foreign merchants, officers of the Guards in green coats and shipmasters wearing short jackets with striped trousers were moving up and down to the incessant sound of a brass band. The ladies sat along the walls, the young ones glittering with all the finery of fashion. Gold and silver glistened on their robes; their slim waists rose from their luxuriant hooped skirts like flower stems; diamonds twinkled in their ears, in their long tresses and around their necks. They cheerfully glanced left and right, waiting for cavaliers and for the dance to begin. The elderly ladies' outfits represented shrewd attempts to combine the new mode of dress with the old styles that were now in disfavour: their headdresses were very like the Tsaritsa Natalya Kirilovna's sable hat,* and their gowns and mantles resembled sarafans and wadded jackets. They attended these newfangled spectacles with more bewilderment, it seemed, than pleasure, and looked askance at the wives and daughters of the Dutch skippers who sat in their calico skirts and red blouses, knitting socks, laughing and chatting amongst themselves as if they were at home. Korsakov could not regain his presence of mind. Noticing the newly arrived guests, a servant came up with beer and glasses on a tray.

"*Que diable est-ce que tout cela?*"* said Korsakov to Ibrahim under his breath. Ibrahim could not suppress a smile. The Empress and the Grand Duchesses, glittering with beauty and elegance, walked through the rows of guests, amicably conversing with them. The Emperor was in another room. Korsakov, wishing to show himself to him, had a hard time pushing his way through the constantly moving crowd. In that room sat mostly foreigners, solemnly smoking their clay pipes and emptying their earthenware mugs. Bottles of beer and wine, leather pouches with tobacco, glasses of rum punch and chessboards were placed on the tables. Peter sat at one of them, playing draughts with a broad-shouldered English skipper. The two of them kept zealously saluting each other with salvos of tobacco smoke, and the Emperor was so preoccupied with an unexpected move of his partner's that he did not notice Korsakov, much as he twisted and turned around them. At this moment a massive gentleman with a massive nosegay on his chest came bustling into the room, to announce in a thunderous voice that the dancing had commenced; then he was gone again, and many of the guests, among them Korsakov, followed after him.

Korsakov was struck by an unexpected sight. Along the whole length of the ballroom, resounding with peals of the most mournful music, ladies and cavaliers were ranged in two rows, facing one another; the cavaliers bowed low and the ladies curtsied, bending even lower, first straight ahead, then to the right, then to the left, then straight ahead again, to the right again, and so forth. Korsakov stared at this intriguing sport wide-eyed and bit his lip. The bowing and curtseying continued for about half an hour; when it stopped at last, the massive gentleman with the nosegay announced that the ceremonial dance was over, and ordered the musicians to play a minuet. Korsakov rejoiced and prepared to shine. One of the young ladies present attracted him particularly. She was about sixteen, dressed expensively but tastefully; she sat by an elderly man of dignified and stern appearance. Korsakov scampered up to her and asked her to do him the honour of dancing with him. The young beauty looked at him with embarrassment, not knowing, it seemed, what to say to him. The man sitting next to her knitted his brows, looking even more stern. Korsakov stood waiting for her answer, but the gentleman with the nosegay came up to him, led him into the centre of the ballroom, and said gravely: "My dear sir, you have committed a breach of etiquette: first you went up to this young person without the required triple obeisance; secondly, you took it upon yourself to select her, though in the minuet the right of choice belongs to the lady, not to the cavalier; for which reasons you are to be severely punished, namely you must drain the *goblet of the Great Eagle*."

Korsakov grew more and more astonished. The guests instantly surrounded him, loudly demanding the immediate execution of the sentence. Peter, hearing the laughter and shouts, and very fond of personally participating in such punishments, came out of the adjacent room. The crowd made way for him and he entered the circle where the marshal of the assembly stood facing the culprit with an enormous goblet filled with malmsey. He was vainly trying to persuade the condemned to submit to the law voluntarily.

"Aha!" said the Emperor, seeing Korsakov, "you've been caught, brother! Please be so good as to quaff it down, monsieur, and don't let me see you wince."

There was no way to escape. The poor fop drained the whole goblet in one gulp and handed it back to the marshal.

"Listen, Korsakov," Peter said to him, "the breeches you're wearing are made of velvet, of a kind even I don't wear, though I am much richer than you. This is extravagance; watch that I don't fall out with you."

Having listened to this censure, Korsakov wanted to leave the circle, but he lost his balance and almost fell down, to the indescribable joy of the Emperor and the whole merry company. This episode not only did not stop the company from enjoying the whole occasion together, but enlivened it further. The cavaliers began scraping and bowing, and the ladies curtseying and tapping their heels, with even greater zeal, no longer paying any attention to the rhythm of the music. Korsakov was unable to participate in the general merriment. The lady he had chosen went up to Ibrahim under orders from her father, Gavrila Afanasyevich, and, casting her blue eyes down, timidly gave him her hand. He danced a minuet with her and led her back to her seat; then he went to look for Korsakov, led him out of the ballroom, put him in a carriage and took him home. On the way home Korsakov began muttering inaudibly, "Accursed assembly! Accursed goblet of the Great Eagle!" but he soon fell into a deep slumber, unaware of how he arrived home and how he was undressed and put to bed; the next morning he woke up with a headache and could only vaguely remember the scraping and curtseying, the tobacco smoke, the gentleman with his nosegay, and the goblet of the Great Eagle.

4

Our forebears weren't such speedy eaters,
nor did the jugs and silver bowls
that held the wine and foaming ale
pass speedily along the tables.

– Ruslan and Lyudmila*

I MUST NOW ACQUAINT my gracious reader with Gavrila Afanasyevich Rzhevsky. Descendant of an ancient family of boyars, he possessed an enormous estate, was a generous host, loved falconry, and had numerous servants. In other words he was a true gentleman of the Russian soil; to use his own expression, he could not endure an alien spirit, and in his household he made every effort to preserve the cherished customs of olden times.

His daughter, Natalya Gavrilovna, was seventeen years old. She had been brought up in the old way – that is, surrounded by nurses and nannies, companions and maidservants. She knew how to do gold embroidery, but she was illiterate. On the other hand her father, despite his aversion to everything foreign, gave in to her desire to learn European dances from a captive Swedish officer who lived in their house. This worthy dance teacher was about fifty years old; his right leg had been shot through at Narva* and was not therefore quite up to minuets and courantes, but with his left leg he could execute even the most difficult steps with amazing skill and lightness. His pupil did honour to his efforts. She was renowned as the best dancer at the assemblies, which had indeed been one of the things that led Korsakov to his faux pas. The latter came to Gavrila Afanasyevich to offer his apologies the next day, but the easy manner and dandyish appearance of the young fop did not please the haughty boyar, who subsequently gave him the witty nickname of French monkey.

One festive day Gavrila Afanasyevich was expecting several relatives and friends. A long table was being laid in the ancient hall.

The guests arrived, accompanied by their wives and daughters, who had at last been freed from their domestic seclusion by the Emperor's decrees and personal example. Natalya Gavrilovna went up to each guest with a silver tray laden with gold cups, and the men emptied their cups, regretting that the kiss that used to accompany such occasions was no longer a custom. They sat down to table. In the place of honour, next to the master of the house, sat his father-in-law, Prince Boris Alexeyevich Lykov, a seventy-year-old boyar; the other guests sat according to the rank of their families, thereby evoking the happy old days of the order of precedence.* The men were seated on one side, the women on the other. At the end of the table were placed, as usual, the housekeeper in her old-fashioned headgear and bodice, a midget – a prim and wrinkled little darling of thirty – and the captive Swede in his time-worn blue uniform. The table, laden with a great number of dishes, was attended by numerous bustling domestics, among whom the butler was clearly distinguishable by his stern expression, large stomach and majestic immobility. During the first minutes of the dinner, attention was devoted exclusively to the products of our old-fashioned cuisine; only the clatter of the plates and assiduously labouring spoons disturbed the prevailing silence. At last the host, judging that it was time to divert his guests with pleasant conversation, turned around and asked, "And where is Yekimovna? Call her here."

Several servants were ready to dash off in different directions, but just at that moment an old woman with a powdered and rouged face, bedizened with flowers and trinkets and wearing a damask robe with deep décolletage, danced into the room humming a tune. Her appearance evoked general delight.

"Good day, Yekimovna," said Prince Lykov. "How are you doing?"

"Never felt better, my good friend: singing and dancing, bridegrooms enticing."

"What have you been up to, old goose?" asked the host.

"I've decked myself out, friend, for your dear guests, for the holy day, by the Tsar's command, by the boyars' demand, to give the world a laughing fit with my foreign outfit."

These words were greeted with loud laughter, and the jester took up her position behind her master's chair.

"The nonsense a fool talks will sometimes make sense," said Tatyana Afanasyevna, the master's elder sister, whom he sincerely respected. "Today's fashions really make the whole world laugh. Now that even you men have shaved off your beards and put on cut-off caftans, there is little to be said about women's rags; yet, I'll vow, one can't help missing the sarafan, the maiden's ribbon and the married woman's headdress. Look at today's beauties – you have to laugh and weep at once. The poor things' hair is all fluffed up like tow, greased and bespattered with French flour; their tummies are laced in so tight it's a wonder they don't break into two; and with their petticoats hitched on hoops, they have to get into carriages sideways, and lean over to get through a door. No way to stand, sit, or breathe. Veritable martyrs, the poor darlings."

"My dear Tatyana Afanasyevna," said Kirila Petrovich T., a former administrative official of Ryazan, who had in that capacity acquired by hook or crook three thousand serfs and a young wife, "in my opinion, let the wife dress as she will; I don't mind if she looks like a scarecrow or a Chinese emperor as long as she doesn't order new dresses every month, throwing away old ones that are still perfectly good. It used to be that the granddaughter was given her grandmother's sarafan in her trousseau, but look at the latest robes: you see them on the lady today, on her serving girl tomorrow. What can you do? It's simply ruining the Russian gentry. A disaster, no two ways about it." As he spoke these words, he looked with a sigh at his Marya Ilyinichna, who did not seem to be pleased either by his praise of the olden days or by his railing against the latest customs. The other beauties present shared her discontent but kept silent, because in those days modesty was considered an indispensable attribute of a young woman.

"And who is to blame?" asked Gavrila Afanasyevich, filling up his mug with frothy sour kvass. "Aren't we to blame ourselves? The young wenches are playing the fool, and we let them have their way."

"But what can we do if it's not our choice?" rejoined Kirila Petrovich. "There's many a husband would be glad to lock his wife in the women's quarters, but she's summoned to the assembly by drums and clarion. The husband grabs after the whip, the wife grabs after her frippery. Oh, these assemblies! The Lord has inflicted them on us as a punishment for our sins."

Marya Ilyinichna was on tenterhooks: she was itching to speak. Finally she could not bear it any longer and, turning to her husband, she asked him with an acid smile just what it was that he found wrong with the assemblies.

"I'll tell you what's wrong with them," answered her husband, flushed. "Since they've begun, husbands have been unable to cope with their wives. Wives have forgotten the Apostle's words, 'let the wife see that she reverence her husband';* their minds are on new dresses, not on the household – what they care about is catching the eyes of feather-brained officers, not pleasing their husbands. And is it becoming, my dear lady, for a Russian noblewoman to consort with alien pipe-smokers and their working women? Whoever heard of dancing into the night and parleying with young men? Not with relatives, mind you, but with strangers who haven't even been introduced."

"'I'd have a little say, but the wolf's on his way,'" said Gavrila Afanasyevich, frowning, "but I confess, the assembly is not to my taste either: it doesn't take long before you run into a drunkard or find yourself forced to drink till you become a public laughing stock. If you don't watch out, some scamp will start playing pranks at the expense of your daughter. Today's young generation's been so utterly spoilt it's beyond belief. Look at the son of the late Yevgraf Sergeyevich Korsakov, for instance: he created such a scandal with Natasha at the last assembly that it made me blush. The next day, I suddenly notice, somebody's driving straight into my courtyard. Who in the name of Heaven could this be, I say to myself; it isn't Prince Menshikov, is it? And who do you think it was? Ivan Yevgrafovich! Do you think he could have stopped at the gate and troubled himself to come up to the porch on foot? No, not he! And then? You should have seen how he flew into the house, bowed and scraped, and gibble-gabbled.

The fool Yekimovna can imitate him capitally; which reminds me: come, old goose, show us the monkey from overseas."

Yekimovna, the jester, seized the lid of a dish, put it under her arm as if holding a hat, and began making grimaces, bowing and scraping to all sides, and muttering words that resembled *monsieur, ma'mselle, assemblée, pardon*. Once more, general and prolonged laughter testified to the guests' delight.

"The spitting image of Korsakov, as like as two peas," said old Prince Lykov, wiping away the tears of laughter, as calm was gradually restored. "There's no concealing the fact: he's not the first, nor will he be the last, to come back a clown from those foreign lands to holy Russia. What do our children learn out there? To scrape with their feet and prattle in God knows what tongue, to treat their elders with disrespect and to dangle after other men's wives. Of all the young people educated abroad (God forgive me), the Tsar's Negro's the one that's most like a human being."

"Indeed so," remarked Gavrila Afanasyevich, "he is a solid, respectable man; you can't compare him with that good-for-nothing... But who is this now driving through the gate into the courtyard? It isn't that foreign monkey again, is it? What are you gawking here for, idiots?" he continued, addressing his servants. "Run and turn him away, and tell him that in the future, too—"

"Are you raving, greybeard?" the jester, Yekimovna, interrupted him. "Are you blind? It's the Imperial sled, the Tsar has come."

Gavrila Afanasyevich hastily rose from the table; everyone dashed to the windows and indeed beheld the Emperor, who was ascending the steps, leaning on his orderly's shoulder. There was a great commotion. The master of the house rushed to meet the Emperor; the servants ran in all directions as if bereft of reason; the guests were terrified, some of them even wondering how to slip away at the earliest opportunity. Then suddenly Peter's thunderous voice could be heard from the entrance hall; all fell silent, and the Tsar came in, accompanied by the master of the house, who was struck dumb with joy.

"Good day, ladies and gentlemen," said Peter with a cheerful expression on his face. They all bowed low. The Tsar glanced over the crowd quickly, seeking out the host's young daughter; he called her to him. She approached him quite boldly, though she blushed, not only to the ears but down to the shoulders.

"You're becoming prettier by the day," the Emperor said to her, kissing her, as was his habit, on the head. Then he turned to the guests: "Have I disturbed you, ladies and gentlemen? You were eating your dinner – please sit down again; and as for me, Gavrila Afanasyevich, would you offer me some aniseed vodka?"

The host dashed to the majestic-looking butler, snatched the tray from his hands, filled a gold goblet himself and proffered it to the Emperor with a bow. Peter, having downed his drink, ate a pretzel and asked the guests once more to continue their dinner. All resumed their former places, except for the midget and the housekeeper, who did not dare remain at a table honoured by the Tsar's presence. Peter sat down by the master of the house and asked for some cabbage soup. His orderly handed him a wooden spoon inlaid with ivory and a small knife and fork with green bone handles, for he never used anybody's cutlery except his own. The dinner party, which had been noisy and lively with good cheer and conversation only a minute before, now continued in silence and constraint. The host, overawed and overjoyed, ate nothing and the guests were all stiff, reverentially listening as the Emperor spoke in a foreign language with the captive Swede about the campaign of 1701. The jester, Yekimovna, to whom the Emperor put several questions, answered with a kind of timid coldness, which (I might say in passing) did not at all testify to innate stupidity. At last the dinner was over. The Emperor, and after him all the guests, rose to their feet.

"Gavrila Afanasyevich," he said, "I would like to have a private word with you." And, taking his host by the arm, Peter led him into the drawing room, locking the door behind them. The guests remained in the dining room, discussing the unexpected visit in a whisper; then, not wishing to appear intrusive, they soon began to leave one by one, without thanking their host for his hospitality. His father-in-law, daughter and sister saw the guests off quietly, and finally remained by themselves in the dinning room, waiting for the Emperor to emerge.

5

*I shall find a wife for thee,
or a miller I won't be.*

– Ablesimov, from the opera *The Miller**

I N HALF AN HOUR the door opened and Peter came out. He acknowledged the threefold bow of Prince Lykov, Tatyana Afanasyevna and Natasha with a solemn inclination of the head and went straight through to the entrance hall. The host helped him on with his red fur coat, accompanied him to his sled and on the porch thanked him once more for the honour. Peter left.

As he returned to the dining room, Gavrila Afanasyevich looked very worried. He curtly ordered the servants to clear the table fast, sent Natasha to her room and, informing his sister and father-in-law that he needed to talk to them, led them to the bedroom where he usually rested after dinner. The old Prince lay down on the oak bed and Tatyana Afanasyevna sat in an ancient damask-upholstered armchair with a little footstool under her feet. Gavrila Afanasyevich locked all the doors, sat on the bed at Prince Lykov's feet, and in a low tone began the conversation with the following words:

"It was not for nothing that the Emperor came to see me: guess what it was his pleasure to speak to me about?"

"How could we know, dear brother?" asked Tatyana Afanasyevna.

"Did the Tsar command you to govern a province?" asked the father-in-law. "It was high time. Or did he offer you an ambassadorship? Why not? After all, men of nobility, not only scribes, can sometimes be sent to foreign monarchs."

"No," answered the son-in-law, knitting his brow. "I am a man of the old school; our services are not needed these days, though it is quite reasonable to think that an Orthodox Russian nobleman is worth as much as today's upstarts, pancake peddlers and infidels – but that's another story."

"Then was he pleased to talk to you about for such a long time, brother?" asked Tatyana Afanasyevna. "You haven't come upon some adversity, have you? The Lord preserve us and have mercy on us!"

"Adversity or no adversity, I must confess it gave me a start."

"But what is it, brother? What is the matter?"

"It concerns Natasha: the Tsar came to arrange a marriage for her."

"Thank God," said Tatyana Afanasyevna, making the sign of the cross. "The girl is marriageable, and if the matchmaker is anything to judge by, the bridegroom cannot be unworthy either. God grant them love and good counsel; the honour is great. And for whom does the Tsar seek her hand?"

"Hum," grunted Gavrila Afanasyevich, "for whom? That's just it, for whom."

"Who is it then?" repeated Prince Lykov, who had been on the point of nodding off.

"Try to guess," said Gavrila Afanasyevich.

"My dear brother," responded the old lady, "how could we guess? There are many eligible men at court; any of them would be glad to take your Natasha. It's not Dolgoruky, is it?"

"No, not Dolgoruky."

"It's just as well; he's so terribly arrogant. It is Shein then, or Troyekurov?"

"No, neither the one nor the other."

"I'm not keen on them either: frivolous young men, too much imbued with the alien spirit. Well, is it Miloslavsky?"

"No, not he, either."

"Let him be: rich and stupid. Who then? Yeletsky? Lvov? Neither? It's not Raguzinsky, is it? For Heaven's sake, I'm at my wit's end. Who is it that the Tsar is asking Natasha's hand for?"

"The Negro, Ibrahim."

The old lady gasped and clasped her hands. Prince Lykov lifted his head from the pillows and repeated with amazement, "The Negro, Ibrahim!"

"Brother, my dearest," said the old lady in a tearful voice, "don't destroy the issue of your own flesh and blood, don't throw Natashenka into the clutches of that black devil."

"But how can I refuse the Emperor," objected Gavrila Afanasyevich, "when he is promising to reward me with his favour, both me and my whole family?"

"How now," exclaimed the old Prince, whose drowsiness had entirely disappeared, "to give Natasha, my granddaughter, in marriage to a bought Negro!"

"He is not of common birth," said Gavrila Afanasyevich. "He is the son of a black sultan. The Muslims captured him and sold him in Constantinople; our ambassador rescued him and gave him to the Tsar. His elder brother came to Russia with a sizable ransom and—"

"Gavrila Afanasyevich, dear brother," the old lady interrupted him, "we have heard the tales of Bova the King's Son and Yeruslan Lazarevich.* Tell us rather what you answered to the Emperor's proposal."

"I said that he ruled over us, and that it was our duty as his vassals to obey in all things."

At this moment a noise could be heard behind the door. Gavrila Afanasyevich went to open it but felt something obstructing it; he gave it a strong push, and when the door opened, they saw Natasha lying prostrate in a swoon on the blood-splattered floor.

When the Emperor had locked himself in with her father, her heart had sunk. Some premonition had whispered to her that the matter concerned her. When Gavrila Afanasyevich sent her off, declaring that he had to speak with her aunt and grandfather, she could not resist the promptings of feminine curiosity and quietly stole through the inner apartments to the door of the bedroom. She did not miss one word of the whole horrifying conversation; when she heard her father's last words, the poor thing lost consciousness, and as she fell, she hit her head against the iron-plated chest in which her trousseau was kept.

The servants came running; they lifted Natasha up, carried her to her room, and put her on the bed. After a while she came to and opened her eyes, but she could not recognize either her father or her aunt. A high fever developed. In her delirious state she kept talking about the Tsar's Negro and a wedding, and suddenly let out a piercing wail: "Valerian, dear Valerian, my treasure! Save me, here they come, here they come!" Tatyana Afanasyevna anxiously glanced at her brother, who blanched, bit his lip and left the room without a word. He returned to the old Prince who, unable to climb the stairs, had remained below.

"How is Natasha?" he asked.

"Unwell," answered the distressed father. "Worse than I thought: in her unconscious state she is raving about Valerian."

"Who is this Valerian?" asked the grandfather, alarmed. "Could it be that orphan, the musketeer's son, whom you took into your house?"

"The very same one," answered Gavrila Afanasyevich. "To my misfortune, his father saved my life at the time of the rebellion,* and the Devil put it into my head to take the accursed wolf cub into my house. Two years ago, when he voluntarily enlisted in a regiment, Natasha, saying goodbye to him, burst into tears, and he stood as if petrified. This seemed suspicious to me, and I discussed it with my sister. But since that time Natasha has not mentioned him, and nothing whatever has been heard of him. I thought she had forgotten him, but evidently she hasn't. This decides the matter: she's to marry the Negro."

Prince Lykov did not contradict him: it would have been in vain. The Prince returned home; Tatyana Afanasyevna remained at Natasha's bedside; Gavrila Afanasyevich, having sent for the physician, locked himself in his room, and the house grew silent and gloomy.

The unexpected marriage proposal surprised Ibrahim at least as much as it had Gavrila Afanasyevich. This is how it had happened. One time, as Peter was working with Ibrahim, he said to him, "I notice, brother, that you've grown a little listless. Tell me frankly, is there anything you want?"

Ibrahim assured the Emperor that he was happy with his situation and wished for nothing better.

"All right," said the Emperor, "if you feel melancholy for no reason, then I know how to cheer you up."

When they finished their work, he asked Ibrahim, "Did you like the girl with whom you danced the minuet at the last assembly?"

79

"She is charming girl, Your Majesty; and she struck me as a modest and good-natured one, too."

"In that case I'll see to it that you get to know her better. Would you like to marry her?"

"I, Your Majesty?"

"Listen, Ibrahim, you are a solitary man, without kith or kin, a stranger to everyone except me. If I should die today, what would become of you tomorrow, my poor Negro? You must get settled down while there is still time; you must find support in new connections, entering into alliance with the Russian gentry."

"Your Majesty, I am blessed with your highest protection and favour. God grant me that I may not survive my Tsar and benefactor: I ask for no more. But even if I were inclined to marry, would the young lady and her relatives consent? My appearance—"

"Your appearance! What nonsense! You're a fine young man in every way. A young girl must obey the wishes of her parents, and we'll see what old Gavrila Rzhevsky says when I come as your matchmaker." With these words, the Emperor sent for his sleigh and left Ibrahim plunged in profound thought.

"To marry!" mused the African. "And why not? Or am I destined to spend my life in solitude, never experiencing the greatest joys and most sacred obligations of a man, just because I was born below the fifteenth parallel?* I cannot hope to be loved, but that is a childish objection. Can one trust love in any case? Does it exist at all in the fickle heart of a woman? Having given up sweet libertinage forever, I have succumbed to other allurements, more significant ones. The Emperor is right: I must ensure my future. Marriage with the Rzhevsky girl will affiliate me with the proud Russian gentry, and I will no longer be a newcomer in my adopted fatherland. I will not demand love from my wife: I shall be content with her fidelity. As for her friendship, I will win it by unfailing tenderness, trust and indulgence."

Ibrahim wanted to get down to work as usual, but his mind wandered. He abandoned his papers and went for a stroll along the embankment of the Neva. Suddenly he heard Peter's voice; turning around he saw the Emperor, who had dismissed his sleigh and was coming after Ibrahim with a cheerful expression on his face.

"It's all accomplished, brother," he said, taking Ibrahim by the arm. "I've asked for her hand on your behalf. Tomorrow pay a visit to your father-in-law, but make sure to honour his boyar pride: leave your sleigh at his gate, go across the courtyard on foot, speak about the services he has rendered his country and about the prominence of his family, and he'll become devoted to you. And now," he continued, shaking his cudgel, "walk with me to that scoundrel Menshikov's house; I must talk to him about his latest pranks."

Ibrahim, having sincerely thanked Peter for his fatherly solicitude, saw him to the gate of Prince Menshikov's magnificent palace and returned home.

6

A SANCTUARY LAMP BURNED QUIETLY before the glass case holding the family's ancient icons in their glittering gold and silver frames. The lamp's flickering flame cast a faint light on the curtained bed and on the little table covered with labelled medicine bottles. A maidservant sat at a spinning wheel close to the stove; the light whirr of her spindle was the only sound that disturbed the silence of the bedroom.

"Who is here?" said a weak voice. The maid rose immediately, went to the bed and gently raised the curtain. "Will it soon be daylight?" asked Natalya.

"It's already noon," answered the maid.

"My God, why is it so dark then?"

"The windows are shuttered, miss."

"Bring me my clothes quickly."

"I can't, miss; it's against doctor's orders."

"Am I sick then? Since when?"

"It's been two weeks already."

"Has it? To me it seems as if I'd gone to bed only yesterday."

Natasha fell silent, trying to collect her scattered thoughts. Something had happened to her, but exactly what it was she could not remember. The maid still stood in front of her, waiting for her orders. At that moment an indistinct rumble could be heard from downstairs.

"What's that?" asked the sick girl.

"Their Honours have finished dinner," answered the maid. "They're getting up from table. Tatyana Afanasyevna will come up here now."

Natasha, it seemed, was pleased; she feebly moved her hand. The maid pulled the curtain to and sat down at her spinning wheel again.

In a few minutes a head wearing a broad white cap with dark ribbons appeared in the doorway and a subdued voice asked, "How's Natasha?"

"Hello, auntie," said the invalid softly, and Tatyana Afanasyevna hastened to her.

"The young mistress has revived," said the maid, cautiously drawing an armchair to the bed.

The old lady, with tears in her eyes, kissed her niece's pale, languid face and sat down by her. Soon after, the German physician in his black coat and scholar's wig entered the room, felt Natasha's pulse and announced, first in Latin and then in Russian, that the danger had passed. He asked for paper and ink, wrote out a new prescription and left. The old lady got up, kissed Natalya once more and went downstairs to tell Gavrila Afanasyevich the good news.

In the drawing room sat the Tsar's Negro, in uniform, with sword by his side and hat in his hand, respectfully conversing with Gavrila Afanasyevich. Korsakov, stretched out on a soft divan, was listening to them absent-mindedly while teasing a venerable wolfhound; when he had grown tired of that occupation, he went up to a mirror – his usual refuge from boredom – and in the mirror caught sight of Tatyana Afanasyevna, who was vainly trying to signal to her brother from the doorway.

"You're wanted, Gavrila Afanasyevich," said Korsakov, turning to his host and interrupting Ibrahim. Gavrila Afanasyevich promptly went to his sister and closed the door behind him.

"I marvel at your patience," said Korsakov to Ibrahim. "Not only do you listen a whole blessed hour to these ravings about the Rzhevskys' and Lykovs' ancient lineage, but you even add your own virtuous commentary! If I were you, *j'aurais planté là** the old prattler and his whole tribe, including Natalya Gavrilovna, who is putting on airs, pretending to be sick, *une petite santé...** Tell me honestly, can you be in love with this little *mijaurée*?* Listen, Ibrahim, take my advice just this once: honestly, I am wiser than I seem. Give up this freakish idea. Don't marry. It seems to me that your fiancée has no particular liking for you. Anything can happen in this world. For instance, it goes without saying that

I cannot complain about my looks; but I have had occasion to deceive husbands who were, I swear, no worse than I. And you yourself... Don't you remember our Parisian friend Count D.? One cannot rely on woman's fidelity; lucky the man who can contemplate the matter with indifference. But you? Should you, with your passionate, brooding and suspicious nature, with your flat nose and thick lips, and with that coarse wool on your head, throw yourself into all the danger of matrimony?"

"I thank you for the friendly advice," Ibrahim interrupted him coldly, "but you know the saying: it's not your chore to rock other people's babies."

"Take care, Ibrahim," answered Korsakov, laughing, "take care not to let it happen that you should illustrate this proverb in a literal sense."

Meanwhile, the conversation going on in the adjacent room was becoming heated.

"You're going to kill her," the old lady was saying. "She will not survive the sight of him."

"But think of it yourself," argued the obstinate brother. "He's been coming here as her bridegroom for two weeks, yet hasn't seen his bride once. After all, he may think that her illness is a mere fabrication, that we're only stalling for time in order to find some way to get rid of him. And what will the Tsar say? He has already sent inquiries about Natalya's health three times. Say what you like, I've no intention of quarrelling with him."

"The Lord be merciful," said Tatyana Afanasyevna, "what will the poor thing come to? Let me at least prepare her for the visit." To this Gavrila Afanasyevich agreed, and he returned to the drawing room.

"Thank God," he said to Ibrahim, "the danger has passed. Natalya is much better. If I weren't embarrassed to leave my dear guest, Ivan Yevgrafovich, all by himself, I would take you upstairs for a glimpse of your bride."

Korsakov rejoiced over the news and, assuring Gavrila Afanasyevich that he had to leave, asked him not to worry about him. He ran out into the entrance hall, giving his host no chance to see him off.

Meanwhile, Tatyana Afanasyevna hastened to prepare the invalid for the frightening guest's arrival. Entering the bedroom, she sat down, out of breath, by the bed and took Natasha's hand; but before she was able to utter a word, the door opened. Natasha asked who it was. The old lady, horror-stricken, lost her faculty of speech. Gavrila Afanasyevich drew the curtain aside, looked at the patient coldly, and asked how she was. She tried to smile at him, but she could not. Struck by her father's stern glance, she felt apprehensive. Presently it seemed to her that somebody was standing at the head of her bed. She raised her head with an effort and suddenly recognized the Tsar's Negro. This brought everything back to her mind, and all the horror of the future presented itself to her imagination. But her exhausted body did not register a visible shock. She let her head fall back on the pillow and closed her eyes... Her heart beat feebly. Tatyana Afanasyevna signalled to her brother that the patient wished to go to sleep, and everybody left the room quietly, except for the maidservant, who set to work again at her spinning wheel.

The unlucky beauty opened her eyes and, no longer seeing anyone by her bed, called the maid to her and sent her to fetch the midget. At that same moment, however, the rotund old elf was already rolling towards her bed like a ball. "Little Swallow" (as the midget was called) had run up the stairs behind Gavrila Afanasyevich and Ibrahim as fast as her short legs could carry her, and had hid behind the door, in keeping with the inquisitive nature of her sex. As soon as Natasha saw her, she sent the maid away, and the midget sat down on a little stool by the bed.

Never has such a small body contained such a lively spirit. She meddled in everything, knew everything, fussed about everything. Her shrewd mind and ingratiating manner earned her the love of her masters and the hatred of the rest of the household, over which she ruled despotically. Gavrila Afanasyevich listened to her denunciations, complaints and petty requests; Tatyana Afanasyevna perpetually asked for her opinion and took her advice; and Natasha had a boundless attachment to her, entrusting her with all her thoughts and all the stirrings of her sixteen-year-old heart.

"You know, Little Swallow," said Natalya, "Father is going to marry me to the Negro."

The midget sighed deeply and wrinkled up all the more her already wrinkled face.

"Is there no hope?" continued Natasha. "Is Father not going to take pity on me?"

The midget shook her little cap.

"Isn't Grandpa or Auntie going to intercede for me?"

"No, miss. While you've been sick the Negro has succeeded in charming them all. The master is devoted to him, the Prince raves about him and Tatyana Afanasyevna says, 'What a pity he's black; otherwise we couldn't wish for a better bridegroom.'"

"Oh my God, my God," groaned Natasha.

"Don't grieve, my beauty," said the midget, kissing Natalya's weak hand. "Even if you have to marry the Negro, you will have your freedom. Today it's not as it used to be: husbands don't lock their wives up. The Negro, they say, is rich; your house will be like a cup brimming over; you'll live in clover..."

"Poor Valerian," said Natasha so softly that the midget could guess more than hear her words.

"That's just it, miss," she said, confidentially lowering her voice. "If the musketeer's orphan weren't quite so much on your mind, you wouldn't rave about him in a fever, and your father wouldn't be angry."

"What?" said the frightened Natasha. "I raved about Valerian, Father heard me, Father is angry?"

"That's exactly the trouble," answered the midget. "After this, if you start asking him not to marry you to the Negro, he will think that the reason is Valerian. There is nothing to be done: you must submit to his paternal will and accept what fate brings you."

Natasha did not utter a single word in protest. The thought that her secret love was known to her father produced a powerful effect on her mind. Only one hope remained for her: to die before the hateful marriage came to pass. The idea comforted her. She submitted to her fate with a faint, sorrowful heart.

A T THE ENTRANCE to Gavrila Afanasyevich's house, to the right of the passageway, there was a tiny cubicle with one small window. In it stood a simple bed covered with a flannel blanket, and in front of the bed a little deal table, on which a tallow candle burned and some sheets of music lay open. A soldier's old blue coat and a three-cornered hat of the same age hung on the wall; above the hat, a print showing a mounted Charles XII* was fastened to the wall with three nails. Notes from a flute resounded through the humble dwelling. Its solitary inhabitant, the captive dance teacher in his nightcap and nankeen dressing gown, was enlivening the monotony of the winter evening by playing old Swedish marches, which reminded him of the gay time of his youth. Having devoted two hours to this exercise, he took his flute apart, put it away in a box, and started undressing.

Just then the latch on his door was lifted, and a tall handsome young man in uniform entered the room.

The Swede rose to his feet, surprised, before the unexpected visitor.

"You don't recognize me, Gustav Adamych," said the young visitor with feeling. "You don't remember the boy whom you drilled in Swedish musketry and with whom you almost started a fire in this same little room, shooting off a toy cannon."

Gustav Adamych looked at his visitor intently.

"Ah!" he cried at last, embracing him, "god dag to you, so are du here now? Sitt down, you old scamp, so shall ve speak."*

THE GUESTS WERE
ARRIVING AT THE DACHA...*

(1828–30)

T HE GUESTS WERE ARRIVING at the dacha of X. The drawing
room was filling up with ladies and men, all driving over at
the same time from the theatre, where they had just seen a new
Italian opera. Order was gradually established: the ladies settled
on the sofas, with the men forming circles around them; parties of
whist were set up; only a few young people remained standing. A
perusal of Parisian lithographs replaced the general conversation.

Two men sat on the balcony. One of them, a Spanish traveller,
seemed to be greatly charmed by the northern night. He looked
with admiration at the clear pale sky, at the majestic Neva, il-
luminated by mysterious light, and at the neighbouring dachas,
whose silhouettes showed in the transparent twilight.

"How splendid is your northern night," he said at last. "I shall
miss its charms even under the skies of my own country."

"One of our poets," answered the other man, "has compared it
with a tow-haired Russian beauty.* I must confess that a swarthy,
black-eyed Italian or Spanish woman, full of liveliness and south-
ern sensuality, captures my imagination far more. But of course
the old controversy between *la brune et la blonde* has not been
settled. Incidentally, do you know what explanation a foreign lady
offered me for the strictness and purity of Petersburg morals? She
declared that our winter nights were too cold and our summer
nights too bright for amorous adventures."

The Spaniard smiled. "So it is owing to the climate," he said,
"that Petersburg is the promised land of beauty, amicability and
purity."

"Beauty is a matter of taste," answered the Russian, "but as far
as amicability is concerned, we have little to boast about. It's not
in vogue: nobody has the least inclination to be amicable. Women
are afraid to be thought flirts, and men to lose their dignity. Eve-
ryone strives, with taste and decorum, to be nothing. As for the

purity of morals, one should not take advantage of a foreigner's trustfulness, so let me tell you an anecdote…"

With this the conversation took a most decidedly satirical turn.

Just then the door of the drawing room opened, and Volskaya came in. She was in the first bloom of youth. Her even features, her large black eyes, her lively movements, even her eccentric dress – everything compelled attention. The men greeted her with a certain jocular affability, and the women with marked hostility. Volskaya herself noticed none of this; while giving haphazard answers to the customary questions, she absently looked about her on every side. Her face, changeable as a cloud, expressed vexation. She sat down next to the stately Princess G. and, as the expression goes, *se mit à bouder.**

Suddenly she shuddered and turned towards the balcony. She got up, passed by the armchairs and tables, stopped for a moment behind the chair of old General R., and without acknowledging his subtle compliment, slipped out onto the balcony.

The Spaniard and the Russian rose to their feet. She walked up to them and said a few words in Russian with embarrassment. The Spaniard, assuming he was superfluous, left them and returned to the drawing room.

The stately Princess G. followed Volskaya with her eyes and said to her neighbour in a low tone, "This sort of thing is just not done."

"She's terribly frivolous," answered he.

"Frivolous? More than that. Her behaviour is inexcusable. She's free to have as little self-respect as she wishes, but society ought not to be treated with such disdain. Minsky should give her a hint."

"*Il n'en fera rien, trop heureux de pouvoir la compromettre.** For all that, I bet you their conversation is perfectly innocent."

"I'm convinced of that… But since when have you become so charitable?"

"I must confess I take an interest in the fate of that young woman. There's much more good and much less bad in her than people think. But passion will ruin her."

"Passion! What a big word! What is passion? You don't really imagine, do you, that she has an ardent heart and a romantic disposition? She's simply had a bad upbringing... What lithograph is that? Is it a portrait of Hussein Pasha?* Would you pass it to me?"

The guests were leaving; there was not one lady left in the drawing room. The hostess alone, with unconcealed displeasure, stood by the table at which two diplomats were finishing their last game of *écarté*. Volskaya, suddenly noticing that it was getting light, hastened to leave the balcony, where she had spent some three uninterrupted hours alone with Minsky. The hostess said goodbye to her coldly and did not so much as deign to look at Minsky. Several guests were waiting for their carriages at the entrance; Minsky helped Volskaya into hers.

"It looks like it's your turn," said a young officer to him.

"Not at all," he answered. "She is otherwise engaged; I'm simply her confidant or call it what you like. But I love her sincerely: she's excruciatingly funny."

Zinaida Volskaya had lost her mother before she was six. Her father, a busy and dissipated person, entrusted her to the care of a French governess, hired tutors of all kinds for her, and paid no further attention to her. By the age of fourteen she had grown beautiful and was writing love letters to her dance teacher. Her father learnt of this, dismissed the dance teacher and, considering her education completed, brought her out in society. Her appearance on the social scene created a great sensation. Volsky, a wealthy young man who usually let his feelings be governed by the opinions of others, fell head over heels in love with her: Adjutant General Y. had stated dogmatically at some court ball that Zinaida was the most beautiful woman in Petersburg and that the Sovereign had once met her on the English Embankment and talked with her a full hour. Volsky began to court her. Her father was glad to get the fashionable debutante off his hands. Zinaida burned with impatience to marry in order to be able to see the whole of Petersburg in her drawing room. Besides, Volsky was not repugnant to her, and thus her fate was soon sealed.

At first her spontaneity, unexpected pranks and childish frivolity made a favourable impression: even high society was grateful to her for breaking the decorous monotony of its aristocratic circles. They laughed at her antics and kept talking about her strange sallies. But years went by, and Zinaida still remained a fourteen-year-old at heart. People began to grumble. It was decided that Volskaya did not possess the sense of decency appropriate to her sex. The women began to avoid her, while the men drew closer to her. Zinaida comforted herself with the thought that she was none the worse off for it.

Rumour began to ascribe lovers to her. Calumny, even without proof, leaves almost indelible marks. According to the code of high society, plausibility equals verity, and to be the target of slander lowers us in our own estimation. Volskaya, shedding tears of indignation, resolved to rebel against the authority of unjust society. An opportunity soon presented itself.

Among the young men of her circle, Zinaida singled out Minsky. Evidently a certain similarity in character and circumstances must have drawn them to each other. In his early youth Minsky, too, had incurred society's disapprobation and was punished by slander. He left society, pretending to be indifferent. For a while passionate affairs muted the anguish of his wounded pride, but eventually, humbled by experience, he reappeared on the social scene, this time bringing with him not the ardency of his incautious youth, but the condescension and outward decorum of self-centredness. He did not like society, yet did not scorn it, knowing how important it was to secure its approbation. With all this said, it must be remarked that, though he respected society in general, he did not spare it in particular instances and was ready to make any of its members victims of his rancorous vanity. He liked Volskaya for daring to despise certain conventions that he hated. He goaded her on with encouragement and advice, assumed the role of her confidant, and soon became indispensable to her.

B. had appealed to her imagination for some time.

"He's too shallow for you," Minsky said to her. "All his ideas derive from *Les Liaisons dangereuses*,* and all his genius is filched from Jomini.* When you get to know him better, you'll grow to despise his oppressive immorality, just as military men despise his trivial pronouncements."

"I'd like to fall in love with R.," said Zinaida.

"Nonsense!" he answered. "What makes you want to get involved with a man who dyes his hair and repeats with rapture every five minutes, '*Quand j'étais à Florence*'.* They say his insufferable wife is in love with him. Leave them alone; they're made for each other."

"Well, how about Baron W.?"

"That's a little girl in an officer's uniform. What do you see in him? But you know what? Fall in love with L. He'll appeal to your imagination: he's just as exceptionally clever as he's exceptionally ugly. *Et puis c'est un homme à grands sentiments.** He'll be jealous and passionate; he'll torment you and amuse you: what more would you wish?"

But Volskaya did not take his advice. Minsky guessed in which direction her heart was inclining, and his vanity was flattered. Not suspecting that frivolity could be joined with fierce passions, he foresaw a liaison without any significant consequences, an augmentation by one more name of the list of his flighty mistresses, and he coolly contemplated his impending conquest. It is likely that if he had anticipated the storms awaiting him, he would have declined the victory, because a man of high society readily sacrifices his pleasures – and even his vanity – for convenience and seemliness.

FRAGMENT 2

Minsky was still in bed when a letter was brought to him. He broke the seal with a yawn and, shrugging his shoulders, unfolded two sheets covered to the last square inch with the minutest feminine handwriting. The letter began in the following way:

I wasn't able to express to you everything that was on my mind: in your presence I couldn't give form to the ideas that are now so vividly haunting me. Your sophisms don't allay my suspicions, but they silence me, which proves that you're invariably superior to me, but that is not enough for happiness, for the tranquillity of my heart...

Volskaya reproached him for his coldness, his distrust and the like; she complained and entreated, not knowing herself what about; showered on him a profusion of tender, affectionate assurances – and made an assignation to meet him in her box at the theatre that evening. Minsky answered her in a couple of lines, excusing his terseness on the plea of tedious but unavoidable business, and promising to come to the theatre without fail.

FRAGMENT 3

"You are so open and kind," said the Spaniard, "that I feel encouraged to ask you to solve a riddle for me. I have wandered all over the world, have been introduced at all the European courts and frequented high society everywhere; but nowhere have I felt as constrained and awkward as I do in your accursed aristocratic circles. Every time I enter Princess V.'s drawing room and see these speechless and motionless mummies, which bring to mind Egyptian burial grounds, I feel frozen to the bone. There's no one with any moral authority among them, nor has fame impressed anyone's name on my memory – why then do I feel so timid?"

"Because of an air of malice," answered the Russian. "It is an aspect of our culture. Among simple people it finds expression in a jeering disposition; among the higher circles, in coldness and inattention. Besides, our ladies receive a very superficial education, and nothing European ever captivates their minds. Of men there's nothing to say at all: politics and literature do not exist for them, and wit has been banned as a sign of levity. What can they all talk about? About themselves? No, they are too well-bred for that. What remains for them is a kind of domestic, petty, private conversation, comprehensible only to a few – to the select. And the person who does not belong to this small herd is received as an alien – not only if he is a foreigner, but even if he is Russian."

"Forgive me for all these questions," said the foreigner, "but I shall hardly find another opportunity to obtain satisfactory answers, and therefore I hasten to take advantage of you. You have mentioned your aristocracy: what does aristocracy mean in Russia? Studying your laws, I see that in your country there is no hereditary aristocracy founded on the indivisibility of landed property. There exists, it seems, a civil equality among your nobility, and access to its ranks is not limited. What, then, is your so-called aristocracy founded on? On ancient lineage alone?"

The Russian laughed. "You are mistaken," he answered. "The ancient Russian nobility, precisely for the reasons you have mentioned, has fallen into obscurity and has formed a kind of third estate. This noble underclass of ours, to which I myself belong, considers Ryurik and Monomakh its forefathers.* I can tell you, for instance," continued the Russian with an air of self-satisfied unconcern, "that the roots of my family reach back into the dark, distant past; you come across the names of my forefathers on every page of our history. Yet if it entered my head to call myself an aristocrat, many people would probably laugh. As for our actual aristocrats, they can scarcely name their grandfathers. The ancient families among them trace their lineage back to the reigns of Peter and Elizabeth. Orderlies, choristers, Ukrainians – those are the kind of forefathers they have. I am not saying this with disapproval: merit, after all, will always remain merit, and the interests of the state demand that it be rewarded. Only it is ridiculous to see in the insignificant grandsons of pastry vendors, orderlies, choristers and sextons a haughtiness befitting the Duke of Montmorency, first Christian baron, or Clermont-Tonnerre.* We are so pragmatic that we get down on our knees before the accident of the moment, before success, and before... well, in any case, no fascination with antiquity, no gratitude for past accomplishments, no respect for moral virtues exists among us. Karamzin* has recently narrated our history for us, but we hardly listened. We pride ourselves not on the glory of our forefathers, but on the rank of some uncle or other, or on the balls our cousin gives. A lack of respect for one's forefathers, mark my word, is a fundamental indication of barbarity and immorality."*

A NOVEL IN LETTERS*

(1829)

1. LIZA TO SASHA

Pavlovskoye village*

Dear Sashenka,

You must have been surprised at my unexpected departure for the country. I hasten to explain it all candidly. My dependent position has always been painful to me. It goes without saying that Avdotya Andreyevna brought me up as an equal with her niece. Yet in her house I always remained a ward: you cannot imagine how many petty grievances are attached to that title. I had to put up with a great deal, to yield in many things and close my eyes to others, while my vanity assiduously took note of the remotest hint of a slight. My very equality with the Princess was a burden to me. When we appeared at a ball in identical dresses, it annoyed me that she wore no pearls. I felt that the only reason why she had not put them on was that she didn't want to be different from me, and this very tactfulness offended me. Does she presume envy or any such childish meanness of spirit in me, I asked myself. The way men treated me, however polite they might have been, wounded my vanity every minute. The coldness of some and the affability of others both suggested a lack of respect for me. In short, I was an extremely unhappy creature, and my heart, though tender by nature, was becoming more and more hardened. Have you not noticed that all young girls who have the status of wards, distant relatives, *demoiselles de compagnie* and the like are usually either base sycophants or insufferable eccentrics? The latter I respect and exonerate with all my heart.

Exactly three weeks ago I received a letter from my poor grandmother. She complained of her lonely life and urged me to come and live with her in the country. I decided to take this opportunity. I had great difficulty in persuading Avdotya Andreyevna to let me go, and I had to promise to return to Petersburg for the winter; but I have no intention of keeping my word. Grandmama was overwhelmed with joy: she had not really thought I would come.

I cannot tell you how much I was moved by her tears. I have grown to love her with all my heart. At one time she belonged to the best society, and she has retained much of the courtesy of those days.

Now that I am living *at home*, I am the mistress of the house, and you will not believe what a heartfelt pleasure this is to me. I grew used to country life in next to no time, and the lack of luxury doesn't seem strange to me at all. Our property is truly charming. An ancient house on a hill, a garden, a lake and pine forests all around – all this is somewhat melancholy in the autumn and winter, but must seem like paradise on earth in the spring and summer. We have few neighbours, and so far I haven't seen anyone. I love solitude – just as it is sung in the elegies of your Lamartine.*

Write to me, my angel; your letters will bring great comfort to me. How are your social gatherings and our common acquaintances? Although I have become a recluse, I have not given up all the vanities of the world: news about it will be entertaining to me.

2. SASHA'S REPLY

*Krestovsky Island**

My dear Liza,

Just imagine how astonished I was when I heard about your removal to the country. Seeing Princess Olga by herself, I thought you were unwell, and I couldn't believe what she told me. Then, the next day, I get your letter. Congratulations, my angel, on your new way of life. I'm glad you like it. Your complaint about your previous situation moved me to tears, though it sounded unduly harsh. How can you compare yourself with wards and *demoiselles de compagnie*! Everybody knows that Olga's father was obligated to yours for everything he had, and that their friendship was as sacred as the closest family tie. It seemed that you were content with your lot. I would never have guessed that you were so oversensitive. Confess: isn't there another, secret reason for your hurried departure? I suspect... But you're being terribly discreet with me and I don't want to anger you with my conjectures from a distance.

What can I tell you about Petersburg? We are still at our dacha, but almost everybody else is already gone. The balls will start in a couple of weeks. The weather is wonderful. I walk a great deal. The other day we had some guests for dinner: one of them asked me if I had any news of you. He said that your absence is as noticeable at the balls as a broken string in a piano – and I completely agree with him. I keep hoping that this fit of misanthropy will not last long. Come back, my angel: otherwise I'll have nobody this winter with whom to share my simple-hearted observations and the epigrams born in my heart. Farewell, dear – give it some thought and change your mind.

3. LIZA TO SASHA

Your letter cheered me up no end. It reminded me of Petersburg so much; it seemed as if I were hearing your voice. How ridiculous are your perpetual speculations! You suspect in me some deep, arcane feelings, some unhappy love, don't you? Calm down, my dear, you're wrong: I resemble a heroine only in that I live in a remote village and pour cups of tea like Clarissa Harlowe.*

You say you won't have anybody this winter with whom to share your satirical observations. But what is our correspondence for? Write to me about anything that attracts your attention: I repeat I have not at all given up society, and everything connected with it interests me. As proof, let me ask you who the person was that found my absence so noticeable. Was it our warm-hearted chatterbox, Alexei R.? I am sure I've guessed right... My ears were always at his service, which was all he wanted.

I have become acquainted with the X. family. The father is a buffoon and a great host, the mother a fat, well-humoured matron, very fond of playing whist, and the daughter a slender melancholy girl of seventeen, brought up on novels in the fresh air. She is in the garden or in the fields with book in hand all day, surrounded by dogs from the farmyard, she speaks about the weather in a sing-song and offers you jam with affection. I found a whole bookcase full of old-fashioned novels in her room. I intend to read them all, and I have already begun with Richardson. Only if you live in the country do you get the opportunity to read the vaunted *Clarissa*. Crossing myself, I began with the translator's preface and, finding in it an assurance that though the first six parts were a bit on the dull side the last six would fully reward the reader's patience, I bravely set about the task.* I read the first, the second, the third volumes... at last I reach the sixth one: dull beyond endurance. Well, thought I, now I shall be rewarded for my pains. And what happened? I read about the deaths of Clarissa and Lovelace, and that was the end of it. Each volume contained two parts, and I did not notice the transition from the six boring to the six entertaining ones.

Reading Richardson led me to some reflections. What a frightful difference between the ideals of the grandmothers and those of the granddaughters! What is there in common between Lovelace and Adolphe?* Yet at the same time the role of women has not changed. Clarissa, except for some ceremonious curtseyings, is very like heroines in the latest novels. Is this because man's attractiveness depends on fashion, on attitudes of the moment, while that of women is based on an emotional make-up and natures that are enduring?

You see, I'm chattering on with you as usual. Please don't be any less generous in your epistolary conversations with me. Write to me as often as possible and as much as possible: you cannot imagine how much one looks forward in the country to the day the post comes. Looking forward to a ball cannot be compared with it.

4. SASHA'S REPLY

You are mistaken, my dear Liza. I declare, in order to humble your pride, that R. does not notice your absence at all. He has attached himself to Lady Pelham, an Englishwoman recently come for a visit. He never leaves her side. She responds to his remarks with a look of ingenuous surprise and with the little exclamation: "Oho!" He is in raptures. Let me tell you: the person who has been enquiring after you and is missing you with all sincerity is your faithful Vladimir Y. Are you satisfied? I imagine you are, and let me presume, in my usual way, that you didn't need my help to guess who it was. Joking aside, Y. is very much preoccupied with you. If I were you I'd draw him out as much as I could. Why not? He is a highly eligible young man... There is no reason why you shouldn't marry him: you would live on the English Embankment, throw parties on Saturday nights, and drive by to pick me up every morning. Stop being silly, my angel: come back and marry Y.

K. gave a ball the other day. There were swarms of people. The dancing went on until five in the morning. K.V. was dressed very simply: a white crepe dress, without even any lace trim, but on her head and around her neck half a million's worth of diamonds – that's all! Z. as usual was dressed in an excruciating fashion. Wherever does she get her outfits? She had, instead of flowers, some sort of dried mushrooms sewn on her dress. Did you by any chance send them to her from the country, my angel? Vladimir Y. did not dance. He is going on leave. The S.s came (probably the very first), sat through the night without dancing, and were the last to leave. The oldest of the girls, I fancied, had put on some rouge – it is high time too... The ball was a great success. The men were not satisfied with the supper, but then men always have to be dissatisfied with something. I had a very good time, even though I danced the cotillion with that insufferable diplomat, St., whose innate stupidity is reinforced by a blasé manner, imported from Madrid.

Thank you, sweetheart, for your report on Richardson. Now I have some notion about him. With my impatience I have little hope of ever reading him: I find superfluous pages even in Walter Scott.

That reminds me: Yelena N.'s romance with Count L. seems to be drawing to a conclusion; at least he looks so crestfallen and she is giving herself such airs that a wedding date appears to have been fixed. Farewell, my precious one, are you satisfied with my chatter today?

5. LIZA TO SASHA

No, my dear matchmaker, I am not about to leave the country and come back to attend my wedding. I admit frankly that I did like Vladimir Y., but it never entered my mind to marry him. He is an aristocrat, and I am a humble democrat. I hasten to explain and proudly remark, like a true heroine of a novel, that by lineage I belong to the most ancient Russian nobility, while my cavalier is the grandson of an unshorn millionaire. But you know what aristocracy means with us.* Be that as it may, Y. is certainly a man of good society and he may even like me, but he will never forgo a rich bride and an advantageous connection for my sake. If I ever marry, I'll choose a forty-year-old landowner right here. He will get involved in his sugar-refining plant, I in my household – and I'll be happy, even though I will not be dancing at the house of Count K. and will not be giving Saturday evening parties on the English Embankment.

Winter has arrived: in the country *c'est un événement*. It radically changes one's way of life. Solitary walks come to an end; bells are tinkling; hunters ride out with their dogs – everything becomes brighter and gayer with the first snow. I never expected it to be this way. Winter in the country used to frighten me. But everything on earth has its good side.

I have become better acquainted with Mashenka X. and have grown fond of her; she has many good qualities and much originality. I've learnt quite by accident that Y. is a close relation of theirs. Mashenka has not seen him for seven years but is enchanted with him. He once spent a summer with them, and Mashenka still cannot stop talking about all the details of what he did then. As I read her novels I come across his faintly pencilled marginalia: it is obvious that he was still a child back then. At this time he was struck by ideas and sentiments that he would of course laugh at now; but at least his remarks show a fresh, impressionable mind. I read a great deal. You can't imagine how strange it is to read in 1829 a novel that was written in 1775. It seems as if you suddenly stepped out of your drawing room into an ancient, damask-wainscoted hall, sat down in a satin-covered upholstered armchair, and saw around you old-fashioned costumes yet familiar faces, in which you recognized your uncles and grandmothers, grown young. Most of these novels have no other merit. The action is entertaining, and the plot skilfully tangled, but Bellecour stammers and Charlotte stutters.* A clever man could adopt these ready-made plots and characters, amend the style, eliminate the absurdities, supply the missing links – and the result would be a splendid, original novel. Pass this on to that ungrateful R. from me. It is time he stopped wasting his wits on conversations with English women. Embroidering new designs on old canvas, he should present us, in a small frame, with a picture of our society and people, which he knows so well.

Masha is well versed in Russian literature – generally, belles-lettres occupy people here more than in Petersburg. They receive the journals, take a lively interest in the squabbles therein, trust each side in turn, and become indignant on behalf of their favourite author if the critics tear him to pieces. Now I understand why Vyazemsky and Pushkin* are so fond of provincial misses: they are their true reading public. I myself thought I'd take a look at some journals, and started reading critical reviews in the *European Herald*, but the banality and boorish tone of these writings struck me as repulsive: it is ludicrous when a work of literature that we have all read – we, the touch-me-nots of Petersburg! – is being pompously accused of immorality and indecency by a former seminary student.*

6. LIZA TO SASHA

My dear, I cannot pretend any more; I need the help and advice of a friend. He from whom I have fled, whom I fear as the plague, Vladimir Y., is here. What am I to do? My head is swimming; I am at a loss; for Heaven's sake decide for me what I should do. Let me tell you all about it.

You noticed last winter how he would never leave my side. He did not visit us at home, but he and I saw each other everywhere. I armed myself with coldness, even with scornful looks, but all in vain: there was no way for me to get rid of him. At balls he always managed to find a place next to me; on our walks we always ran into him; and at the theatre his lorgnette was always directed at our box.

At first this appealed to my vanity. It is possible that I made that all too obvious to him. At least he fancied he had acquired new rights over me and kept speaking to me about his feelings, now voicing jealousy, now complaining... I asked myself with alarm what all this was leading to, and acknowledged with a sense of despair that he had power over my heart. I left Petersburg in order to prevent calamity while it was not too late. The decisive step I had taken and the conviction that I had done the right thing were beginning to calm my heart; I was already thinking of him with greater equanimity and less grief. Then, suddenly I see him!

Yes, I have seen him. Yesterday there was a name-day party at the X.s' house. I arrive just before dinner. As I come into the drawing room I find a whole crowd of guests; I see uhlan officers' uniforms; the ladies surround me; I exchange kisses with them all. Noticing nothing, I sit down next to the hostess and lift my eyes: Y. is right in front of me. I was stunned... He said a few words to me with such a look of tender, genuine joy that I could not gather enough strength to hide either my confusion or my pleasure.

We went into the dining room. He sat just across the table from me; I did not dare to look at him but noticed that everybody else's eyes were fixed on him. He was silent and distracted. At another time it would have very much amused me to see such a general desire to attract the attention of a newcomer – and officer of the Guards – such unease on the part of young ladies and such awkwardness in the men, roaring with laughter over their own jokes, and at the same time such cool politeness and total indifference on the part of the company... After dinner he came up to me. Feeling obliged to say something, I asked him rather unfelicitously whether some business had brought him to our part of the world.

"I've come on a business on which the happiness of my life depends," answered he in an undertone, moving away from me immediately. He sat down to play Boston with three old ladies (Grandmama among them); as for me, I went upstairs to Mashenka's room and lay on her bed until evening on the pretext of a headache. Indeed I felt worse than ill. Mashenka did not leave my side. She is enraptured with Y. He is going to stay with them a month or more. She will be spending all day with him. The truth of the matter is that she is in love with him – may Heaven grant that he, too, fall in love with her. She is slender and enigmatic – just the two traits that men want.

What am I to do, my dear? I shall not be able to avoid his relentless attentions here. He has already succeeded in charming Grandmama. He will be coming to see us – and the confessions, laments, vows will pour forth anew: *but to what end?* He will obtain my love, my confession; then he will consider the disadvantages of marrying me, will go away under some pretext, abandon me, and I... What a terrible prospect! For Heaven's sake, hold your hand out to me! I am sinking.

7. SASHA'S REPLY

Isn't it much better to have unburdened yourself with a full confession? You should have done it a long time ago, my angel! Why on earth did you not admit to me what I had already known, that Y. and you are in love? And what's the great misfortune about that? Enjoy it. You have a knack of looking at things from extraordinary angles. You're asking for misfortune: take care not to bring it on yourself. Why not marry Y.? Where do you see insurmountable obstacles? He's rich and you're poor – that's immaterial. He's rich enough for two: what else do you want? He is an aristocrat; but aren't you one also by both name and upbringing?

Some time ago I heard a discussion concerning ladies of the best society. R., as I learnt during the discussion, had once declared himself on the side of the aristocrats because they wore nicer shoes. Isn't it clear, if we follow his logic, that you are an aristocrat from top to toe?

Forgive me, my angel, but your pathetic letter made me laugh. Y. had arrived in the country in order to see you. What horror! You're at your wits' end, you ask for my advice. I fear you've really become a provincial heroine. My advice is this: hold the wedding at your wooden church as soon as possible, and move to Petersburg in order to take the part of Fornarina* in the tableaux vivants that are just being organized at the S.s' house. Your cavalier's gesture has touched me, I'm not joking. Of course, in the old days a lover went to fight in the Holy Land for three years in order to win a charitable smile, but in our day and age if a man travels five hundred versts from Petersburg in order to see the one who rules his heart it truly means a great deal. Y. deserves a reward.

8. VLADIMIR Y. TO A FRIEND

Do me a favour, spread the rumour that I am on my deathbed; I intend to extend my leave, but I want to do it observing propriety in every possible way. I've already been here in the country for two weeks, but I've scarcely noticed how time flies. I am taking a rest from my Petersburg life, which had really got on my nerves. Only the pupil of a convent school, just freed from her cell, or an eighteen-year-old gentleman of the Emperor's bedchamber can be forgiven for not loving the countryside. Petersburg is the entrance hall, Moscow is the maidservants' quarters, the village is our study room. A man of good breeding goes through the entrance hall by necessity and drops by the maids' quarters on occasion, but he sits in his study. And that's what I'll end up doing. I am going to retire from the service, get married and settle in my village near Saratov. The occupation of a landowner is also a service. To manage three thousand serfs, whose welfare depends entirely on us, is more important than to command a platoon or to copy diplomatic dispatches...

The state of neglect in which we leave our peasants is inexcusable. The more rights we have over them, the greater our obligations towards them. Yet we leave them to the mercy of some scoundrel of a steward, who oppresses them and robs us. We use up our future income in payment of debts; we ravage our property; old age catches us in need and worry.

This is the reason for the rapid decline of our nobility: the grandfather was rich, the son lives in want, the grandson goes a-begging. Ancient families come to insignificance; new ones rise, but in the third generation disappear again. Estates merge, and not one family is conscious of its ancestry. What does such political materialism lead to? I don't know. But it is time to put some obstacles in its path.

I have never been able to contemplate the degradation of our historic families without sorrow: nobody cherishes them in our country, not even those who belong to them. Indeed what pride of the past can you expect from a people whose national monument is inscribed with the words: "In memory of Citizen Minin and Prince Pozharsky"? * Which Prince Pozharsky? What does Citizen Minin signify? There was a privy councillor called Prince Dmitry Mikhaylovich Pozharsky, and a citizen named Kozma Minych Sukhoruky, elected representative of the state. But the fatherland has forgotten even the correct names of its liberators. The past does not exist for us. A wretched people!

No aristocracy based on service can replace a hereditary aristocracy. The gentry's family traditions should be the nation's historical heritage. But what family traditions are there for the children of a collegiate assessor?

When I speak out in favour of the aristocracy, I'm not trying – like the diplomat Severin, grandson of a tailor and a cook* – to pose as an English lord; my origin, though it is nothing to be ashamed of, gives me no right to do that. But I agree with La Bruyère's statement: "*Affecter le mépris de la naissance est un ridicule dans le parvenu et une lâcheté dans le gentilhomme.*"*

I've arrived at all this wisdom by living in someone else's village and watching petty landowners manage their estates. These gentlemen are not in the service, and they do manage their small villages, but I confess I wish they would go to ruin just like you and me. What barbarity! As far as they are concerned, Fonvizin's times have not yet passed. Prostakovs and Skotinins* are still flourishing among them.

This, by the way, does not refer to the relative I'm staying with. He is a very kind man, his wife a very kind woman, and their daughter a very kind little girl. You can see I've become very kind myself. In truth, since I've been living in the country I've grown exceedingly benign and forbearing – the effect of a patriarchal way of life and of the presence of Liza A. I had truly been missing her. I came to persuade her to return to Petersburg. Our first meeting was splendid. It was at my aunt's name-day party. The whole neighbourhood had assembled. Liza came too, and could hardly believe her eyes when she saw me… She couldn't in all honesty not realize that I had come here solely for her sake. At least I did my best to let her perceive it. My success here has surpassed all my expectations (which means a lot). The old ladies are enraptured with me, and the young ones run after me "because they're patriots".* The men are distinctly annoyed with my *fatuité indolente*,* which is still a novelty in these parts. They're all the more furious because I am exceedingly polite and proper: although they sense that I am insolent, they cannot quite say what that insolence consists of. Goodbye. What are our friends doing? *Servitor di tutti quanti*.* Write to me at the village of U.

9. THE FRIEND'S REPLY

I have carried out your commission. Last night I announced at the theatre that you had succumbed to a nervous fever and in all likelihood had already given up the ghost; so enjoy life until resurrected.

Your ethical reflections on the management of estates make me rejoice on your behalf. They are long overdue.

> *Un homme sans peur et sans reproche,*
> *Qui n'est ni roi, ni duc, ni comte aussi.**

The position of the Russian landowner, in my opinion, is most enviable.

Ranks in Russia are a necessity, if only for the sake of post stations where you cannot get a horse unless you have rank.*

*   *   *   *   *   *   *

Indulging in these weighty considerations I quite forgot that your mind is not on them just now: you are busy with your Liza. Whatever makes you imitate Monsieur Faublas* and get entangled with women all the time? It's not worthy of you. In this respect you are behind your times, behaving like one of those outdated husky guards officers from 1807. Right now this is only a shortcoming, but soon you'll become even more ridiculous than General G. Wouldn't you do better if you got used to the austerity of mature age in good time and voluntarily gave up your fading youth? I realize I am preaching in the wind, but that is my destiny.

All your friends send their greetings and are deeply upset by your untimely demise. Count among them your former mistress, too, just back from Rome and in love with the Pope. How very like her, and how very thrilled you must be to hear it! Won't you return in order to compete *cum servo servorum dei*?* That would be very like you. I shall expect your arrival any day.

10. VLADIMIR Y. TO HIS FRIEND

Your censures are totally unjust. Not I, but you have fallen behind your times, by a whole decade. Your grave metaphysical musings belong to the year 1818. At that time an austere code of behaviour and political economy were in vogue. We made our appearance at balls without taking our swords off; we were ashamed to dance, and had no time to devote to the ladies. I have the honour to report to you that all this has now changed. The French quadrille has replaced Adam Smith;* all flirt and make merry as best they can. I adapt to the spirit of the time; it is you who are hidebound, you outdated stereotype of a man. Aren't you tired of sitting all by yourself, glued to the bench of the opposition? I hope Z. will guide you in the right direction: I hereby entrust you to her Vatican-style coquetry. As for me, I have entirely abandoned myself to a patriarchal way of life: I go to bed at ten o'clock in the evening, ride out with local landowners, tracking down the game in the fresh snow, play Boston for copeck stakes with old ladies, and get upset if I lose. I see Liza every day, falling deeper and deeper in love with her. She's captivating in many ways. Her mien has something quiet, dignified, harmonious about it, showing the grace of the best Petersburg society, and yet there is in her a spontaneity, a capacity for tolerance and (as her grandmother puts it) a constitutional good humour. You never notice anything sharp or uncharitable in her judgements, and she doesn't scowl when faced with a new impression, like a child before taking rhubarb. She listens and understands – a rare virtue among our women. I have often been struck by a dullness of intellect or by an impurity of imagination in otherwise perfectly well-bred ladies. Frequently they will take the most subtle joke, the most poetic compliment, either for an impertinent epigram or for an indecent banality. On such occasions the frigid countenance they affect is so atrociously repulsive that even the most ardent love cannot survive it undamaged.

I experienced just this with Yelena N., with whom I was madly in love. When I addressed a tender phrase to her, she took it for an insult and complained to a girl friend about me. That incident dashed all my illusions about her. In addition to Liza, I have Mashenka X. here to amuse myself with. She is sweet. These girls, brought up by nannies and nature among apple trees and haystacks, are much more appealing than our stereotyped beauties, who cling to their mothers' opinions until their weddings and to those of their husbands ever after.

Farewell, my dear friend; what's new in society? Tell everybody that I have at last plunged into poetry. The other day I composed an inscription for Princess Olga's portrait (for which Liza scolded me very charmingly):

As stupid as the truth, as boring as perfection.

Or would this be better?

As boring as the truth, as stupid as perfection.

Both versions look as if there was some thought in them. Ask V. to furnish a rhyme for the next line and to consider me a poet from now on.

NOTES OF A YOUNG MAN*

(1829 / 1830)

I WAS COMMISSIONED AN OFFICER on 4th May 1825, and on the 6th received an order to join a regiment in the small town of Vasilkov.* On the 9th I left Petersburg.

Only a few days ago I was still a cadet; only a few days ago they were still waking me at six o'clock in the morning, and I was still learning my foreign-language lesson amid the unceasing noise of the military school. Now I am an ensign, I have 475 roubles in my satchel, I can do what I like, and am travelling at a gallop with relay horses to the small town of Vasilkov, where I shall sleep till eight and shall never utter a single foreign word again.

My ears are still ringing with the noise and shouts of cadets playing, and with the monotonous murmur of industrious students repeating the vocabulary lessons: *"le bluet, le bluet* – cornflower; *amarante* – amaranth – *amarante, amarante…"* Now the only noise disturbing the tranquil scene around me is the rumble of the cart and the tinkling of bells… I still can't get used to this silence…

The thought of my freedom, of the pleasures of the journey, and of the adventures awaiting me filled me at first with a sense of inexpressible joy, approaching ecstasy. Calming down somewhat, I began to observe the motion of the front wheels and made some mathematical calculations. This occupation gradually tired me out, and the journey no longer seemed as pleasant as it had at the beginning.

Arriving at a wayside station, I handed my order for fresh horses to the one-eyed superintendent, and demanded to be served as soon as possible. But to my indescribable annoyance, I was told that there were no horses available. I looked at the station register: an official of the sixth class, travelling from the city of X. to Petersburg, had taken twelve horses for himself and for an unidentified future companion; the wife of General B. had taken eight; two teams of three had gone off with the mail; and the remaining two horses had been put at the disposal of an ensign like your humble servant. Only the team reserved for courier duty stood in the yard, and the superintendent could not give me that one. If a courier or special emissary should unexpectedly gallop up and find no horses, what would happen to the superintendent? There would be a calamity: he might lose his position and have to go begging. I tried to bribe him, but he remained steadfast and resolutely rejected my twenty-copeck piece. There was nothing I could do. I resigned myself to the unavoidable.

"Would you like some tea or coffee?" the superintendent asked.

I thanked him and started looking at the pictures that adorned his humble dwelling. They depicted the parable of the Prodigal Son.* In the first one, a venerable old man, in nightcap and dressing gown, was bidding farewell to a restless youth who was hastily accepting his blessing and a bag of money. The second one depicted the corrupt young man's dissolute behaviour in vivid colours: he was seated at a table surrounded by false friends and shameless women. Further on, the ruined youth, in a French robe and with a three-cornered hat on his head, was tending swine and sharing their meal. Deep sorrow and repentance were reflected in his features; he was remembering his father's house, where *how many hired servants*, etc.* At last his return to his father's house was shown. The warm-hearted old man, in the same nightcap and dressing gown, was running forward to meet him. The Prodigal Son was kneeling; in the background, the cook was killing the fatted calf, and the elder brother was asking the servants with annoyance about the cause of all the rejoicing. Verses in a foreign language were printed under each picture. I read them with enjoyment and copied them in order to translate them in some future hour of leisure.

The other pictures have no frames and are affixed to the wall with small nails. They depict *The Cat's Burial*, *The Quarrel between Red Nose and Mighty Frost*, and the like – none deserving the attention of an educated man either from an ethical or from an artistic point of view.

I sat down by the window. There was nothing to look at: just a compact row of uniform cottages, one leaning against the other.

One or two apple trees here and there, and a couple of rowans, surrounded by a decrepit fence. And a cart without horses, with my suitcase and hamper in it.

The day was hot. The drivers had gone off in various directions. In the street little boys with golden heads and smeared faces were playing knucklebones. Across the street a forlorn old woman sat before a cottage. Cocks crowed occasionally. Dogs rolled around in the sun, or wandered about with tongues stuck out and tails hanging limp; piglets ran out from under a gate, squealing, and scurried off without any apparent cause.

What boredom! I went for a walk among the fields. A tumble-down well. A shallow puddle beside it. Little yellow ducklings gambolling in it under the eyes of a stupid-looking mother duck, like spoilt children left in charge of a governess.

I set out along the main highway: there was a field of scrubby winter corn on the right; brushwood and a swamp on the left. A flat expanse all around. Nothing but striped verst posts* ahead. A slow-moving sun in the sky; a cloud here and there. What boredom! Having gone to the third verst post and ascertained that it was twenty-two more versts to the next station, I turned back.

Returning to the station I tried to have a chat with my driver, but he, as though deliberately avoiding a decent conversation, would answer my questions only with phrases like "I couldn't tell, Your Honour", "God only knows", "that may be"...

I sat down by the widow once more and asked the fat serving woman, who was continually running by me on her way either to the back porch or to the storeroom, whether she could find something for me to read. She brought out a few books. Delighted, I opened them eagerly. But my joy vanished at once when I discovered a worn primer and an arithmetic book published for elementary schools. The superintendent's son, a nine-year-old little ruffian, used these books, as the woman said, "to study all the sciences", and he had stubbornly pulled out each page he had memorized, for which, in accordance with the law of natural retribution, he had had his hair pulled...

MY FATE IS SEALED: I AM GETTING MARRIED...*

(1830)

*Translated from the French**

M Y FATE IS SEALED: I am getting married...
She whom I have doted on for two whole years, whom my eyes have sought out first wherever I have been, and with whom a simple encounter has seemed like bliss – she is, by God, almost mine.

Waiting for a decisive answer has been one of the most painful experiences of my life. Watching for a long-expected card to turn up, suffering pangs of conscience, or sleeping before a duel are nothing compared with this experience.

Being rejected was not the only thing I was afraid of. One of my friends used to say, "I don't understand how anybody can propose if he knows for sure that there is no chance of rejection."

To get married – easy to say! Most people see in marriage no more than shawls bought on credit, a new carriage and a pink dressing gown.

Others expect a dowry and a settled life...

Still others marry just to be doing it – since everybody else is doing it, and since they have reached the age of thirty. If you ask them what matrimony means, they will answer you with a banal epigram.

For me, marrying means sacrificing my independence – my carefree, whimsical independence – my extravagant habits, aimless wanderings, solitude and inconstancy.

I am about to take upon myself two lives, though even the one I have had has not been complete. I have never chased after happiness – I could do without it. Now I need it for two: where am I to get it?

While I am still not married, what are my obligations? I have an ailing uncle,* whom I hardly ever see. If I come to visit him, he is pleased to see me; if I do not come, he excuses me: "The scapegrace is young, he has other things on his mind." I do

123

not correspond with anybody, and I pay my bills every month. I get up when I like in the morning and receive whom I like. If I feel like going out, I have my clever and tame jenny saddled, and ride down side streets, looking through windows of squat little houses; here a family is sitting around a samovar; there a servant is sweeping the rooms; behind still another window a little girl is learning to play the piano, with her drudge of a music teacher seated beside her. She turns her absent gaze on me, while her teacher scolds her; I slowly ride by... When I come back home, I sort out some books and papers, tidy up my dressing table, and dress either carelessly – if I am going visiting – or with painstaking care – if I am to dine at a restaurant, where I read a new novel or journals. If Walter Scott and Cooper* have written nothing new, and if no criminal case is reported in the papers, I order a bottle of champagne on ice, watch the glass frost over, and drink slowly, rejoicing over the fact that the dinner is costing me seventeen roubles and that I can afford such an extravagance. I go to the theatre and seek out in some box a striking attire and black eyes; we trade glances, and this keeps me busy until it is time to leave. I spend the evening either in noisy society, where the whole town is crowding together, where I see everyone and everything, and where nobody takes any notice of me; or else in a cherished circle of the select, where I speak about myself and where they listen to me. I return home late; I fall asleep reading a good book. The next day I ride around the side streets again, past the house where the little girl was playing the piano. She is repeating yesterday's lesson. She looks at me as at an acquaintance and laughs. My life as a bachelor!...

I was thinking: if I am rejected, I will go abroad – and I was already imagining myself on board a steamer. Everybody around me is bustling, saying goodbye, carrying suitcases, looking at the clock. The steamer sets off: fresh sea air blows in my face; I look at the receding shore for a long time: "My native land, adieu."* A young woman standing close to me is beginning to feel nauseated, which lends her pale face an expression of languid tenderness... She asks me to bring her some water. Thank God, I shall have something to do until we reach Kronstadt...

At that moment a note was handed to me: it was an answer to my letter. My fiancée's father was amiably asking me to come over... Without any doubt, my proposal had been accepted. Nadenka, my angel – she is mine!... All my melancholy doubts disappeared at that heavenly thought. I throw myself into my carriage and go at a gallop; here is their house; I enter the ante-room; the bustling reception given me by the servants already shows that I am betrothed. This embarrasses me: these people see into my heart and talk about my love in their lowly tongue!

Her father and mother were sitting in the drawing room. The former met me with open arms. He drew a handkerchief from his pocket and wanted to weep but could not; he decided to blow his nose instead. Her mother's eyes were red. Nadenka was sent for: she came in pale and ill at ease. Her father went out and brought in the icons of Nicholas the Miracle-Worker and the Kazan Mother of God. We were blessed. Nadenka gave me her cold, unresponsive hand. Her mother started speaking about the dowry, and her father about a village in the Saratov Province: I was engaged.

And so, this is no longer the secret of two hearts. Today it is domestic news; tomorrow it will be broadcast through the streets.

In the same way a verse tale, conceived in solitude during the summer nights in the moonlight, is later sold at the bookstore and is criticized in the journals by fools.

*   *   *   *   *   *   *

Everybody is glad of my happiness, everybody is congratulating me, all have grown fond of me. Each is offering his services: one would let me have his house, another would lend me money, and a third one recommends a Bukhara merchant who sells shawls. There is even a person who worries about the size of my future family and is offering me twelve dozen pairs of gloves with the image of Mlle Sontag* on them.

Young people are beginning to stand on ceremony with me: they treat me with respect and no longer as a friend. The ladies, to my face, praise me for my choice, but behind my back they express their pity for my fiancée: "Poor thing! She's so young, so innocent, and he is such a wayward, unprincipled man..."

I must confess that all this is beginning to get on my nerves. I like the custom, prevalent in some ancient tribes, of the bridegroom secretly spiriting away his bride. The next day he could introduce her to the town tattlers as his wife. In our society, preparations for family happiness involve printed announcements, gifts known to the whole city, formal letters and visits – in other words, ostentation of all kinds...

A FRAGMENT*

(1830)

D ESPITE ALL THE GREAT ADVANTAGES enjoyed by versifiers (it must be admitted that apart from the privilege of using the accusative instead of the genitive case after a negative verb and one or two other acts of so-called poetic licence, we do not know of any particular advantages Russian versifiers could be said to enjoy) – however that may be, despite all their advantages these people are subject to a great deal of trouble and unpleasantness. There is no need to mention their usually low social prestige and poverty, which has become proverbial, or the envy and slander to which their own peers subject them if they attain fame, and the contempt and ridicule showered on them from all sides if their works are not liked; but I ask you what can be comparable to the misfortune none of them can avoid – I mean being judged by fools. Even this grief, however, great as it may be, is not the worst visited on them. The most bitter and intolerable bane of the poet is his title, his sobriquet, with which he is branded and of which he can never rid himself. The reading public look on him as though he were their property, and consider themselves entitled to hold him to account for the smallest step he takes. In their opinion, he was born for their pleasure and draws his breath solely in order to pick out rhymes. If his circumstances require him to spend some time in the country, when he returns the first person he runs into will ask him, "Have you brought with you something new for us?" If he visits the army in order to see friends and relatives, the public will inevitably demand that he writes an epic about the latest victory, and the journalists will get angry with him for making them wait for it too long.* If he is sunk in thought about his tangled finances, matrimonial intentions or the illness of someone close to his heart, this will immediately provoke the inane exclamation, accompanied by an inane smile, "No doubt you are composing something!" Should he fall in love, the lady of his heart will promptly buy an album and be ready to receive an elegy. If he visits his neighbour on business or simply in order to be diverted from his work, the neighbour will call in his young son, ordering him to recite *some* poetry, and the lad will treat the poet, in most doleful tones, to the latter's own verses with distortions. And these occasions are only what might be called his triumphs. What must the pains of his profession be like? I am not sure, but it seems to me that they must be easier to bear. At least, one of my young friends, a well-known poet, has confessed that all those salutations, enquiries, albums and little boys have irritated him so much that he has constantly had to be on his guard lest he make some rude response, and has had to tell himself repeatedly that these good people probably do not intend to exasperate him…

Although a poet, my friend was the simplest and most ordinary of people. When he felt that nonsense approach (which was what he called inspiration), he locked himself in his room and wrote lying in bed from morning till late night; he would dress hastily in order to dine at a restaurant, go out for about three hours, then, returning, get back into bed and write until the cocks crowed. This would last about two or three weeks, a month at the most, and occurred only once a year, always in the autumn. He assured me that he knew true happiness only at such times. The rest of the time he led his dissipated life, reading little, writing nothing, and perpetually hearing the inevitable question, "When will you present us with a new creation of your pen?" The esteemed public would have had to wait for long periods at a time before they received a new gift from my friend if it had not been for the booksellers, who paid fairly high prices for his poetry. Since he was always short of money, he published his words as he wrote them, and then had the pleasure of reading critical judgements of them in the press (as mentioned above), which he in his pithy parlance called "eavesdropping on the pothouse, to learn what the lackeys are saying about you".

My friend was descended from one of our ancient noble families, a matter on which he prided himself with all the simplicity of his heart. Three lines of a chronicle mentioning one of his forebears were as dear to him as three stars on the chest of an uncle are to a fashionable gentleman of the bedchamber. Although he was poor – as is most of our ancient nobility – he asserted, turning his nose up, that he would sooner not marry than take a wife who was not a direct descendant of the princely line of Ryurik. He even insisted he would take one of the Yeletsky princesses, whose fathers and brothers, as is well known, plough their own land nowadays and, meeting one another among the furrows, shake the mud off their ploughs with the words:

"Lord bless you, Prince Antip Kuzmich, how much has Your Princely Healthiness ploughed today?"

"I thank you, Prince Yerema Avdeyevich…"

Apart from this foible, which by the way we attribute to a wish to imitate Lord Byron, who also sold his poems very well, my friend was *un homme tout rond*, a perfectly rounded man as the French say, or a *homo quadratus*, a square person according to the Latin expression – that is, in plain Russian, a very decent man.

With very, very few exceptions, he did not like the company of his fellow men of letters. He thought they had too many pretensions, some to a sharp wit, others to a fiery imagination, still others to sensibility, melancholy, disillusionment, profundity, philanthropy, misanthropy, irony, and so on, and so forth. Some seemed to him tedious in their stupidity, others insufferable in tone, still others repulsive in their baseness or dangerous in their double line of business* – and all of them too vain, exclusively preoccupied with themselves and their own work. He preferred the company of women and of people belonging to high society, who, seeing him daily, no longer stood on ceremony with him and spared him conversations about literature as well as the famous question, "Have you written a new little something?"

We have expatiated on our friend for two reasons: first, because he is the only man of letters with whom we have had occasion to become closely acquainted, and second, because it was from him that we have heard the story herewith offered to the reader.

* * *

This fragment seems to have constituted a preface to a story that either has not been written or has been lost. We did not want to destroy it…

IN THE CORNER OF A SMALL SQUARE...*

(1830 OR 1831)

1

Votre cœur est l'éponge imbibée de fiel et de vinaigre.

– Correspondance inédite*

IN THE CORNER OF a small square, in front of a little wooden
house, there stood a carriage – an unusual phenomenon in this
remote area of the city. The driver lay asleep on the coach box,
while the postilion played snowballs with some serving boys.

A pale lady, no longer in the first bloom of youth but still beau-
tiful, dressed with great refinement, lay on a sofa strewn with
cushions, in a room appointed with taste and luxury. A young man
of about twenty-six sat in front of the fireplace, leafing through
an English novel.

The pale lady's black eyes, deep-set and blue-shadowed, were
fixed on the young man. It was getting dark and the fire was going
out, but he continued his reading. At last she said:

"Has anything happened, Valerian? You're angry today."

"I am," he answered, without raising his eyes from the page.

"With whom?"

"With Prince Goretsky. He's giving a ball today to which I'm
not invited."

"Did you very much want to attend his ball?"

"Not in the least. The Devil take him and his ball. But if he
invites the whole town, he must invite me too."

"Which Goretsky is this? Prince Yakov?"

"Not at all. Prince Yakov's been dead for a long time. It's his
brother, Prince Grigory, the well-known jackass."

"Who's his wife?"

"She's the daughter of that chorister, what's his name?"

"I haven't gone out for so long that I'm beginning to forget
who's who in your high society. In any case, do you so highly value
whatever attention Prince Grigory, a well-known scoundrel, pays

to you, and whatever favour his wife, the daughter of a chorister, bestows upon you?"

"Of course I do," answered the young man heatedly, tossing his book on the table. "I'm a man of aristocratic society and don't want to be slighted by any one of its members. What their lineage or morality may be is none of my business."

"Whom do you call aristocrats?"

"Those with whom the Countess Fuflygina shakes hands."

"And who's this Countess Fuflygina?"

"A stupid and insolent woman."

"Are you saying that being slighted by people whom you despise can upset you so much?" she asked after a brief silence. "Do confess, there must be some other reason."

"So that's what you're driving at: suspicions and jealousy, all over again! God be my witness, this is intolerable."

With these words he rose and picked up his hat.

"Are you leaving already?" the lady asked anxiously. "Don't you want to have dinner with me?"

"No, I've another engagement."

"Do have dinner with me," she resumed in an affectionate and timid voice. "I've had some champagne bought for the occasion."

"And what did you do that for? Do you think I'm some kind of Moscow gambler who can't do without champagne?"

"Last time you found fault with my wine and were cross because women don't know anything about wines. There's no way to please you."

"I'm not asking anybody to please me."

She made no answer. The young man immediately regretted the rudeness of his last words. He stepped up to her, took her hand, and said with tenderness:

"Zinaida, forgive me: I'm just not myself today; I'm angry with everybody for everything. At such times I should sit at home. Forgive me: don't be angry with me."

"I'm not angry, Valerian. But it hurts me to see how much you've changed lately. You come to visit me as if out of duty, not because your heart draws you here. You're bored with me. You don't talk, you don't know what to do, you just leaf through books and find fault with everything in order to quarrel with me and be able to go away. I'm not reproaching you: our feelings are not in our power, but I…"

Valerian was no longer listening to her. He was pulling at his glove which he had put on long before, and was impatiently looking out into the street. She fell silent with an air of restrained irritation. He squeezed her hand, uttered some meaningless words, and ran out of the room like a restless schoolboy from a classroom.

Zinaida went to the window and watched him waiting for his carriage, then climbing in and leaving. She stayed at the window for a long time, pressing her burning forehead against the icy pane. At length she said aloud:

"No, he doesn't love me!"

She rang for her maid, told her to light the lamp, and sat down at her desk.

2

*Vous écrivez vos lettres de 4 pages plus vite que je ne puis les lire.**

X. HAD SOON FOUND OUT that his wife was unfaithful. It threw him into great perplexity. He did not know what to do: it seemed to him that to pretend not to notice anything would be stupid; to laugh at this so very common misfortune would be despicable; to get angry in earnest would be too scandalous; and to complain with an air of deeply offended feeling would be too ridiculous. Fortunately, his wife came to his aid.

Having fallen in love with Volodsky, she conceived the kind of aversion to her spouse that is characteristic only of women and is understandable only to them. One day she walked into his study, locked the door behind her, and declared that she loved Volodsky, that she did not want to deceive and secretly dishonour her husband, and that she was resolved to divorce him. X. was alarmed by such candour and precipitousness. Giving him no time to collect himself, she removed herself from the English Embankment to Kolomna* that same day, and sent a brief note about it all to Volodsky, who had expected nothing of the kind...

He was thrown into despair. He had never meant to tie himself down with such bonds. He hated boredom, feared every obligation, and valued his egotistical independence above all else. But it was a *fait accompli*. Zinaida was left on his hands. He pretended to be grateful, but in fact he faced the pains of his liaison as if performing an official duty or getting down to the tedious task of checking his butler's monthly accounts... *

ROSLAVLEV*

(1831)

As I was reading *Roslavlev** I realized with astonishment that its plot is based on a real-life incident all too well known to me. At one time I was a close friend of the unfortunate woman whom Mr Zagoskin has made the heroine of his novel. He has drawn anew the attention of the public to a forgotten event, reawakening feelings of indignation that time had lulled and disturbing the tranquillity of a grave. I will undertake to defend her shade, and trust that the reader, bearing in mind the sincerity of my motives, will excuse the feebleness of my pen. I shall be compelled to speak quite a lot about myself, because my poor friend's fate was closely linked with mine for a prolonged period.

I was brought out in the winter season of 1811. I shall not go into the details of my first impressions. It is easy to imagine the feelings of a girl of sixteen who has just exchanged her school-room and teachers for an uninterrupted series of balls. Not yet a thinking person, I threw myself into the whirl of gaiety with all the liveliness of my years… This was a pity, because those times were worth observing.

Among the debutantes who were brought out with me that season, Princess N. was particularly notable. (Since Mr Zagoskin gave her the name Polina, I will call her the same.) She and I soon became friends as a result of the following circumstances.

My brother, a fine fellow of twenty-two, belonged to the smart set of the time; he was listed as an employee at the Ministry of Foreign Affairs but lived in Moscow, dancing and sowing his wild oats. He fell in love with Polina, and asked me to effect a closer friendship between her family and ours. My brother was the idol of our whole family, and he could make me do whatever he liked.

Having formed closer ties to Polina as a favour to my brother, I soon grew genuinely attached to her. There was much in her that seemed strange, but even more that was appealing. I was not yet able to understand her, but I already loved her. Unconsciously, I began to look at the world with her eyes and her thoughts.

Polina's father was a man who had rendered the state consider-able service – in other words, he rode around with a team of six horses and was decorated with a key and a star*– though actu-ally he was a frivolous and simple-minded fellow. Her mother, by contrast, was a sensible woman, distinguished by dignity and good judgement.

Polina was present at all the social functions; she was surrounded by admirers; everybody paid court to her. But she was bored, and boredom lent her an air of haughtiness and coldness. This suited her Grecian profile and dark eyebrows extremely well. I felt triumphant whenever my satirical observations brought a smile to those regular features frozen by boredom.

Polina read exceptionally large numbers of books, without at all discriminating. She kept the key to her father's library, which consisted of works by eighteenth-century authors. She was well versed in French literature from Montesquieu to the novels of Crébillon. She knew Rousseau* by heart. The library contained no Russian books, except the works of Sumarokov,* which Polina never opened. She told me she could hardly make out the Russian script; she evidently never read anything in Russian, not even the doggerel presented to her by Moscow versifiers.

Here I will allow myself a brief digression.* It has been, by God's mercy, some thirty years since they started scolding us poor Rus-sian women for not reading in Russian and allegedly not being able to express ourselves in our native tongue. (NB: It is unjust on the part of the author of *Yury Miloslavsky* to repeat these banal accusations. We have all read his novel, and if I am not mistaken, he is indebted to one of us for its French translation.)* The truth is that we would be glad to read in Russian, but our literature, as far as I know, goes back only as far as Lomonosov* and has until now been extremely limited in scope. It has, of course, presented us with some excellent poets, but you cannot expect all readers to have an exclusive taste for poetry. In prose, all we have is Karamzin's *History*.* It is true that the last two or three years have seen the appearance of the first two or three Russian novels; but look at France, England and Germany, where one remarkable book comes out after the other. We do not even see Russian translations; and if we do, well, say what you like, I still prefer the originals. Our journals are of interest only to our men of letters. We are forced to derive everything – both information and concepts – from foreign books, and therefore we also think in a foreign language (those of us that is, who do think and keep up with the ideas of humankind). Our best-known literati have admitted this much to me. Our writers' perpetual lamentations about our neglect of Russian books are like the complaints of the Russian tradeswomen who resent our buying our hats at Sichler's instead of contenting ourselves with the creations of milliners in Kostroma.* But let us return to our subject.

Recollections of society life, even of a historical epoch, are usually vague and insignificant. But the arrival of one lady visitor in Moscow did leave a deep impression on my mind. This visitor was Madame de Staël.* She arrived in the summer, when the majority of Moscow's inhabitants had already left for the country. Yet a great bustle of Russian hospitality arose; people went all out to entertain the famous foreigner. It goes without saying that there were dinner parties in her honour. Ladies and gentlemen gathered to gape at her, but most went away dissatisfied with her. All they saw in her was a fat woman of fifty, whose dress was inappropriate for her years. Her manners did not please; people found her speeches too long and her sleeves too short. Polina's father, who had met Madame de Staël in Paris, gave a dinner for her, convoking all our Moscow wits. It was at this dinner party that I met the author of *Corinne*. She sat in the place of honour, resting her elbows on the table, furling and unfurling a piece of paper between her lovely fingers. She seemed to be in low spirits; made several attempts at conversation, but could not warm to her theme. Our wits ate and drank their measure, appearing more satisfied with the Prince's fish soup than with Madame de Staël's conversation. The ladies looked all starched. Convinced of the insignificance of their thoughts and overawed by the presence of a European celebrity, the guests in general spoke very little. Polina was on tenterhooks all through dinner. The attention of the guests was divided between the sturgeon and Madame de Staël. All the while they were waiting for her to toss out a bon mot; at last a double entendre, and rather a daring one at that, escaped her lips. Everyone snatched it up, bursting out in laughter; a general murmur of amazement went round the table; the Prince was beside himself with rapture. I glanced at Polina. Her face was aflame, and tears appeared in her eyes. The guests rose from the table entirely reconciled to Madame de Staël: she had made a pun they could carry all over town at a gallop.

"What's the matter with you, *ma chère*?" I asked Polina. "Could that joke, admittedly a rather bold one, have embarrassed you to such a degree?"

"Oh, my dear," answered Polina, "I am in despair! How insignificant our high society must have seemed to this unusual woman! She is used to being surrounded by people who understand her, on whom a brilliant remark, a powerful sentiment, an inspired word are never lost; she is used to fascinating conversations in the most highly cultured circles. But here – my God! Not one thought, not one memorable word in the course of three hours! Dull faces, dull pomposity and nothing else! How bored she was! How weary she seemed! She realized what they needed, what these apes of civilization were capable of understanding, and she tossed them a pun. How they threw themselves on it! I burned with shame and was ready to burst into tears... But let her," continued Polina heatedly, "let her go away thinking of our aristocratic rabble what it deserves. At least she has seen our good-natured simple people and understands them. You heard what she said to that insufferable old buffoon who, trying to play up to a foreigner, started cracking jokes at the expense of Russian beards: 'People who were able to defend their beards* a hundred years ago will be able to defend their heads today.' How charming she is! How I love her! How I hate her persecutor!"*

I was not the only one to notice Polina's embarrassment. Another pair of penetrating eyes rested on her at that same moment: the dark eyes of Madame de Staël. I do not know what she thought was the matter, but after dinner she came over to my friend and engaged her in a long conversation. A few days later she sent her the following note:

*Ma chère enfant, je suis toute malade. Il serait bien aimable à vous de venir me ranimer. Tâchez de l'obtenir de Mme votre mère et veuillez lui présenter les respects de votre amie. de S.**

This note has survived in my safekeeping. Despite all my curiosity Polina never told me what further contact she had with Madame de Staël; but she certainly adored this distinguished woman, who was as kind-hearted as she was gifted.

How people love to slander! Just recently, I recounted all this at a highly respectable social gathering.

"It is quite possible," I was told, "that Madame de Staël was nothing but a spy for Napoleon, and Princess N. was supplying her with information she needed."

"For pity's sake," said I, "Madame de Staël, who had been hunted by Napoleon for ten years; the kind, noble Madame de Staël who had barely managed to escape under the Russian Emperor's protection; Madame de Staël the friend of Chateaubriand and Byron – would Madame de Staël become Napoleon's spy?"

"Quite, quite possible," rejoined the sharp-nosed Countess B. "Napoleon was such a devil, and Madame de Staël such a cunning creature."

At the time Madame de Staël visited Moscow everybody was talking about the impending war and, as far as I remember, talking rather light-heartedly. Aping French manners of the time of Louis XV was in fashion. Love of one's fatherland seemed like pedantry. The savants of the day glorified Napoleon with fanatical obsequiousness and jested over our defeats. Unfortunately, those who championed the fatherland were somewhat simple-minded; they were ridiculed rather amusingly, and had no influence. Their patriotism was limited to violent denunciations of the use of French in society, to a condemnation of foreign loan words, to fearful sallies against the Kuznetsky Bridge,* and the like. Young people spoke about everything Russian either with contempt or with indifference, and jokingly predicted that Russia would become another Confederation of the Rhine.* In other words, society was rather repugnant.

Suddenly we were staggered by the news of the invasion, and the Emperor's appeal. Moscow was shaken up. Count Rastopchin's folksy posters* appeared; fury gripped the masses. The high-society jesters grew humble; the ladies were frightened. The detractors of the French language and Kuznetsky Bridge were decisively taking the upper hand, and the drawing rooms became filled with patriots: some poured French tobacco out of the snuffboxes and started sniffing a Russian brand; others burned at least ten French brochures; still others renounced Château Lafite and took to drinking sour kvass. All swore to abstain from the French language; all started shouting about Pozharsky and Minin* and advocating a people's war, while at the same time getting ready to leave for their estates in the Saratov Province.*

Polina could not hide her contempt any more than she had been able to hide her indignation before. Such an expeditious change of tune and such cowardice made her lose patience. She deliberately spoke French on the boulevards and by the Presnya Ponds;* and over the dinner table, in the presence of servants, she deliberately disputed vainglorious patriotic claims, deliberately spoke of the large number of Napoleon's troops and of his military genius. Those present blanched, fearing a denunciation, and hastened to censure her for her devotion to the enemy of the fatherland. Polina smiled with contempt. "May God grant," she would say, "that all Russians should love their fatherland as I do."

She astonished me. I had always known her to be modest and quiet, and could not understand what made her so audacious.

"For goodness' sake," I said to her once, "why on earth should you meddle in matters that don't concern us? Let men fight and shout about politics; women don't go to war and have nothing to do with Bonaparte."

Her eyes flashed. "Shame on you," she said. "Don't women have fatherlands? Don't they have fathers, brothers and husbands? Is Russian blood alien to us? Or do you suppose we were born only to be whirled around in Scottish square dances and to sit at home embroidering little dogs on canvas? No, I know how much influence a woman can have on public opinion, or at least, if you please, on the heart of one man. I do not accept the humble position to which they try to relegate us. Consider Madame de Staël: Napoleon fought against her as he would fight an enemy force. And my uncle has the face to laugh at her when she is frightened of the approach of the French army! 'Be reassured, Madame: Napoleon is fighting against Russia, not against you…' Yes, indeed! If Uncle fell into the hands of the French, they would let him walk about the Palais Royal,* but if they caught Madame de Staël, she would die in a state prison. And how about Charlotte Corday? And our Mayoress Marfa? And Princess Dashkova?* In just what way am I inferior to them? Surely not in daring of spirit and resoluteness!"

I listened to Polina in amazement. I had never suspected so much ardour and so much ambition in her. But alas! Where did the extraordinary qualities of her soul and the masculine loftiness of her mind lead her? My favourite writer was correct to say: "*Il n'est de bonheur que dans les voies communes.*"*

The arrival of the Emperor increased the general agitation. At last patriotic fervour took possession of the best society too. Drawing rooms turned into debating chambers. Everywhere there was talk about patriotic contributions to the war effort. Young Count Mamonov's* immortal speech, pledging the whole of his fortune, was being recited. After that some mammas remarked that the Count was no longer such an attractive match, but *we* all idolized him. Polina raved about him.

"What are *you* pledging?" she once asked my brother.

"I have not yet come into possession of my estate," answered my rakish brother. "All I have is a debt of thirty thousand roubles; I will offer it as a sacrifice on the altar of the fatherland."

Polina lost her temper. "To some people," she said, "honour and fatherland are mere trifles. While their brothers are dying on the battlefields, they play the fool in drawing rooms. I wonder if any woman would sink so low as to allow such a buffoon to pretend to be in love with her."

My brother coloured. "You expect too much, Princess," he rejoined. "You demand that everyone see a Madame de Staël in you and declaim tirades to you from *Corinne*. You should realize that, just because a man jokes with a woman, he may not be inclined to jest when it comes to his fatherland or its enemies."

With these words he turned away. I thought they had quarrelled for ever, but I was wrong: my brother's insolence appealed to Polina. His noble outburst of indignation made her forgive him for his clumsy joke; and when she heard a week later that he had joined Mamonov's regiment, she herself asked me to bring about a reconciliation between them. My brother was in raptures. He asked for her hand immediately. She gave her consent, but postponed the wedding until after the war. The next day my brother set off for his regiment.

Napoleon was marching on Moscow; our troops were retreating; the city grew alarmed. Its citizens fled one after another. The Prince and Princess persuaded my mother to accompany them to their estate in X. Province.

We arrived at Y., a large agricultural settlement twenty versts from the provincial capital. We had lots of neighbours all around, mostly recent arrivals from Moscow. There were daily social gatherings: our life in the provincial town resembled city life. Letters from the front came almost every day; old ladies searched for a place called *bivouac* on the map and were angry when they could not find it. Polina devoted herself exclusively to politics, reading nothing but newspapers and Rastopchin's posters, and not opening a single book. Surrounded by people whose understanding was limited, and perpetually hearing preposterous conclusions and unfounded reports, she fell into a deep depression; a weariness took possession of her spirit. She despaired of the deliverance of her fatherland; it seemed to her that Russia was fast approaching final collapse; every report received deepened her despondence; and Count Rastopchin's police bulletins drove her out of her mind. Their jocular tone struck her as the height of indecency, and the measures he took as intolerable barbarity. She could not comprehend the strategy of that period, that strategy so utterly appalling, but whose bold execution was to save Russia and liberate Europe.* She spent hours on end with her elbow on the map of Russia, counting versts and tracing the rapid movement of troops. Strange notions would sometimes enter her mind. Once she informed me of her intention to abscond from town, present herself in the midst of the French army, find a means to get close to Napoleon, and kill him with her own hands. It was not difficult to convince her of the madness of such an undertaking. But the thought of Charlotte Corday haunted her mind for a long time.

Her father, as you already know, was a rather frivolous man, whose only concern in the country was to live as far as he possibly could in the Moscow style. He gave dinners, set up a *théâtre de société** that staged representations of French fables, and employed every other means to vary our entertainments. Some captive officers arrived in town. The Prince, glad to see new faces, persuaded the governor to quarter them in his house.

There were four of these prisoners of war – three of them rather insignificant people, fanatic champions of Napoleon and insufferable braggarts, who had, it must be admitted, paid for their boastfulness by honourable wounds. The fourth one was an exceptional, remarkable man.

He was twenty-six years old at the time. He came from a good family. He had a pleasant face and excellent manners. We singled him out at once. He received our kindness with dignified modesty. He spoke little, but his remarks were always sound. He found favour with Polina as the first person able to give her clear explanations of military manoeuvres and troop movements. He set her mind at ease, assuring her that the retreat of the Russian army was not a senseless flight, and that it worried the French as much as it embittered the Russians.

"And what about you?" Polina asked him. "Aren't you confident of your Emperor's invincibility?"

Sénicour (I will call him by the name given by Mr Zagoskin) thought for a while, then answered that in his situation it would be awkward for him to be frank. Polina persisted in demanding an answer. Sénicour eventually divulged his opinion that the French army's thrust into the heart of Russia could prove to be a dangerous move, and that the campaign of 1812 appeared to be over, though it had not produced any decisive results.

"Over?" retorted Polina. "Over, when Napoleon is still advancing and we are still retreating?"

"All the worse for us," answered Sénicour, and changed the subject.

Polina, who was tired of both the fearful predictions and the stupid braggadocio of our neighbours, avidly listened to these conclusions, based on knowledge and objectivity. From my brother I received letters that one could not make head or tail of. They were filled with jokes – some clever, others flat – with questions about Polina, with banal protestations of love, and the like. Reading them, Polina grew irritated and shrugged her shoulders.

"You must admit," she said, "your Alexei is the most trivial man. Even under the present circumstances, from the very fields of battle, he manages to write letters totally lacking in meaning. What sort of conversation will he have for me in the course of quiet family life?"

She was mistaken. My brother's letters were trivial, not because he himself was empty-headed, but because of a prejudice that, by the way, is most offensive to us: he supposed it incumbent on him, when addressing women, to adapt his language to their feeble understanding, and imagined that serious matters did not concern us. Such an opinion would be boorish anywhere in the world; in our country it is also stupid. There is no doubt that in Russia the women are better educated, read more and think more than the men, who are preoccupied with Heaven knows what.

News of the Battle of Borodino arrived. Everybody talked about it; everybody had his own most reliable information and his own list of the dead and wounded. My brother was not writing. We were extremely worried. At last one of those news-mongers arrived to inform us that he had been taken prisoner; to Polina, however, he whispered the news of his death.* Polina was deeply distressed. She was not in love with my brother and had often been annoyed with him, but at that moment she saw him as a martyr and a hero, and wept over him, hiding her grief from me. I caught her with tears in her eyes several times. This did not surprise me, since I knew how keenly she felt the plight of our suffering land. I did not suspect this additional cause of her grief.

One morning I was walking in the garden; Sénicour accompanied me, and we talked about Polina. I noticed how deeply he appreciated her unusual qualities, and what a strong impression her beauty had made on him. I hinted jokingly that his situation was most romantic. Captured by the enemy, the wounded knight falls in love with the castle's noble proprietress, touches her heart and eventually wins her hand.

"No," said Sénicour, "the Princess sees in me an enemy of Russia, and will never consent to leaving her fatherland."

At that moment Polina appeared at the end of the avenue, and we went to meet her. She approached us with hasty steps. I was struck by her paleness.

"Moscow has been taken," she said to me without acknowledging Sénicour's bow. My heart sank, and tears started streaming from my eyes. Sénicour kept silent, casting his eyes down.

"The noble, enlightened French," she continued in a voice trembling with indignation, "have celebrated their triumph in a befitting manner. They have set Moscow on fire. Moscow has been burning the last two days."

"What are you saying?" cried Sénicour. "That is impossible."

"Wait until night," she answered drily, "and you may be able to see the glow."

"My God! He is done for," said Sénicour. "How can you fail to see that the burning of Moscow means the destruction of the whole French army, that Napoleon will have nothing to hold on to, nothing to sustain his troops with, and will be compelled to retreat as fast as he can across a ravaged wasteland with a disorganized and disaffected army under the threat of approaching winter? How could you believe that the French would have dug their own grave? No, no, it was the Russians; the Russians set Moscow on fire! What horrifying, barbarous prodigality! Now it's all decided: your country is out of danger. But what will become of us, and what will happen to our Emperor?"

He left us. Polina and I could not recover our senses.

"Could he," she said, "could Sénicour be right? Could the burning of Moscow be the work of our own hand? If that is so... Oh, then I can feel proud to be a Russian woman! The whole world will marvel at such tremendous sacrifice! Now even our ruin cannot daunt me, since our honour has been saved: never again will Europe dare fight against our people who hack their own hands off and set their own capital on fire."

Her eyes flashed and her voice had a metallic ring to it. I embraced her; we blended our tears of noble exaltation and fervent prayers for the fatherland.

"You don't know," said Polina with an inspired look on her face, "but your brother... he is happy, he is not a prisoner of war. Be glad: he had died for the deliverance of Russia."

I cried out and fell into her arms unconscious...

A NOVEL AT A CAUCASIAN SPA*

(1831)

O N ONE OF THE FIRST DAYS of April 181– there was a great commotion in the house of Katerina Petrovna Tomskaya. All the doors were wide open; the ante-room and the hall were piled high with trunks and suitcases; the drawers were pulled out of all the chests; the servants continually ran up and down the stairs; and the maids bustled and argued. The head of the household herself, a forty-five-year-old lady, sat in her bedroom, going over the accounts brought to her by her corpulent steward, who was now standing in front of her with his hands behind his back and with his right foot thrust forward. Katerina Petrovna pretended to be fully conversant with all the ins and outs of the management of her estate, but her questions and suggestions revealed the ignorance of a noblewoman about such affairs: they occasionally brought a barely perceptible smile to the steward's dignified face, though he nonetheless embarked in detail on all the required explanations with great indulgence. At this time a servant announced the arrival of Praskovya Ivanovna Povodova. Katerina Petrovna, glad to have an opportunity to interrupt her consultations, gave orders to have her guest shown in and dismissed her steward.

"Mercy on us, my dear," said an old lady, entering, "you're about to take the road! So where's God carrying you off to?"

"To the Caucasus, my dear Praskovya Ivanovna."

"To the Caucasus! So Moscow has really been saying the truth for the first time in my life, and I didn't believe it. To the Caucasus! But that's frightfully far. What can possess you to go tramping Heaven knows where and Heaven knows why?"

"What else am I to do? The doctors have advised that my daughter, Masha, needs the mineral waters, and that my health requires hot baths. I've been suffering for a year and a half; perchance the Caucasus will help."

"May God grant it. And how soon are you leaving?"

"In another four days or so; perhaps a week, no more. Everything is ready. My new carriage was delivered yesterday, and what a carriage! It's a toy, it's a beauty to behold; it's full of drawers and everything you could ask for: it has a bed, a dressing table, a provisions hamper, a medicine cabinet, a kitchen with crockery – do you want to see it?"

"Please, my dear."

Both ladies went out on the porch. The coachmen pulled the carriage out of the shed. Katerina Petrovna told them to open the doors; she got in and rummaged through everything, turning up all the cushions, pulling out all the drawers, revealing all the secrets and conveniences, letting up all the blinds, displaying all the mirrors, and turning all the pouches inside out – in other words, she acted very nimbly and energetically for a sick woman. Having admired the equipage, the two ladies returned to the drawing room, where they talked some more about the impending journey, about coming back to Moscow, and about plans for the following winter.

"I certainly hope to return in October," said Katerina Petrovna. "I shall be at home two evenings a week, and I hope, dear, that you will transfer your Boston parties to my house."

At this moment a girl of about eighteen, graceful and tall, with a beautiful pale complexion and fiery black eyes, entered the room quietly, kissed Katerina Petrovna's hand, and dropped a curtsey for Povodova.

"Did you sleep well, Masha?" asked Katerina Petrovna.

"Very well, mama; I've only just got up. You're probably surprised to hear about such laziness, Praskovya Ivanovna, but I can't help it. It's an invalid's privilege."

"Sleep, my dear, sleep, to your heart's content," Povodova replied. "But mind that you come back to me from the Caucasus rosy-cheeked and healthy, and, God willing, married."

"What do you mean, married?" rejoined Katerina Petrovna, laughing. "Whom should she marry in the Caucasus? A Circassian prince?"

"A Circassian! The Lord save her! All these Turks and Bukharans are infidels. They'd shave her head and lock her up."

"If God grant her good health," Katerina Petrovna said with a sigh, "suitors will be found. Masha, Heaven be thanked, is still young, and she has a dowry. And if a good man grows fond of her, he'll take her even without a dowry."

"It's still better to have a dowry," said Praskovya Ivanovna, getting up. "Let us say goodbye, Katerina Ivanovna; I shan't see you before September: it's too far for me to drag myself all the way here, from Basmannaya to Arbat, and I will not ask you to visit me – I know you're busy just now. And goodbye to you too, my beauty: don't forget my advice."

The ladies said farewell, and Praskovya Ivanovna left.

DUBROVSKY*

(1832–1833)

VOLUME ONE

1

A FEW YEARS BACK, there lived on one of his feudal estates a Russian landowner of the old type, Kirila Petrovich Troyekurov. Owing to his wealth, distinguished birth and connections, he carried great weight in the provinces where his estates lay. His neighbours were ready to indulge his slightest whim; provincial officials trembled at the mere mention of his name; he himself accepted all gestures of servility as his due. His house was always full of guests, willing to provide diversion for their lordly host's idle days and participating in his noisy, sometimes even riotous, amusements. No one dared to refuse an invitation from him or to fail to pay their respects at the manor house in Pokrovskoye on certain days. In his domestic circle Kirila Petrovich displayed all the vices of an uncultivated man. Spoilt by his surroundings, he was accustomed to give free rein to every impulse of his fiery nature and to every caprice of his rather limited mind. Despite his exceptionally strong constitution, he suffered from the effects of gluttony once or twice a week and was drunk every evening. In one wing of his house there lived sixteen housemaids, engaged in handicrafts appropriate to their sex. The windows in that wing were protected by wooden bars and the doors padlocked, with the keys in Kirila Petrovich's safe keeping. The young recluses came down into the garden at appointed hours to walk under the eyes of two old women. Every so often Kirila Petrovich married some of them off and new ones took their place. He was severe and arbitrary with his peasants and house serfs; yet they were proud of their master's wealth and reputation, and in their turn took many a liberty with their neighbours, trusting in their master's powerful protection.

Troyekurov usually spent his time riding about his extensive estates, feasting at length and playing pranks, newly invented by the day, whose victims as a rule were new acquaintances, though even old friends were not always spared – with the one exception of Andrei Gavrilovich Dubrovsky. The latter, a retired lieutenant of the Guards, was Troyekurov's nearest neighbour and the owner of seventy serfs. Troyekurov, haughty in his relations with people of the highest rank, treated Dubrovsky with respect despite the latter's humble circumstances. They had at one time been together in the service, and Troyekurov knew from experience how impetuous and determined his friend was. They had been separated by circumstances for a long time. Dubrovsky, with his property in disarray, had been forced to retire from the service and settle in his last remaining village. Having heard of this, Kirila Petrovich offered him his good offices, but Dubrovsky, though expressing his gratitude, preferred to remain poor and independent. A few years later Troyekurov, retiring with the rank of General-in-Chief, came to live on his estate; they met again and were delighted with each other. From that time on they became daily companions; and Kirila Petrovich, who had never in his life condescended to visit anyone else, frequently called unannounced at his old friend's humble abode. Of the same age, born of the same social class and educated the same way, they were to some extent similar in character and disposition. In certain respects, fate too had treated them similarly: both had married for love and soon lost their wives; and each was left with a child. Dubrovsky's son was being educated in Petersburg, while Kirila Petrovich's daughter was growing up under her father's eye. Kirila Petrovich often said to Dubrovsky, "Listen, brother Andrei Gavrilovich: if your Volodka grows into a sensible lad, I'll let him marry Masha; never mind if he's as poor as a plucked falcon."

Andrei Gavrilovich usually shook his head and answered, "No, Kirila Petrovich: my Volodka is no match for your Maria Kirilovna. A poor nobleman like him should marry a poor noblewoman and be the head of his household, rather than become the steward of a spoilt female."

Everybody envied the accord reigning between the haughty Troyekurov and his poor neighbour, and everybody marvelled at the latter's boldness when he unceremoniously announced his opinions at Kirila Petrovich's table, not caring whether they contradicted those of his host. Some attempted to imitate him, stepping outside the bounds of required subservience, but Kirila Petrovich put them in such fear that they lost for ever the desire for any such ventures; and thus Dubrovsky alone remained outside the general law. An unexpected occurrence unsettled and changed all this.

One time, early in the autumn, Kirila Petrovich was preparing to ride out for a hunt. On the eve of the occasion the kennelmen and grooms were given orders to be ready by five o'clock in the morning. A tent and a field kitchen were sent ahead to the place where Kirila Petrovich intended to dine. The host and his guests came out to the kennels, where over five hundred harriers and wolfhounds lived in comfort and contentment, lauding Kirila Petrovich's generosity in their canine tongue. The kennels included a hospital for dogs, supervised by the chief of the veterinary staff, Timoshka, and a maternity ward, where noble bitches whelped and suckled their puppies. Kirila Petrovich was proud of this fine establishment and never omitted an opportunity to show it off to his guests, each of whom had already inspected it at least twenty times. He walked about the kennels, surrounded by his guests and escorted by Timoshka and the chief kennelmen; he stopped in front of some of the kennels, now enquiring after the condition of the sick, now handing out reprimands, more or less strict and just, now calling to him some dogs by name and fondly talking to them. The guests considered it their duty to be enthusiastic about Kirila Petrovich's kennels. Dubrovsky alone kept silent, frowning. He was a passionate hunter; and since his circumstances allowed him to keep only two harriers and one team of wolfhounds, he could not help feeling a certain envy at the sight of this magnificent establishment.

"Why are you frowning, brother?" Kirila Petrovich asked him. "Don't you like my kennels?"

"I do indeed," he answered morosely. "Your kennels are marvellous; I doubt whether your servants live as well as your dogs."

One of the kennelmen felt insulted.

"Thanks God and the master," he said, "we have no complaints; but if the truth be told, there's other gentlemen who'd be better off exchanging their homestead for any one of these kennels. They'd be both fed better and kept warmer."

Kirila Petrovich burst into loud laughter at his serf's insolent remark, and his guests followed suit, even though they felt that the dog-keeper's joke might well have applied to them. Dubrovsky blanched and did not say a word. At this moment some newborn pups were brought to Kirila Petrovich in a basket, and he turned his attention to them, choosing two to keep and ordering the rest to be drowned. In the meantime Andrei Gavrilovich disappeared, unnoticed by anyone.

On returning with his guests from the kennels, Kirila Petrovich sat down to supper, and only then, not seeing Dubrovsky, did he realize that his friend was missing. The servants reported that Andrei Gavrilovich had gone home. Troyekurov gave orders to go after him immediately and bring him back without fail. Never had he ridden out on a hunt without Dubrovsky, who was an experienced and acute judge of canine virtues and an unerring arbiter of all manner of huntsmen's disputes. The servant sent after him came back while the company was still at table, and reported to his master that Andrei Gavrilovich, defying orders, had refused to return. Kirila Petrovich, flushed with liquor as usual, grew angry and sent the same servant off for a second time to tell Andrei Gavrilovich that if the latter did not come at once to spend the night at Pokrovskoye, he would break off all relations with him for ever. The servant galloped off once more, while Kirila Petrovich rose from the table, dismissed his guests and went to bed.

The next morning his first question was whether Andrei Gavrilovich was there. Instead of an answer, they handed him a letter folded into a triangle; he ordered his scribe to read it, and heard the following:

Most gracious sir,

I do not intend to come to Pokrovskoye until you send me your kennelman, Paramoshka, with an admission of his guilt; and it will be my pleasure to punish him or spare him; and I do not intend to tolerate jests from your serfs, nor will I tolerate them from you, for I am not a buffoon but a nobleman of ancient lineage.

I remain your humble servant,

Andrei Dubrovsky

By today's code of etiquette this letter would be considered extremely boorish; what angered Kirila Petrovich, however, was not its strange style and composition, but simply its substance.

"What's this?" thundered Troyekurov, jumping out of bed onto his bare feet. "That I should send him my men with an admission of guilt, and that it should be his pleasure to punish them or spare them! What the Devil's got into him? Who does he think he's locking horns with? I'll show him… I'll make him cry himself blind; I'll teach him what it's like to affront Troyekurov!"

Kirila Petrovich got dressed and rode out in his usual splendour, but the hunt did not turn out well. They saw only one hare the whole day and let even that one escape. The dinner under the tent in a field was unsuccessful, or at least it was not to the taste of Kirila Petrovich, who beat up the cook, tongue-lashed his guests, and on his way home deliberately rode over Dubrovsky's fields with his whole cavalcade.

Several days passed, but the hostility between the two neighbours did not abate. Andrei Gavrilovich continued to stay away from Pokrovskoye; and Kirila Petrovich, bored without him, poured out his annoyance in the most insulting expressions, which thanks to the diligence of the local gentry, reached Dubrovsky's ears with amendments and supplements. Any last hope of a reconciliation was extinguished by a new incident.

One day Dubrovsky was driving about his small estate. Approaching a copse of birches, he heard the sound of an axe and, a minute later, the crash of a falling tree. He rushed into the copse and came upon some peasants from Pokrovskoye, who were calmly stealing his timber. Seeing him, they tried to run away, but he and his coachman caught two of them and brought them back to his house in bonds. Three enemy horses were also among the spoils of the victor. Dubrovsky was exceedingly angry: never before had Troyekurov's men, brigands as everyone knew, dared to play their pranks within the boundaries of his property, since they were aware of his friendly relations with their master. Dubrovsky realized that they were now taking advantage of the breach of friendship that had recently occurred, and he decided, against all military conventions, to teach his prisoners-of-war a lesson with the same switches that they themselves had cut in his copse, and to set the horses to work, adding them to his own livestock.

A report about this incident reached Kirila Petrovich that same day. He flew into a rage, and in the first moment of anger wanted to gather all his men and fall upon Kistenevka (as his neighbour's village was called), raze it to the ground, and besiege the landlord in his manor house. Such exploits were not unusual with him. But his thoughts were soon drawn in a different direction.

Pacing up and down the hall with heavy steps, he accidentally glanced through the window and caught sight of a troika stopped by the gate. A small man in a leather cap and heavy woollen coat climbed out of the wagon and went to see the steward in a wing of the house: Troyekurov recognized the assessor Shabashkin and sent for him. In another minute Shabashkin stood before Kirila Petrovich, scraping and bowing and reverently awaiting his orders.

"Hullo, what's-your-name," said Troyekurov. "What brought you to us?"

"I was driving to town, Your Excellency," answered Shabashkin, "and dropped by Ivan Demyanov's to see if Your Excellency had any instructions for me."

"You came at just the right time, what's-your-name; I need you. Have a glass of vodka and listen to me."

The assessor was pleasantly surprised by such a warm welcome. He refused the vodka and listened to Kirila Petrovich with all his attention.

"I have a neighbour," said Kirila Petrovich. "He's a boor of a smallholder. I want to take away his estate. What do you think?"

"Well, Your Excellency, if there are some documents, or—"

"Nonsense, brother; what documents do you want? What are court orders for? The crux of the matter is precisely to take away his estate without any rights. Wait a minute, though. That estate used to belong to us at one time; it was bought from somebody called Spitsyn and then sold to Dubrovsky's father. Couldn't we make a case out of that?"

"It'd be difficult, Your Excellency: that sale was probably effected in a legal manner."

"Think about it, brother; search around a little."

"If, for instance, Your Excellency could somehow obtain from your neighbour the record or deed that entitles him to his estate, then, of course…"

"I understand, but the trouble is that all his documents were burnt in a fire."

"What, Your Excellency? His documents were burnt? You couldn't wish for anything better! In that case you may proceed according to the law, and you will without doubt find complete satisfaction."

"Do you think so? Well, take good care of the matter. I rely on your zeal, and you can rest assured of my gratitude."

Shabashkin bowed almost to the floor and left. That same day he busied himself with the concocted case, and, thanks to his dexterity, in exactly two weeks Dubrovsky received from town an order to present without delay due clarification concerning his ownership of the village of Kistenevka.

Astonished by the unexpected request, Andrei Gavrilovich wrote a rather rude reply the same day, declaring that the village of Kistenevka had come into his possession after his father's death, that he held it by right of inheritance, that Troyekurov had nothing to do with it, and that any other party's claims to his property amounted to chicanery and fraud.

This letter made a highly agreeable impression on the assessor Shabashkin. He could see, first, that Dubrovsky had little comprehension of legal matters, and second, that it would not be difficult to get such a hot-tempered and incautious man into a very disadvantageous situation. Andrei Gavrilovich, when he had considered the assessor's request with a cool head, did see the need to reply in greater detail and did write quite a business-like communication, but subsequently even this turned out to be insufficient.

The business dragged on. Convinced of the rightness of his case, Andrei Gavrilovich paid little further attention to it. He had neither the desire nor the means to throw money about, and although he had always been the first to crack jokes about the venality of the tribe of scriveners, it never occurred to him that he might become a victim of chicanery. Troyekurov, on his part, cared just as little about winning the case he had initiated. It was Shabashkin who kept busy on his behalf, acting in his name, intimidating and bribing judges, and interpreting every possible edict in whatever way he could.

Anyway, on 9th February 18— Dubrovsky received through the town police a summons to appear before the N. district judge to hear his ruling with regard to the estate contested between him (Lieutenant Dubrovsky) and General-in-Chief Troyekurov, and to sign it, indicating either his agreement or his dissent. Dubrovsky left for town that same day. On the road he was overtaken by Troyekurov. They glanced at each other haughtily, and Dubrovsky noticed a malicious smile on his adversary's face.

2

O N HIS ARRIVAL in town Andrei Gavrilovich stopped at the house of a merchant he knew and spent the night there, and the next morning he presented himself at the district courthouse. No one paid any attention to him. Right after him Kirila Petrovich arrived. The clerks rose and stuck their pens behind their ears. The panel of judges welcomed Troyekurov with abject subservience, pulling up an armchair for him in consideration of his rank, years and portliness; he sat down close to the door, which was left open. Andrei Gavrilovich stood, leaning against the wall. Profound silence ensued, and the secretary began to read the court's ruling in a ringing voice. We cite that ruling in full, assuming that it will be gratifying to every reader to be apprised of one of the means whereby we in Holy Russia can be deprived of property to which we have an indisputable right:

On the 27th day of October in the year 18—, the N. District Court examined the case of the wrongful possession by Lieutenant of the Guards Andrei Dubrovsky, son of Gavrila Dubrovsky, of an estate belonging to General-in-Chief Kirila Troyekurov, son of Pyotr Troyekurov, which comprises the village of Kistenevka situated in P. Province, with X number of serfs of the male sex and Y *desyatinas* of land,* including meadows and appurtenances. From which case it is evident that: on the 19th day of June in the past year of 18—, the said General-in-Chief Troyekurov instituted at this Court a possessory action setting forth that on the 14th day of August 17—, his father, Collegiate Assessor and Cavalier Pyotr Troyekurov, son of Yefim Troyekurov, deceased, who was at that time serving as provincial secretary in the chancery of the Governor-General of S., purchased by an act of sale from the clerk Fadei Spitsyn, son of Yegor Spitsyn, of the nobility, an estate, comprising, in the said village of Kistenevka of R. region (which village, according to census No. X, was called Kistenevo Settlements), a total of Y number of male serfs registered in Census No. 4, with all the peasants' chattels, with a farmstead, with arable and non-arable land, woods, meadows, fishing rights in the Kistenevka River, with all appurtenances attached to the estate, and with a wooden manor house – in other words everything without exclusion that Fadei Spitsyn had inherited from his father, Sergeant Yegor Spitsyn, son of Terenty Spitsyn, of the nobility, and which he held in his possession, excluding not one of his serfs nor any measure of land – for the price of 2,500 roubles, for which a deed of sale was validated the same day at N. courthouse, and after which, on the 26th day of the same month of August, Troyekurov's father was duly placed in possession of the said estate by the N. District Court, and a livery of seizin was executed. And at last on the 6th day of September in the year 17—, his father by God's will deceased, while he, the said Plaintiff, General-in-Chief Troyekurov, from the year 17—, almost from infancy, had been in military service, mostly participating in campaigns abroad, for which reason he received no intelligence either of his father's death or about the estate left after him. Having now finally retired from the service and returned to his father's estates, comprising a total of 3,000 serfs in different villages situated in R. and S. districts of N. and P. Provinces, he finds that one of the said estates with the above-mentioned number of serfs according to Census No. X (of whom, according to the current census, Y number belong to this one estate) is being held, together with its land and all appurtenances, without any legal proof of possession by the aforementioned Lieutenant of the Guards Andrei Dubrovsky; for which reason he, Troyekurov, attaching to his petition the original deed of sale given to his father by the vendor Spitsyn, petitions that the aforementioned estate be removed from Dubrovsky's wrongful possession and placed, according to its proper pertinence, at his, Troyekurov's, disposal in full. As for Dubrovsky's wrongfully entering upon the said estate, from which he has enjoyed revenues, the petitioner prays the Court that, the appropriate interrogatories having been processed, lawful damages be assessed against Dubrovsky, wherewith restitution to Troyekurov be effected.

The investigations conducted by N. District Court with regard to the above cause of action have revealed that: the aforementioned current possessor of the disputed estate, Lieutenant of the Guards Dubrovsky, has deposed before the assessor in charge of affairs of the nobility that the estate currently in his possession, comprising the said village of Kistenevka, with X number of serfs, land, and appurtenances, had been conveyed to him as inheritance after the death of his father, Second Lieutenant of the Artillery Gavrila Dubrovsky, son of Yevgraf Dubrovsky; that his father had acquired it through purchase from the said Plaintiff's father, Troyekurov, who had earlier been a provincial secretary and later a collegiate assessor; and that the said purchase had been effected through the services of Titular Councillor Grigory Sobolev, son of Vasily Sobolev, to whom the Plaintiff's father had given power of attorney on 30th August 17—, notarized at the N. District Court, according to which a deed of sale was to be issued to his, Dubrovsky's, father, because in the said power of attorney as it is stated that he, Troyekurov's father, had sold to Dubrovsky's father the whole estate, comprising X number of serfs and land, bought earlier from the chancery clerk Spitsyn; and that Troyekurov's father had received in full from Dubrovsky's father and had not returned the 3,200 roubles that were due to him according to the sales agreement; and that he wished the aforementioned agent, Sobolev, to convey to Dubrovsky's father the title to the property. Moreover, according to the same power of attorney, Dubrovsky's father, by virtue of having paid the whole sum, was to take possession of the estate bought by him and was to be in charge of it as its full owner even before the transference to him of the said title, and neither the vendor Troyekurov nor anyone else was henceforth to interfere with it. But when exactly and at which court of law the aforementioned deed of sale was issued by the agent Sobolev to his father, this he, Andrei Dubrovsky, did not know, because at that time he was a small child, and because after his father's death he could not find the title; for which reason he supposes that it might have been burnt along with other documents and property in a fire that occurred in their house in the year 17—, about which the inhabitants of the said village also knew. As for the Dubrovskys' undisputed possession of the said estate from the day of its sale by Troyekurov or from the day of the issuance of a power of attorney to Sobolev – that is, from the year 17— till the death of his father in 17— and thereafter – he has called to witness inhabitants of the neighbourhood, who, fifty-two in number, have testified under oath that indeed, as far as they could remember, the said nobleman Dubrovsky came into possession of the aforementioned disputed estate without any dispute some seventy years ago, but that they could not tell by exactly which deed or title. As for the aforementioned previous purchaser of the said estate, former Provincial Secretary Pyotr Troyekurov, they could not remember whether he had owned it. The house of the noblemen Dubrovsky did burn down about thirty years ago in a fire that had started in the village at night; and the witness confirmed the assumption that the estate sued for could produce revenue, counting from that time on, of no less than 2,000 roubles a year.

In response, on 3rd January of the current year General-in-Chief Kirila Troyekurov, son of Pyotr Troyekurov, filed at this Court the pleading that, although the aforementioned Lieutenant of the Guards Andrei Dubrovsky had, in the course of the investigation of the present action, adduced as evidence the power of attorney given by his, the Plaintiff's, father to Titular Councillor Sobolev for effecting the purchase of the said estate, he had not, by this document, shown clear proof – as required by Chapter 19 of the General Regulations and by the edict of 19th November 1752 – either of the actual deed of sale or of its execution at any time. Therefore this power of attorney today, after the death of its issuer, his father, is, according to the decree of the Nth day of May 1818, completely null and void. Moreover: it has been decreed that properties sued for shall be restored to their proprietors – those with deeds under titles, according to the titles, and those without deeds, according to the results of an investigation.

For the said estate, which had belonged to his father, he, Troyekurov, has already shown the deed of sale as proof, and therefore it should, on the basis of the aforementioned laws, be recovered from the said Dubrovsky's wrongful possession and restored to him by right of inheritance. And since the said landowners, having in their possession, with no title whatsoever, an estate that did not belong to them, have also wrongfully enjoyed revenues from it to which they have not been entitled, it should be established according to the law to what sum the said revenues amount, and damages should be assessed against the landowner Dubrovsky, wherewith restitution to him, Troyekurov, be effected.

Having investigated the said cause of action and having considered the Plaintiff's and Defendant's averments as well as the relevant legal statutes, the N. District Court *orders, adjudges, and decrees* as follows:

As is evident from the said action, with regard to the aforementioned estate sued for, which is currently in the possession of Lieutenant of the Guards Andrei Dubrovsky, son of Gavrila Dubrovsky, and which comprises the village of Kistenevka with X number of male serfs according to the latest census, and with land and appurtenances, General-in-Chief Kirila Troyekurov, son of Pyotr Troyekurov, has shown a valid deed of sale, proving that the said estate was conveyed in the year 17— to his late father, provincial secretary and subsequently collegiate assessor, from chancery clerk Fadei Spitsyn, of noble birth; and, furthermore, the said purchaser of the estate, Troyekurov, was, as can be seen from a notation entered on the deed of sale, placed in possession of the said estate by the N. District Court the same year, with a livery of seizin executed. Lieutenant of the Guards Andrei Dubrovsky, on the other hand, has adduced as evidence a power of attorney given by the said purchaser, Troyekurov, deceased, to Titular Councillor Sobolev, authorizing him to issue a deed of sale to his, Dubrovsky's father, but it is forbidden by Edict No. X not only to confirm proprietorship of immovable property, but even to permit temporary possession thereof on the basis of such documentation; moreover, the death of its issuer has rendered the said power of attorney completely null and void. Furthermore Dubrovsky has failed, from the commencement of the present action in 18— to date, to present clear evidence about when and where a deed of sale for the said disputed estate, in accordance with the power of attorney, was actually issued. Therefore this Court orders, adjudges and decrees: that the said estate, with X number of serfs, land and appurtenances, in whatever condition it may now be, shall be confirmed, on the basis of the deed of sale presented by him, as the property of General-in-Chief Troyekurov; that Lieutenant of the Guards Dubrovsky shall be removed from the management of the said estate; and that P. local court shall be instructed duly to place Mr Troyekurov, by virtue of his having inherited the estate, in possession thereof, and to execute a livery of seizin. General-in-Chief Troyekurov has furthermore sued for damages from Lieutenant of the Guards Dubrovsky for having enjoyed revenues from his inherited estate, wrongfully in possession of Dubrovsky; but since the said estate, according to the testimony of inhabitants of long standing, has been in the undisputed possession of the noblemen Dubrovsky for several years; since the evidence as presented does not show that Mr Troyekurov had before now sued Dubrovsky in any way for his wrongful possession of the said estate; and since according to the statute "it is decreed that, if anyone should sow a crop in a tract of land or enclose a farmstead that does not belong to him, and an action be brought, with pretension to direct damages, against him for his wrongfully having taken possession, then the party adjudged right shall have that land with the crop sown in it, and the enclosure, and other improvements"; therefore General-in-Chief Troyekurov shall be denied the damages for which he has sued Lieutenant of the Guards Dubrovsky in view of the circumstances that the estate belonging to him is being restored to his possession without any diminution. At the time the said estate is being taken into possession, no part thereof may be found missing; if, on the other hand, General-in-Chief Troyekurov should have clear and legitimate cause for claims in that regard, he shall have the right to sue separately at the appropriate court.

This decision is to be communicated in advance both to Plaintiff and to Defendant in a legal manner and with opportunity for appeal; and the said Plaintiff and Defendant shall be summoned by the police to this Court in order to hear the decision and sign it, respectively indicating their agreement or their dissent.

The aforegoing decision has been signed by all hereto present members of this Court.

The secretary fell silent; the assessor rose and turned to Troyekurov with a low bow, offering him the document to sign. Troyekurov, triumphant, took the pen from him and signed the court's decision, indicating his complete agreement.

It was Dubrovsky's turn. The secretary brought the document to him. But Dubrovsky remained motionless, with his head lowered.

The secretary for the second time invited him to sign and indicate either his full and complete agreement or his explicit dissent, if, with a clear conscience and against the court's expectations, he felt that his case was just and wished to file an appeal at the appropriate court within the legally allotted time. Dubrovsky remained silent… Then suddenly he raised his head with eyes flashing, stamped his foot, shoved the secretary aside with such force that the man fell to the ground and, seizing an ink pot, hurled it at the assessor. Everyone was terrified.

"What! Dishonouring the church of God! Away with you, you heathen spawn!" Then he turned to Kirila Petrovich and continued: "It's unheard of, Your Excellency: kennelmen bringing dogs into God's church! Dogs are running all over the church. Just wait, I'll teach you…"

The guards, who had run in on hearing the noise, overpowered him with difficulty. They led him out and put him in his sleigh. Troyekurov came out after him, accompanied by the whole court. Dubrovsky's sudden fit of insanity made a powerful impression on him and poisoned his triumph.

The judges, who had been hoping for an expression of gratitude, were not favoured with a single word of appreciation. Troyekurov left for Pokrovskoye the same day. Dubrovsky, meanwhile, lay in bed: the district doctor, who was fortunately not a complete ignoramus, had successfully let his blood and applied leeches and Spanish flies.* By the evening the patient's condition improved, and he regained consciousness. The next day he was driven back to Kistenevka – which hardly belonged to him any more.

3

S OME TIME HAD PASSED, but poor Dubrovsky's state of health was still bad. Although no more fits of madness recurred, he was visibly losing his strength. He began to forget his earlier occupations, rarely left his room and fell into reverie for days at a time. The good-hearted old woman Yegorovna, who had at one time looked after his son, now became his nurse too. She took care of him as if he were a child: reminded him of mealtimes and bedtime, fed him and put him to bed. Andrei Gavrilovich obeyed her quietly, and had no contact with anyone except her. Since he was in no shape to take care of his affairs or manage his estate, Yegorovna thought it necessary to write about it all to the young Dubrovsky, who was in Petersburg at the time, serving in one of the regiments of the Foot Guards. Tearing a page out of a housekeeping book, she dictated a letter to the cook Khariton, who was the only literate person in Kistenevka, and sent it off to town the same day for mailing.

It is time, however, to acquaint the reader with the actual hero of our narrative.

Vladimir Dubrovsky had been educated at a military academy, and after graduation appointed an officer in the Guards. His father spared nothing to support him in proper style, and the young man received more from home than he had a right to expect. Prodigal and ambitious, he indulged himself in extravagant habits, played at cards, got into debt and gave no thought to the future, anticipating that sooner or later he would find a rich bride – the usual dream of poor youths.

One evening, as several officers sat in his apartment, sprawled on sofas and smoking his amber pipes, his valet Grisha handed him a letter, whose address and seal immediately struck the young man. He broke the seal hurriedly and read the following:

Our gracious master, Vladimir Andreyevich – I, your old nurse, have decided to inform you of your dear father's state of health. He is very poorly, sometimes he drivels, and sits all day like an idiot child – but life and death are in the hands of the Lord. Come home to us, my dearest, we'll even send horses for you to Pesochnoye. They say the local court is coming to put us under the control of Kirila Petrovich Troyekurov, because, they say, we are his, but we have always been yours, and I have never even heard such a thing since the day I was born. Living in Petersburg, you could report it to the Tsar, our father, and he would not let us be wronged. I remain your faithful slave and nurse,

Orina Yegorovna Buzyreva

I send my motherly blessing to Grisha; is he serving you well? Here, it has been two weeks already as the rains would not stop, and the shepherd Rodia died close upon St Mikola's Day.

Vladimir Dubrovsky read these rather incoherent lines several times with extreme agitation. He had lost his mother in infancy and, scarcely knowing his father, had been sent to Petersburg in his eighth year. Nevertheless he had a romantic attachment to him, and he loved family life all the more for having never enjoyed its quiet pleasures.

The thought of losing his father lacerated his heart; and the state of the poor sick man, which he could picture to himself from his nurse's letter, appalled him. He imagined his father, forsaken in a remote village, under the care of a foolish old woman and his other domestics, threatened by some calamity and languishing without succour in the midst of both physical and mental torments. Vladimir reproached himself for his criminal neglect. He had not heard from his father for a long time, yet he had not thought of enquiring after him, supposing him to be either travelling about or engrossed in the care of his estate.

He decided to go and see him, and even to retire in case his father's condition should require his presence. His friends noticed his agitation and departed. Left by himself, Vladimir wrote an application for leave of absence, lit his pipe and sank into deep thought.

He handed in his application that same evening, and in another three days was already on the highway.

Vladimir Andreyevich was approaching the post station at which he had to turn off the highway towards Kistenevka. His heart was full of sad forebodings: he feared his father might be dead by the time he reached home; and he imagined the dreary life awaiting him in the country – backwoods, loneliness, poverty and troubles over business, about which he did not know the first thing. When he arrived at the station, he went to ask the superintendant if there were horses available.

The superintendant, learning his destination, told him that a team of horses sent from Kistenevka had been waiting for him for more than three days. Soon the old coachman Anton, who used to take Vladimir around the stables and look after his pony, presented himself to him. Tears welled up in Anton's eyes on seeing him; he bowed to the ground and reported that his old master was still alive. He hurried off to harness the horses. Vladimir Andreyevich refused the breakfast offered him and hastened to depart. Anton drove him along the country lanes, and conversation began between them.

"Please tell me, Anton, what's this business between my father and Troyekurov?"

"Heaven only knows, young master Vladimir Andreyevich... The master, they say, fell foul of Kirila Petrovich, who then took him to court, as if he weren't his own judge anyway! It's not for us serfs to remark on what our masters wish to do, but, by God, your dear father shouldn't have set himself against Kirila Petrovich; you'll never smash an axe head with a whip."

"So evidently this Kirila Petrovich does just what he likes in these parts?"

"Aye, so he does, young master: he snaps his fingers at the assessor, and the local police chief is his errand boy. As for the gentlefolks hereabout, they gather at his house to pay their respect: if I may say so, as long as there's a trough, you'll have no lack of swine."

"Is it true that he's taking away our property?"

"Even so, young master, that's what we hear tell. Just the other day the sacristan from Pokrovskoye said at a christening held at our elder's house: 'The good times are over: you'll see what it's like when Kirila Petrovich takes you in hand.' Mikita the blacksmith answered him: 'Enough of that, Savelich,' he says, 'don't sadden the godfather, don't upset the guests.' Kirila Petrovich is one master, Andrei Gavrilovich another; and we're all in the hands of God and the Tsar. But you can't sew a button on someone else's mouth."

"You don't wish, then, to pass into Troyekurov's possession?"

"To pass to Kirila Petrovich's possession! The Lord save and preserve us from that! His own people have a rough enough deal at times: if he gets his hand on strangers, he'll not only skin them, but tear their very flesh off. Nay, God grant a long life to Andrei Gavrilovich, and if it's His will to gather him to his fathers, then we wish for no other master than you, our provider. Don't abandon us, and we'll stand up for you." With these words, Anton brandished his whip and shook the reins; the horses broke into a brisk trot.

Touched by the old coachman's loyalty, Dubrovsky fell silent and once more gave himself up to reflection. More than an hour passed. Suddenly Grisha awakened him with the exclamation: "Here's Pokrovskoye!" Dubrovsky raised his head. They were riding along the shore of a wide lake drained by a stream that meandered into the distance among hills; on one of these hills there arose, above the dense greenery of a copse, the green roof and belvedere of an enormous stone house; on another one, there stood a five-domed church and an ancient bell tower; and all around were scattered peasant cottages with their vegetable gardens and wells. Dubrovsky recognized all these landmarks: he recalled that on that hill he used to play with little Masha Troyekurova, two years his junior, who was already then promising to grow into a beauty. He wanted to ask Anton about her, but a sense of reserve held him back.

As he drew closer to the manor house, he saw a white dress drifting among the trees of the park. At this moment Anton lashed at the horses and, obeying a vanity common both to country coachmen and city drivers, dashed across a bridge and past the village. Leaving the village behind, they climbed a slope. Vladimir soon caught sight of a birch wood and, in a clearing to its left, a little grey house with a red roof. His heart pounded: he saw before him Kistenevka and his father's humble home.

Ten minutes later he drove into the courtyard. He looked about him with indescribable emotion: he had not seen his home for twelve years. The little birches that had only just been planted along the fence when he was still living there had grown into tall trees with branches spread wide. The yard, which used to be ornamented with three neat flower beds, a well-swept broad path running among them, had by now turned into an unmowed pasture, on which a hobbled horse was grazing. The dogs began to bark but, recognizing Anton, grew quiet, wagging their shaggy tails. The domestics all poured out of the servants' quarters and surrounded their young master with loud manifestations of joy. He was barely able to push his way through the eager crowd in order to ascend the dilapidated porch; in the ante-room Yegorovna met him, embracing her former charge with sobs.

"How are you, nurse? It's so good to see you," he kept repeating while pressing the kind old woman to his heart. "But what about father? Where is he? How is he?"

At this moment a tall old man, pale and thin, wearing a dressing gown and a nightcap, entered the room, though hardly able to drag his feet one after the other.

"Hullo, Volodka!" he said in a weak voice, and Vladimir warmly embraced his father. The joy of seeing his son was too much of a shock for the sick man: he grew faint, his legs gave way under him, and he would have collapsed had his son not caught him.

"Why did you get out of bed?" Yegorovna said to him. "You can't stand on your legs, yet you're itching to go where other folk go."

The old man was carried off to his bedroom. He tried to talk to his son, but his thoughts became confused and his words were incoherent. He fell silent and soon dozed off. Vladimir was dismayed by his condition. He installed himself in his father's bedroom and asked to be left alone with him. The domestics obeyed and now turned to Grisha, whom they carried off to the servants' quarters, giving him a hearty welcome, feasting him in a rustic manner and exhausting him with questions and greetings.

4

*Where was a table spread with food now stands a coffin.**

A FEW DAYS after his arrival, the young Dubrovsky wanted
to turn to business matters, but his father was in no state to
provide the necessary explanations and had no attorney. Going
over his father's papers, Vladimir found only the assessor's first
letter and a draft of Andrei Gavrilovich's answer, from which he
could not derive a clear idea of the lawsuit. He decided to await
further developments, placing his hopes in the rightness of his
family's case.

In the meantime, Andrei Gavrilovich's condition worsened by
the hour. Vladimir saw that the end was not far off, and he never
left the side of the old man, now fallen into a state of complete
infancy.

Meanwhile, the deadline for an appeal lapsed, with none filed.
Kistenevka now belonged to Troyekurov. Shabashkin came to him
with bows and congratulations, asking when it would suit His
Excellency to be placed in possession of his newly acquired estate,
and whether he would wish to participate in the transaction in
person or would prefer to give power of attorney to someone
else. Kirila Petrovich felt embarrassed. He was not avaricious
by nature: his desire for vengeance had carried him too far, and
now he had pangs of conscience. He knew about the condi-
tion of his adversary – the old comrade of his youth – and his
victory brought no joy to his heart. He glanced at Shabashkin
menacingly, searching for some reason to heap curses on him,
but finding no sufficient pretext, angrily said: "Go away, I'm not
in the mood for you."

Seeing that he was indeed not in a good mood, Shabashkin
bowed and hastily withdrew. Left by himself, Kirila Petrovich
started pacing up and down, whistling 'May thou, thunder of

victory, rumble',* which, with him, was always a sign of extraordinary agitation.

At last he gave orders to have the racing droshky harnessed, dressed warmly (it was already the end of September), and rode out, driving himself.

He soon beheld Andrei Gavrilovich's little house, and contradictory feelings filled his heart. Satisfied vengeance and a love of power had smothered his more noble sentiments up to a point, but at long last these latter triumphed. He resolved to make it up with his old neighbour, erasing all traces of the quarrel and returning his property to him. His feelings alleviated by this commendable decision, he approached his neighbour's house at a trot and drove straight into the courtyard.

At this time the sick man was seated by his bedroom window. He recognized Kirila Petrovich, and his face assumed an expression of terrible confusion: a purple flush suffused his usually pale cheeks, his eyes flashed and he uttered some incomprehensible sounds. His son, seated in the same room over some ledgers, raised his head and was struck by the old man's condition. The patient pointed to the courtyard with a look of horror and anger. He hastily gathered the skirts of his dressing gown, preparing to get up from his armchair; he rose… and suddenly collapsed. His son rushed to him. The old man had lost consciousness and was not breathing; he had suffered a stroke.

"Quick, quick, send to the city for a doctor!" Vladimir cried.

"Kirila Petrovich is asking for you," said a servant, entering.

Vladimir threw a dreadful glance at him.

"Tell Kirila Petrovich to clear out of here before I have him thrown out… Off you go!"

The servant gladly rushed from the room to fulfil his master's command. Yegorovna clasped her hands.

"Young master," she said in a squeaky voice, "you're bringing ruin on your head! Kirila Petrovich will swallow us all up!"

"Be quiet, nurse," said Vladimir angrily. "Send Anton to the city for the doctor at once."

Yegorovna left.

There was nobody in the entrance hall: all the servants had gathered in the courtyard to look at Kirila Petrovich. Yegorovna, going out onto the porch, heard the servant deliver his young master's reply to the visitor. The latter heard him out, seated in his droshky. His face turned darker than night, then a contemptuous smile came over it; he glanced at the servants menacingly and slowly drove past the house. He also glanced at the window where Andrei Gavrilovich had been seated but could no longer be seen. The nurse stood on the porch, forgetting her master's order. The servants started a noisy discussion of what had happened. Suddenly Vladimir appeared among his servants and abruptly declared, "There's no need for a doctor; father has died."

There was general confusion. The servants rushed into their old master's room. He lay in the armchair where Vladimir had placed him; his right arm dangled over the floor and his head hung over his chest; there was not the least sign of life left in his body, still warm but already disfigured by death. Yegorovna burst into sobs, and the servants crowded around the corpse left to their care; they washed it, dressed it in a uniform made back in 1797, and laid it out on the same table at which they had served their master for so many years.

5

THE FUNERAL WAS HELD three days later. The poor old man's body lay on the table wrapped in a shroud and surrounded by candles. The dining room was full of servants. They were getting ready for the funeral procession. Vladimir and three servants lifted the coffin. The priest went first, accompanied by the sexton, singing dirges. The master of Kistenevka passed over the threshold of his house for the last time. They carried the coffin through the woods to where the church stood. It was a clear, cold day. The autumn leaves were falling from the trees.

Past the wood, the Kistenevka village church and the cemetery, shaded by old lime trees, came into view. The body of Vladimir's mother lay there, and next to her tomb a new grave had been dug the day before.

The church was full of Kistenevka peasants who had come to pay their last respects to their master. The young Dubrovsky stood in the chancel; he neither wept nor prayed, but his face looked frightening. The sombre service came to an end. Vladimir went up first to take leave of the corpse; all the servants followed after him. The lid was brought in and the coffin nailed shut. The village women wailed loudly, and the men now and then wiped away their tears with their fists. Vladimir and the same three servants, accompanied by the whole village, carried the coffin to the cemetery. The coffin was lowered into the grave; each person present threw a handful of soil on it; they filled the pit, bowed down and dispersed. Vladimir left hastily, before anybody else, and disappeared into the Kistenevka wood.

Yegorovna, in the name of the young master, invited the priest and all the clergy to a funeral dinner, at the same time informing them that he himself would not be present. Father Anton, his wife Fedotovna and the sexton walked back to the house, talking with Yegorovna about the virtues of the departed and discussing what was likely to happen to his heir. The whole neighbourhood already knew about Troyekurov's visit and the reception he got, and every local know-it-all was predicting that the incident would have grave consequences.

"What is to be, will be," said the priest's wife. "It would be a pity, though, if Vladimir Andreyevich weren't to be our landlord. Such a fine fellow, I declare!"

"Who else could be our landlord, if not he?" interrupted Yegorovna. "It's no use Kirila Petrovich getting all worked up. He's not dealing with a child: my precious one can stand up for himself, and, God helping, his protectors won't turn their backs upon him neither. He's uncommon high and mighty, ain't he, Kirila Petrovich! But I'll be sworn he stuck his tail between his legs when my Grishka yelled at him: 'Out with you, old dog! Out of this yard!'"

"Mercy on us, Yegorovna," said the sexton, "it's a wonder Grigory's tongue didn't refuse to obey him. For my part I think I'd sooner consent to bark at the bishop than look askance at Kirila Petrovich. You only have to catch sight of him and you're already cringing with fear and trembling; before you know it, your back is bending double of its own accord, it is."

"'Vanity of vanities',"* said the priest. "One day the burial service will be read over Kirila Petrovich, just as it was over Andrei Gavrilovich this morning; only perhaps the funeral will be more sumptuous and more people will be invited, but isn't it all the same to God?"

"Aye, truly, Father, we too wanted to invite the whole neighbourhood, but Vladimir Andreyevich refused. I'll be sworn we have plenty to do the honours with, but what can you say if he doesn't want to? Even if there's no other people, though, I'll have a nice spread at least for you, dear guests."

This cordial invitation and the hope of laying their fingers on some delectable pies helped quicken the steps of the conversing party; they soon arrived at the house, where the table was already laid and the vodka served.

In the meantime Vladimir, trying to muffle the voice of sorrow in his heart by physical exertion and tiredness, had got himself deep into the thickets. He walked at random, off the beaten path, brushing against branches and getting scratched, while his feet kept sinking into bogs, to none of which did he pay any attention. At length he came upon a little hollow, surrounded by woods on all sides, and a brook that meandered silently under the trees, half-stripped of their leaves by the autumn. He stopped and sat down on the cold turf. His mind was full of thoughts, each one gloomier than the one before. He keenly felt his loneliness. Storm clouds seemed to be gathering over his future. The feud with Troyekurov foretokened new misfortunes. His modest property might pass into another's hands, in which case poverty awaited him. For a long time he sat motionless in the same place, watching the brook's quiet flow as it carried away some withered leaves – a faithful, all-too-familiar image of life. At last he noticed it was getting dark: he rose and set out to find the way home, but it took him a great deal of straggling about unfamiliar woods before he stumbled on the path that led straight to the gate of his house.

It so happened that the priest and his retinue were just then coming up the path. The idea that this was a bad omen crossed Vladimir's mind. He could not help turning aside and hiding behind a tree. Not noticing him, they talked excitedly among themselves as they passed by.

"Depart from evil, and do good,"* the priest was saying to his wife. "There's no reason for us to tarry here. Whatever transpires is not our business."

His wife said something in answer, which Vladimir could not make out.

As he approached his house he saw a great many people: peasants and servants were crowding in the courtyard. Loud voices and much noise could be heard even at a distance. Two carriages stood by the barn. On the porch several strangers in uniform seemed to be discussing something.

"What does all this mean?" he crossly asked Anton, who was running to meet him. "Who are these people and what do they want?"

"Alas the day, young master Vladimir Andreyevich," answered the old man, catching his breath. "The court's come. They're giving us over to Troyekurov, taking us away from Your Honour!"

Vladimir hung his head; the servants crowded around their unfortunate master.

"Father and benefactor," they cried, kissing his hands, "we don't want no master but you; just give us the word and we'll take care of the court. We'd sooner die than betray you."

Vladimir looked at them with strange feelings stirring in his soul. "Just stand quietly," he told them. "I'll talk the matter over with the officials."

"Do, young master, do talk it over," they shouted to him from the crowd. "Awaken their conscience, the dammed rascals!"

Vladimir went up to the officials. Shabashkin, without taking off his cap, stood with his arms akimbo and haughtily looked about him. The local police chief, a tall, corpulent man of about fifty with a red face and whiskers, cleared his throat as he saw Dubrovsky approach and called out in a hoarse voice:

"And so I repeat what I've already told you: by the decision of the district court, from now on you belong to Kirila Petrovich Troyekurov, whose person is represented here by Mr Shabashkin. Obey all his commands; and you, women, love him and respect him, for he's got a great fondness for you."

The police chief burst into laughter over his witty joke; Shabashkin and the other officials followed his example. Vladimir seethed with indignation.

"Allow me to ask," he addressed the merry police officer with pretended calmness, "what all this means."

"What all this means," answered the resourceful official, "is that we have come to place Kirila Petrovich Troyekurov in possession of the estate, and to request *all other parties* to clear out of here while the going is good."

"It seems to me, though, that you might have turned to me before my peasants, and announced to a landowner that he has been deprived of his possessions."

"And who might you be?" asked Shabashkin with an insolent look. "The former landowner, Andrei Dubrovsky, son of Gavrila

Dubrovsky, has passed away by the will of God, and as for you, we neither know you nor desire to."

"Vladimir Andreyevich is our young master," said a voice from the crowd.

"Who was it dared open his mouth over there?" asked the police chief menacingly. "What master? What Vladimir Andreyevich? Your master is Kirila Petrovich Troyekurov, d'ye hear, you blockheads?"

"Not likely," said the same voice.

"But this is a riot!" shouted the policeman. "Hey, elder, come here!"

The village elder stepped forward.

"Find the man at once who dared talk back to me. I'll teach him!"

The elder turned to the crowd, asking who had spoken, but everyone kept quiet. Soon, however, a murmur began to rise from the back of the crowd, and in one minute it had grown into a horrendous uproar. The police chief lowered his voice and tried to calm the crowd down.

"Why take any notice of him?" shouted the servants. "Throw him out, fellows!"

The whole crowd lurched forwards. Shabashkin and the others lost no time in dashing into the ante-room and locking the door behind them. "Grab them, fellows," shouted the voice previously heard, and the crowd began to press on the house.

"Stop!" yelled Dubrovsky. "Idiots! What are you up to? You'll ruin yourselves, and me too. Go back to your cottages and leave me in peace. Don't be afraid: the Sovereign has a kind heart; I will appeal to him. He will not let us be harmed. We're all his children. But how can he protect you if you're rioting and housebreaking?"

The young Dubrovsky's speech, his ringing voice and majestic air, produced the desired effect. The people calmed down and dispersed; the courtyard became empty. The officials sat in the ante-room. At last, Shabashkin cautiously unlocked the door, came out on the porch and, bowing and scraping, thanked Dubrovsky profusely for his kind intervention. Vladimir listened with contempt and made no answer.

"We have decided," continued the assessor, "to spend the night here if you'll allow us: it's already dark, and your peasants might fall upon us on the highway. Do us a great favour: give orders to spread at least some hay on the drawing-room floor for us to sleep on; as soon as the day breaks, we'll be on our way."

"Do what you like," answered Dubrovsky drily. "I'm no longer master here." With these words he retired to his father's room and locked the door behind him.

6

"ALL IS FINISHED, THEN," said Vladimir to himself. "This morning I still had a roof over my head and a piece of bread; tomorrow I shall have to leave the house where I was born and my father died – and leave it to the man who caused his death and made me a pauper." He fixed his eyes on his mother's portrait. The painter had depicted her with her elbow resting on a balustrade, in a white morning dress and with a scarlet rose in her hair. "This portrait, too, will fall into the hands of my family's foe," he thought further. "It will be tossed into a storeroom among broken chairs, or else will be hung in the entrance hall, to be ridiculed and commented on by his kennelmen. In her bedroom, where father died, his steward will take up residence, or his harem will be installed. No, and a thousand times no! He shall not have the woeful house from which he is evicting me." Vladimir clenched his teeth: terrible thoughts came to his mind. He could hear the voice of the officials: they were behaving like masters of the house, demanding now this, now that, and unpleasantly distracting his mind from his melancholy reflections. At last all grew quiet.

Vladimir unlocked the chests and cabinets, and began to sort out his late father's papers. They consisted mostly of accounts and business correspondence. Vladimir tore them up without reading them. Among them, however, he found a package with the inscription "Letters from my wife". His feelings deeply stirred, Vladimir set to reading these: they were written during the Turkish campaign* and addressed from Kistenevka to the army. She described to her husband her lonely life and domestic occupations, gently lamenting their separation and urging him to come home into the arms of a loving wife. In one letter she voiced her anxiety over little Vladimir's health; in another, she expressed her joy over early signs of his abilities, predicting a bright and happy future for him. Vladimir read on and on, letting his memory plunge into a world of family happiness, oblivious to everything else; he did not notice how time passed. The grandfather clock struck eleven. Vladimir put the letters in his pocket, took the candle and left the study. The officials were sleeping on the floor in the drawing room.

Their empty glasses stood on the table, and the whole room smelt strongly of rum. Walking past them with disgust, Vladimir went out into the entrance hall. The outside door was locked. Not finding the key, he returned to the drawing room: it lay on the table. He opened the door and stumbled on a man crouching in the corner; an axe glinted in his hand. Turning the candle towards him, Vladimir recognized Arkhip the blacksmith.

"What are you doing here?" he asked.

"Oh, it's you, Vladimir Andreyevich," whispered Arkhip. "Merciful Lord! It's a good thing you came with a candle!"

Vladimir looked at him in astonishment.

"Why are you hiding here?" he asked.

"I wanted... I came to... to see if they're all inside," answered Arkhip in a low, faltering voice.

"And why are you carrying an axe?"

"An axe? Why, these days a body can't stir abroad without one. These officials, you see, are into such mischief – a man can never tell..."

"You must be drunk. Put away that axe and go sleep it off."

"Me, drunk? Vladimir Andreyevich, young master, as God is my witness I haven't had one drop in my mouth. Nay, how could one think of liquor when the officials want to lay their hands on us; have you ever seen such infamy, chasing our masters off their property?... Snoring in there, aren't they, the damned rascals: I'd put them all away at once, and none would be the wiser."

Dubrovsky frowned.

"Listen, Arkhip," he said after a short pause, "you're barking up the wrong tree. It's not the officials' fault. Light a lantern and follow me."

Arkhip took the candle from his master's hand, found a lantern behind the stove and lit it: both quietly descended the steps and proceeded into the courtyard. Someone on watch began to beat an iron plate, and the dogs started barking.

"Who is on watch?" asked Dubrovsky.

"It's us, young master," answered a thin voice, "Vasilisa and Lukeria."

"Go home," he said, "we don't need you."

"That'll do," added Arkhip.

"Thank you, kind sir," replied the women and went home immediately.

Dubrovsky proceeded further. Two men approached him and called to him. He recognized the voices of Anton and Grisha.

"Why aren't you sleeping?" he asked them.

"How could we sleep?" answered Anton. "What we've lived to see... Who would have thought?"

"Quietly," said Dubrovsky. "Where is Yegorovna?"

"She's at the manor house, in her little corner," replied Grisha.

"Go and bring her here, and get all our people out of the house, leaving not a soul in it except for the officials. And you, Anton, get a cart ready."

Grisha left and soon reappeared with his mother. The old woman had not undressed for the night; except for the officials, nobody in the house had closed an eye.

"Is everybody here?" asked Dubrovsky. "Is there no one left in the house?"

"No one except the officials," answered Grisha.

"Bring some hay or straw," said Dubrovsky.

The servants ran to the stables and returned with their arms full of hay.

"Pile it under the porch. That's right. And now, fellows, give me a light!"

Arkhip opened the lantern, and Dubrovsky lit a splinter. "Wait a minute," he said to Arkhip; "I think in my hurry I locked the door of the entrance hall: go and unlock it quickly."

Arkhip ran up to the entrance hall and found the door unlocked. He locked it with the key, murmuring under his breath, "Unlock it! Not likely!" And he returned to Dubrovsky.

Dubrovsky put the splinter to the hay, which flared up. The

flames soared high, illuminating the whole courtyard.

"Mercy on us," cried Yegorovna in a plaintive voice. "Vladimir Andreyevich, what are you doing?"

"Be quiet," said Dubrovsky. "Farewell, my good people: I'm going where God will guide me. Be happy with your new master."

"Father and provider," answered the servants, "we'd sooner die than leave you: we're coming with you."

The cart drew up; Dubrovsky climbed into it with Grisha – for the others he designated the Kistenevka wood as a meeting place. Anton lashed the horses, and they left the courtyard.

A wind blew up. In one minute the flames engulfed the whole house. Red smoke rose writhing over the roof. The window panes cracked and shattered, flaming beams were falling and plaintive cries and howls could be heard:

"Help, we're burning, help!"

"Not likely," said Arkhip, eyeing the fire with a malicious smile.

"Arkhipushka," called out Yegorovna, "save them, the damned rascals; God will reward you."

"Not likely," answered the blacksmith.

At this moment the officials appeared in the windows, trying to break the double frames. But the roof caved in with a crash just then, and the howls died away.

Soon all the servants poured into the courtyard. The women, crying, rushed to save their pitiable belongings, while little boys and girls jumped up and down, enjoying the fire. The sparks flew in a blazing blizzard, and the cottages caught fire.

"All set, now," said Arkhip. "It's burning nicely, ain't it? A fine sight from Pokrovskoye, I'll vow."

At this moment, however, something new attracted his attention: a cat was running about on the roof of the blazing barn, not knowing where to jump; flames surrounded it on all sides. The poor animal was calling for help with pitiful miaows. Some little boys were killing themselves with laughter, watching her despair.

"You devils, what are you laughing at?" said the blacksmith angrily. "Don't you fear the Lord? God's creature's a-perishing, and you're glad, you blockheads."

With these words he placed a ladder against the burning roof and climbed up to rescue the cat. The animal understood his intention and clutched his sleeve with a look of eager gratitude. The blacksmith, half-burnt, climbed down with his catch.

"Fare you well, good people," he said to the bewildered servants. "There's nothing else for me to do here. Live happily and remember me kindly."

The blacksmith left; the fire raged for some time longer. At last it abated; only heaps of embers glowed flameless but bright in the dark of the night, with Kistenevka's burnt-out inhabitants wandering around them.

7

NEWS OF THE FIRE spread throughout the neighbourhood the next day. Everybody talked about it, offering different guesses and suppositions. Some claimed that Dubrovsky's servants, having got drunk at the funeral feast, had set the house on fire through carelessness; others blamed the officials, who must have had a drop too much as they took possession of the house; still others maintained that Dubrovsky, too, had perished in the flames, together with the officials and all the servants. There were some, however, who guessed the truth, asserting that Dubrovsky himself, driven by spite and despair, was the instigator of the awful calamity. Troyekurov came the very next day to the site of the conflagration and conducted an investigation. It was established that the local police chief and the assessor, scribe and clerk of the district court, as well as Vladimir Dubrovsky, the nurse Yegorovna, the house serf Grigory, the coachman Anton, and the blacksmith Arkhip were all missing. Further, the servants testified that the officials had burnt when the roof caved in; and their charred bones were indeed found in the ashes. The serving women Vasilisa and Lukeria also declared that they had seen Dubrovsky and the blacksmith Arkhip just a few minutes before the fire started. The latter, according to the general testimony, was alive and had been the chief, if not the only instigator of the fire. But strong suspicion fell on Dubrovsky too. Kirila Petrovich sent the governor a detailed account of the incident, and new legal proceedings started.

Soon other reports aroused curiosity and gave rise to gossip. Robbers cropped up in the N. District, spreading terror throughout the environs. The measures the authorities took against them proved ineffective. Robberies, each more spectacular than the last, followed in succession. There was no safety either along the highways or in the villages. Carts filled with robbers criss-crossed the whole province in broad daylight, waylaying travellers and the mail, coming into villages, pillaging landowners' houses and consigning them to flames. The band's chief gained a reputation for intelligence, daring, and a certain magnanimity. Wondrous tales circulated about him. The name of Dubrovsky was on everybody's lips, all being convinced that it was he and no other who commanded the daring brigands. One circumstance that amazed everybody was that Troyekurov's estates were spared: the robbers did not plunder one single barn or waylay one single cart that belonged to him. With his usual arrogance, Troyekurov ascribed this exceptional treatment to the fear he inspired throughout the province, and also to the exceptionally good police force that he had organized in his villages. At first the neighbours chuckled among themselves over Troyekurov's loftiness and daily expected the uninvited guests to arrive in Pokrovskoye, where there was plenty to plunder, but at last they had to come round to his interpretation of the matter and admit that even robbers, inexplicably, showed him respect. Troyekurov was triumphant, and every time he heard about a new robbery by Dubrovsky he showered jibes on the heads of the governor, the police chiefs and the platoon commanders, from whom Dubrovsky invariably got away unharmed.

Meanwhile, the 1st of October, which was celebrated in Troyekurov's village as the patron saint's day, arrived. But before we embark on a description of this celebration or relate the ensuing events, we must acquaint the reader with certain personages who are either new to him or have been mentioned only fleetingly at the start of our narrative.

8

IN ALL LIKELIHOOD the reader has already guessed that Kirila Petrovich's daughter, about whom we have so far said only a few words, is the heroine of our tale. At the time we are describing she was seventeen years old, in the full bloom of her beauty. Her father loved her to distraction but treated her with his usual capriciousness, now trying to indulge her every wish, now frightening her with his stern, sometimes even cruel, ways. Although sure of her affections, he could never gain her confidence. She developed the habit of concealing her feelings and thoughts from him, because she could never be sure how he would receive them. Growing up in solitude, she had no friends. The neighbours' wives and daughters rarely came to Kirila Petrovich's house, because his usual conversation and amusements called more for male company than for the presence of ladies. Seldom did our young beauty appear among guests feasting with Kirila Petrovich. The huge library, consisting mostly of French authors of the eighteenth century, was placed at her disposal. Her father, who never read anything except *The Complete Art of Cookery*, could not guide her in her choice of books, and Masha, having sampled works of all kinds, naturally gave her preference to novels. It was with their aid that she completed her education, begun at one time under the guidance of Mademoiselle Mimi, whom Kirila Petrovich completely trusted and favoured, and whom he was obliged in the end to transfer surreptitiously to another of his estates, since the consequences of his friendship had become all too apparent. Mademoiselle Mimi left behind a rather pleasant memory. She was a good-hearted girl who never abused the influence she obviously had over Kirila Petrovich, in which respect she greatly differed from his other mistresses, who had replaced each other in quick succession. It seemed that Kirila Petrovich himself loved her more than the others, for a black-eyed naughty little boy of nine, whose face recalled Mademoiselle Mimi's southern features, was being brought up in the house as his son, even though a great many other barefooted little children, all the spit and image of Kirila Petrovich, were running about under his windows, regarded as house serfs. Kirila Petrovich had a French tutor sent down from Moscow for his little Sasha; and this tutor arrived in Pokrovskoye just at the time of the events we are describing.

Kirila Petrovich was favourably impressed with the tutor's pleasant appearance and simple conduct. The Frenchman presented him his credentials and a letter from a relative of the Troyekurovs at whose house he had served as a tutor for four years. Kirila Petrovich looked at all this carefully, and was dissatisfied only with the Frenchman's youth: not because he thought this enviable shortcoming indicated that the young man would lack the patience and experience so very necessary in a tutor's unfortunate profession, but because he had doubts of his own, which he decided to voice at once. To this end, he sent for Masha. (Since he himself did not speak French, she served as an interpreter for him.)

"Come here, Masha: tell this monsieur that, all right, I'll take him on, but only under the condition that he doesn't start running after my girls, or else I'll teach him, the son of a bitch... Translate this for him, Masha."

Masha blushed and, turning to the tutor, said to him in French that her father counted on his modest and proper behaviour.

The Frenchman bowed and answered that he hoped he would deserve respect, even if he did not win favour.

Masha translated his answer word for word.

"Very well, very well," said Kirila Petrovich. "He needn't bother about either favour or respect. His business is to look after Sasha, and teach him grammar and geography. Translate this for him."

Maria Kirilovna softened her father's rude expressions in her translation, and Kirila Petrovich let his Frenchman proceed to the wing of the house where a room had been assigned to him.

Masha paid no attention to the young Frenchman: brought up with aristocratic prejudices, she regarded tutors as a kind of servant or artisan, who were not men in her eyes. She noticed neither the impression she made on Monsieur Desforges, nor his embarrassment, nor his trembling, nor his changed voice. During the days following his arrival she met him quite frequently, but did not bestow any greater attention on him. As a result of an unexpected incident, however, she formed an entirely new idea of him.

Several bear cubs were usually being raised at Kirila Petrovich's house, serving as one of the chief sources of amusement for the master of Pokrovskoye. When still little, they were brought into the living room daily, where Kirila Petrovich played with them for hours at a time, setting them at cats and puppies. When they grew up, they were put on a chain, awaiting the real baitings they were destined for. From time to time they were led out in front of the windows of the manor house, where an empty wine barrel studded with nails was rolled out towards them: the bear would sniff at the barrel, then gently touch it, which would hurt its paw; angered, it would push the barrel with greater force, and the pain would become greater. It would get into a blind rage and keep throwing itself on the barrel with growls until at last they separated the poor beast from the target of its futile frenzy. At other times a pair of bears would be harnessed to a cart, and some guests, put in the cart against their will, would be driven off Heaven knows where. But the joke Kirila Petrovich considered best was the following.

A hungry bear would be locked in an empty room, tied with a rope to a ring screwed into the wall. The rope would be long enough to reach to any point in the room except the opposite corner, which would be the only place safe from the ferocious beast's attack. Some unsuspecting person would be led up to the door of this room, suddenly pushed inside, and the door locked behind him, leaving the hapless victim alone with the shaggy hermit. The poor guest, with the skirt of his coat torn and he himself bleeding from scratches, would soon find the safe corner, but would be compelled, sometimes for as long as three hours, to stand there, two steps from the bear, flattening himself against the wall, and from this position to watch the frenzied beast growl, leap and rear up, tearing at its rope and straining to reach him. Such were the noble pastimes of a Russian gentleman! Some days after the tutor's arrival it occurred to Troyekurov to entertain him, too, with a visit to the bear's room. With this purpose in mind, he summoned the Frenchman one morning and led him along some dark corridors. Suddenly a side door opened, two servants pushed the Frenchman in and locked the door after him. The Frenchman, unruffled, did not flee, but awaited the attack. When the bear came close, he pulled a small pistol from his pocket, held it to the hungry beast's ear and fired. The bear rolled over. People came running to open the door; Kirila Petrovich appeared, astonished by the outcome of his joke. He demanded a full explanation of the whole business, wanting to know if someone had alerted Desforges to the practical joke set up for him, and if not, why was he carrying a loaded pistol in his pocket. Masha was sent for. She came running and translated her father's questions to the Frenchman.

"I had not heard of the bear," answered Deforges, "but I always carry a pistol on me because I do not intend to tolerate offences for which, in view of my position, I cannot demand satisfaction."

Masha looked at him in amazement and translated his words for Kirila Petrovich. The latter made no answer. He gave orders to have the bear removed and skinned, and then, turning to his men, said, "Quite a character, isn't he! He didn't funk, did he, I'll be sworn."

From that time on he took a liking to Desforges and never thought of testing him again.

The incident made an even deeper impression on Maria Kirilovna. It stirred her imagination: she kept seeing in her mind's eye the dead bear and Desforges, as he calmly stood over it and calmly conversed with her. She came to realize that courage and proud self-respect were not the exclusive attributes of one social class; and from that time on she began to show the young tutor her esteem, which was fast turning into favour. A certain relationship was established between them. Masha had a beautiful voice and great musical talent; Desforges offered to give her lessons. The reader will easily guess that after this Masha fell in love with the Frenchman, though for the time being she did not confess it even to herself.

VOLUME TWO

9

T HE GUESTS BEGAN TO ARRIVE the day before the holiday.
Some stayed at the manor house or in one of its wings; others
were put up at the steward's, or at the priest's, or at the houses of
well-to-do peasants. The stables were full of horses, the yards and
barns crowded with carriages of different shapes and sizes. At nine
o'clock in the morning the bells rang for mass: everyone streamed
towards the new stone church, built by Kirila Petrovich and annu-
ally improved by his new gifts. It was filled with such a large crowd
of the honourable faithful that the simple peasants could not get
in and had to stand either at the porch or in the churchyard. The
mass had still not begun: they were waiting for Kirila Petrovich.
At length he arrived in a coach-and-six and solemnly took his
place, accompanied by Maria Kirilovna. The eyes of both men
and women turned on her, the former marvelling at her beauty,
the latter carefully examining her dress. The mass commenced;
the landlord's private singers sang in the choir, reinforced by his
own voice now and then. Kirila Petrovich prayed, looking neither
to the right nor to the left, and bowing to the ground with proud
humility when the deacon referred, in a thunderous voice, to *the
founder of this house of God*.

The mass was over. Kirila Petrovich went up to kiss the crucifix
first. Everyone lined up after him; then all the neighbours filed
by him to pay their respects. The ladies surrounded Masha. On
leaving the church, Kirila Petrovich invited everybody to dine
at his house, got into his carriage and drove home. The whole
crowd followed him. The rooms were soon filled with guests.
New people arrived every minute and could hardly push their way
through to the master of the house. The ladies, dressed according

to yesterday's fashion, in expensive but worn garments, and be-decked with pearls and diamonds, sat decorously in a semi-circle, while the men crowded around the caviar and the vodka, talking in loud, discordant tones. In the hall, the table was laid for eighty. The servants were busily rushing about, arranging bottles and decanters and smoothing out tablecloths. At last the butler an-nounced, "Dinner is served," and Kirila Petrovich went to take his place at the table first. The ladies followed after him, the matrons solemnly taking their places according to a system of seniority, while the unmarried girls huddled together like a flock of timid little goats and chose places next to one another. The men seated themselves on the opposite side. The tutor sat at the end of the table, next to little Sasha.

The waiters began to serve the dishes according to rank, resorting in case of doubt to guesses based on Lavater's system,* and almost always hitting the mark. The clinking of plates and spoons mingled with the guests' loud conversation. Kirila Petrovich looked merrily round the table, fully enjoying his happy role as the generous host. At this moment, a coach-and-six drove into the courtyard.

"Who is that?" asked the host.

"It's Anton Pafnutych," answered several voices.

The door opened and Anton Pafnutych Spitsyn, a fat man of fifty with a round, pockmarked face adorned with a triple chin, burst into the room, bowing and smiling, and ready to offer his apologies.

"Set a place right here," cried Kirila Petrovich. "Welcome, Anton Pafnutych; sit down and tell us what the meaning of all this is: you didn't come to my mass and are late for dinner. This is most unlike you, for you're both pious and fond of your stomach."

"Forgive me, please," answered Anton Pafnutych, tucking his napkin into a buttonhole of his pea-coloured coat. "Excuse me, dear sir, Kirila Petrovich: I did set out early for the journey, but I'd scarcely travelled ten versts when the rim on one of my front wheels broke into two: what was there to do? Fortunately, we weren't too far from a village, but even so, by the time we'd dragged the carriage there, sought out the blacksmith and made repairs as best we could, full three hours had passed, there was no helping it. Not daring to drive straight across Kistenevka wood, I made a detour—"

"Aha!" interrupted Kirila Petrovich, "I see you're not a valiant knight. What are you afraid of?"

"What indeed, dear sir Kirila Petrovich! Dubrovsky, that's what! You can never tell when you might fall into his clutches. He's nobody's fool: he doesn't let people off lightly; and especially me, Heaven help me – he would skin me twice."

"Why, brother, such a distinction?"

"Why indeed, dear sir Kirila Petrovich! For the lawsuit, of course, against the late Andrei Gavrilovich. Wasn't I the one who, in order to please you – that is, according to my conscience and the truth – testified that the Dubrovskys held possession of Kistenevka without any rights, thanks merely to your generosity? Already the late Andrei Gavrilovich (may he rest in peace) promised to have a word with me in his own fashion; do you think his son won't keep his father's promise? By God's grace I've been spared until now. So far they've plundered only one of my granaries, but you can never tell when they might find their way to the manor house."

"And when they do, they'll have a merry time," remarked Kirila Petrovich. "The little red coffer, methinks, is full to the brim."

"How could it be, my dear sir, Kirila Petrovich? It used to be full, but by now it's entirely empty."

"Enough of fibbing, Anton Pafnutych. We know you all too well: what would you be spending money on? You live at home like a pig in a sty, never inviting anybody and fleecing your peasants; you do nothing but scrape and save, I'll vow."

"Surely, most worthy sir, Kirila Petrovich, you are but jesting," muttered Anton Pafnutych with a smile. "God is my witness, I've been ruined."

Anton Pafnutych proceeded to swallow down his host's high-handed joke with a greasy mouthful of fish pie. Kirila Petrovich let him be and turned to the new police chief, a guest at his house for the first time, who was seated at the far end of the table, next to the tutor.

"Well, Mr Superintendent, will you at last catch Dubrovsky?"

The police chief winced, bowed, smiled, and said at length in a faltering voice, "We will do our best, Your Excellency."

"Hm, do your best. All of you have been doing your best for a long time, yet we've seen no results. And why should you wish to catch him, come to think of it? His robberies are sheer blessings for senior policemen: journeys, investigations, expeditions, all of it bringing grist to the mill. Why snuff out such a benefactor? Isn't that true, Mr Superintendent?"

"That is the plain truth, Your Excellency," answered the superintendent, totally confused.

The guests burst into laughter.

"I like the lad for his sincerity," said Kirila Petrovich. "It's a pity they burned our late superintendent, Taras Alexeyevich: the neighbourhood would be more peaceful with him around. By the way, what do you hear about Dubrovsky? Where was he seen last?"

"At my house, Kirila Petrovich," resounded a lady's booming voice. "He dined at my house last Tuesday."

All eyes turned towards Anna Savishna Globova, a simple-hearted widow whom everybody loved for her kind and cheerful disposition. Everyone waited for her story with interest.

"I should mention that three months ago I sent my steward to the post office to forward some money to my Vanyusha. I don't indulge my son, and wouldn't have the means for it even if I wanted to; but as you all know, an officer of the Guards must live decently, and so I try to share with my Vanyusha what little income I have. This time I sent him two thousand roubles. Dubrovsky did cross my mind more than once, but I said to myself: the town's close by, a mere seven versts; the money'll get through with God's help. But, come evening, there was my steward returning pale, all tattered, and on foot. 'Aah!' I cried. 'What's the matter? What's happened to you?' 'Dear Anna Savishna ma'am,' says he, 'the bandits robbed me, they all but killed me; Dubrovsky himself was there – he wanted to hang me, but took pity on me and let me go, but not before robbing me clean, and taking away even the horse and cart.' My heart stood still: gracious goodness heavens, what'll my Vanyusha do? But there was no helping it: I wrote my son a letter, telling him all about it and sending him my blessing without as much as half a copeck.

"A week went by, then another – suddenly a carriage drives into my yard. Some general's asking if he could see me: welcome, show him in. A man enters, aged about thirty-five, swarthy, with black hair, whiskers and beard, just like a portrait of Kulnev;* introduces himself as a friend and former comrade of my late husband Ivan Andreyevich. He was riding by, says he, and couldn't miss visiting his friend's widow, knowing that I lived here. I treated him to whatever was in the house, and we talked about this and that, mentioning at last Dubrovsky, too. I told him about my misfortune. My general frowned. 'That's strange,' says he. 'What I've heard is that Dubrovsky attacks, not just anybody, but only men known for their riches; and even with them he divides the spoils, not robbing them clean; and as for murder, he's never been accused of that. Isn't there some mischief in this? Pray send for your steward.' We sent for the steward; he appeared; seeing the general he just stood rooted to the ground. 'Would you mind telling me, brother, just how it was Dubrovsky robbed you and wanted to hang you?' My steward went all a-tremble and threw himself at the general's feet. 'Gracious sir, I am guilty: it was the Devil's work – I lied.' 'If that's so,' replied the general, 'then please be good enough to tell your lady how the whole thing happened, while I listen.' The steward could not recover his senses. 'Well,' continued the general, 'do tell us: where was it you met Dubrovsky?' 'At the two pines, my gracious sir, at the two pines.' 'And what did he say to you?' 'He asked me, whose man are you, where are you going, and what for?' 'Very well, and then?' 'And then he demanded the letter and the money.' 'Well?' 'I gave him the letter and the money.' 'And he? Well, and what did he do?' 'Gracious sir, I am guilty.' 'But what did he do?' 'He returned the money and the letter to me, saying, move on, and God be with you; take them to the post office.' 'And what did you do?' 'Gracious sir, I am guilty.' 'I'll settle with you, friend,' said the general menacingly. 'And you, madam, be so good as to give orders to have this rascal's trunk searched; as for him, give him to me, I'll teach him a lesson. I want you to know that Dubrovsky used to be an officer of the Guards himself, and he would do no wrong to a former comrade.' I guessed who His Excellency was, but I wasn't going to enter into a discussion on that score. His coachman tied the steward to his carriage box. The money was found; the general stayed to dine with me, and left right after dinner, taking the steward with him. They found the steward the next day in the woods, tied to an oak and stripped like a lime sapling."

Everybody, especially the young ladies, listened to Anna Savishna's story with bated breath. Many of them wished Dubrovsky well, seeing a romantic hero in him; this was especially true of Maria Kirilovna, an ardent dreamer, brought up on Radcliffe's mysterious horrors.*

"And you suppose, Anna Savishna, that it was Dubrovsky himself who visited you?" asked Kirila Petrovich. "You couldn't be further from the truth. I don't know who visited you, but it certainly wasn't Dubrovsky."

"How now, my dear sir? Who else if not Dubrovsky would take to the highways, stopping and searching travellers?"

"I don't know, but surely not Dubrovsky. I remember him as a child: he may have become dark-haired since, though at that time he was a little boy with curly blond hair. But this I do know, that he was five years older than my Masha: consequently he's not thirty-five, but about twenty-three."

"Exactly so, Your Excellency," declared the police chief. "I have in my pocket Vladimir Dubrovsky's description, and it says precisely that he's in his twenty-third year."

"Ah!" said Kirila Petrovich. "Would you read that description while we listen: it wouldn't be amiss to know his distinctive features, in case we run into him; we wouldn't want to let him slip away, would we?"

The police chief drew from his pocket a rather soiled sheet of paper, solemnly unfolded it and read in a singsong voice:

"Vladimir Dubrovsky's distinctive features, taken down from the words of his former house serfs: He is in his twenty-third year of life, of medium *height*, with a clear *complexion*; he shaves his *beard*, his *eyes* are brown, his *hair* dark blond and his *nose* straight. *Special distinctive features*: said to have none."

"And that's all," said Kirila Petrovich.

"That is all," replied the police chief, folding up the paper.

"Congratulations, Mr Superintendent. What a splendid document! It'll indeed be a simple matter to find Dubrovsky by these distinctive features. Who else, after all, is of medium height, with dark-blond hair, straight nose and brown eyes! I'll bet you could talk with Dubrovsky himself for three full hours and not guess with whom fate has thrown you together. Clever fellows, these officials, I must say!"

The police chief meekly put the document in his pocket and silently turned to his goose and cabbage. The servants, in the meantime, had gone around the table several times, filling up glasses. Several bottles of Caucasian and Tsimlyanskoye* wines had been popped open and graciously accepted under the name of champagne; the faces began to glow and the conversation grew more and more noisy, disconnected and merry.

"No," continued Kirila Petrovich, "we'll never see another superintendent like the late Taras Alexeyevich! You couldn't catch him out, he was no fool. It's a pity they burnt the lad: he wouldn't have let a single one get away from the whole band. He'd have caught them to a man; even Dubrovsky himself couldn't have slipped away from him or bribed his way out. Taras Alexeyevich would have got the money from him all right, and wouldn't have let him go either: such was the character of the deceased. There's no other way, it seems: I'll have to take the matter into my own hands and go after the robber with my own servants. I'll dispatch twenty men to begin with; they'll clean up the robbers' woods, for they're not what you might call timid fellows: each will take on a bear single-handed, so they're not likely to turn tail on some robbers."

"How is your bear, dear sir Kirila Petrovich?" asked Anton Pafnutych, reminded of a shaggy acquaintance and a certain practical joke of which he had once been the victim.

"Misha has succumbed," replied Kirila Petrovich. "He died an honourable death, at the hands of an adversary. And there sits his vanquisher." Kirila Petrovich pointed at Desforges. "You should get yourself an icon of the Frenchman's patron saint, for he's avenged your… craving your pardon… Do you remember?"

"How could I not remember?" said Anton Pafnutych, scratching himself. "I do, only too well. So Misha's dead. I'm sorry for him, upon my word I am. What a jester he was! And what a clever fellow! You'll never find another bear like him. And why did m'sieur kill him?"

Kirila Petrovich launched with great pleasure into the story of his Frenchman's exploit, for he had the happy faculty of priding himself on everything that surrounded him. The guests listened attentively to the tale of Misha's demise and looked with surprise at Desforges, who, not suspecting that the subject of conversation was his courage, calmly sat in his place, handing out admonitions to his restive charge.

The dinner, which had lasted about three hours, came to an end; the host put his napkin on the table, everyone rose and repaired to the drawing room, where coffee and cards were awaiting them, along with a continuation of the drinking, so famously commenced in the dining hall.

10

ABOUT SEVEN O'CLOCK in the evening some of the guests wanted to leave, but the host, merry with drink, gave orders to lock the gates and made it clear that nobody was to leave the house till morning. Soon, the thunderous notes of music were heard; the doors were opened into the hall and the dancing commenced. The host and his intimate circle sat in a corner, drinking glass after glass and watching with delight the gaiety of the young. The old ladies played cards. As usual (except where a brigade of uhlans is quartered), there were fewer cavaliers than ladies, and therefore every man at all fit to dance was recruited. The tutor distinguished himself above the rest, dancing more than anyone; the young ladies kept choosing him, and found him an adroit waltzing partner. He whirled around with Maria Kirilovna several times, so much so that the other young ladies began to make derisive comments about them. At length, around midnight, the tired host stopped the dancing, giving orders to serve supper, while he himself retired to bed.

Kirila Petrovich's absence lent a freer and livelier spirit to the company. The cavaliers took the liberty of sitting next to their ladies, the girls laughed and whispered comments to their neighbours and the married women loudly conversed across the table. The men drank, argued, and roared with laughter – in other words, the supper turned out to be exceedingly merry, leaving behind many pleasant memories.

There was only one person who did not take part in the general festivities: this was Anton Pafnutych, sitting in his place, gloomy and silent, eating absently and looking extremely worried. All the talk about robbers had stirred up his imagination. As we shall soon see, he had plenty of reason to fear them.

He had not sworn falsely in invoking God as his witness that his little red coffer was empty: it indeed was empty, because the money he used to keep in it had been transferred to a leather pouch, which he was wearing under his shirt around his neck. Only by this precaution was he able to still his suspicions and constant fear. Compelled to spend the night in a strange house, he was afraid that he might be assigned a bed somewhere in a remote room easily accessible to thieves. He looked around for a room-mate to protect him, and his choice fell on Desforges. The Frenchman's appearance, exuding strength, and even more, the courage he had displayed in his encounter with the bear – a creature that Anton Pafnutych could not recall without trembling – were the decisive factors in his choice. When everybody rose from the table, Anton Pafnutych started circling around the young French-man, coughing and clearing his throat, until at last he turned to him with his request:

"Hm, hm, couldn't I, m'sieur, spend the night in your little room, because, you see…"

"*Que désire monsieur?*"* asked Desforges with a polite bow.

"Ach, it's a pity you haven't learnt Russian yet, m'sieur. Jer ver, mua, shey voo cooshey,* d'you understand?"

"*Monsieur, très volontiers,*" replied Desforges. "*Veuillez donner des ordres en conséquence.*"*

Anton Pafnutych, highly satisfied with his ability to communicate in French, immediately went off to make the necessary arrangements.

The guests wished one another goodnight, each going to the room assigned to him. Anton Pafnutych proceeded with the tutor to his wing. It was a dark night. Desforges lit the way with a lantern, and Anton Pafnutych followed behind him quite cheerfully, occasionally pressing the secret sum against his chest in order to be sure that the money was still there.

Arriving at the room, the tutor lit a candle, and both started undressing. In the meantime, Anton Pafnutych walked about the room to check on the door locks and the windows, shaking his head at the disheartening results of his inspection. The only lock on the door was a latch, and the windows had not yet been fitted with double frames. He tried to complain about it to Desforges, but his knowledge of French was insufficient to convey such a complex matter; since the Frenchman did not understand him, he was compelled to stop complaining. Their beds stood opposite each other; both men lay down, and the tutor blew out the candle.

"Poorkua voo tooshey, poorkua voo tooshey?"* cried Anton Pafnutych, trying somehow to conjugate the Russian verb *tushit'* – "extinguish" – in a French manner. "I can't *dormir** in the dark."

But Desforges did not understand his exclamations and wished him goodnight.

"Damned infidel," grumbled Spitsyn, wrapping himself in his blanket. "Why did he have to blow out that candle? So much the worse for him. I can't sleep without a light. M'sieur, m'sieur," he went on, "jer ver avek voo parley."*

But the Frenchman did not answer and soon started snoring.

"Snoring, the French beast!" said Anton Pafnutych to himself. "And I can't even think of sleep. Thieves might come in through the unlocked door or climb through the window, and this beast couldn't be waked with a cannon."

"M'sieur! Hey, m'sieur! The Deuce take you!"

Then Anton Pafnutych fell silent: fatigue and the effects of the alcohol gradually overcame his fear; he dozed off and soon fell into a deep slumber.

A strange awakening came upon him. He felt, still in sleep, that someone was gently pulling at the collar of his shirt. Opening his eyes, he saw Desforges before him in the pale light of the autumn dawn: the Frenchman was holding a pocket pistol in one hand and unfastening the cherished treasure with the other. Anton Pafnutych's heart stood still.

"Kes ker sey, m'sieur, kes ker sey?"* he uttered in a trembling voice.

"Hush, be quiet," answered the tutor in pure Russian. "Be quiet, or you're done for. I am Dubrovsky."

11

W E SHALL NOW ask the reader for permission to explain the last events of our tale by certain previous occurrences that we have not yet had occasion to relate.

One day at the P. post station, inside the house of the superintendent whom we have mentioned earlier, there sat in a corner a traveller with a meek and patient air, which betrayed either a member of the third estate or a foreigner* – in any case a person unable to assert his rights on the mail route. His carriage stood in the yard, waiting to be greased. A small suitcase – a meagre token of less-than-comfortable circumstances – lay in the carriage. The traveller did not ask for either tea or coffee; he just looked through the window and whistled – an action that greatly annoyed the superintendent's wife, who was sitting behind the partition.

"The Lord blessed us with a whistler," she muttered. "Ugh, he does whistle, may he be struck dumb, the damned infidel."

"Surely now," said the superintendent, "it's no great matter: let him whistle."

"No great matter?" rejoined his wife crossly. "And don't you know what they say?"

"What do they say? That whistling drives money away? Nay, Pakhomovna, with us whistling makes no difference: there's no money in any case."

"But let him go anyway, Sidorych. What makes you keep him here? Give him some horses and let him go to the Devil!"

"He can wait, Pakhomovna: I've only three teams of horses in the stables, the fourth is resting. You can never tell, some better sort of traveller may turn up: I don't want to stick my neck out for a Frenchman. Ha! Just as I said! Here they come galloping. And how fast, too! As I live, it's a general!"

A carriage stopped by the porch. A footman jumped off the box and opened the door: soon a young man in a military coat and white cap came in to see the superintendent; the footman brought in a travelling box after him and put it on a window sill.

"Horses!" said the officer in a imperious voice.

"In just one moment," answered the superintendent. "May I have your order?"

"I don't carry an order. I'm travelling by side roads. Don't you recognize me?"

The superintendent began to bustle about and ran to hurry the coachmen. The young man paced up and down the room, then went behind the partition and softly asked the superintendent's wife who the other traveller was.

"Heaven knows," she answered. "Some sort of Frenchman. He's been waiting for horses these five hours, whistling. I'm sick to death of the damned fool."

The young man addressed the traveller in French.

"May I ask where you are going?" he inquired.

"To the town nearby," replied the Frenchman, "and from there to a landowner who's hired me unseen as a tutor. I thought I'd reach my destination today, but evidently monsieur the superintendent has decided otherwise. It's hard to find horses in this part of the world, officer."

"And who among the local landowners has hired you?" asked the officer.

"Mr Troyekurov," replied the Frenchman.

"Mr Troyekurov? What sort of man is this Troyekurov?"

"*Ma foi, mon officier…** I've heard little good about him. They say he's a proud and wilful gentleman, cruel in his treatment of those in his service; apparently no one can get along with him, everyone trembles at the very sound of his name, and he's reported not to stand on ceremony with his tutors (*avec les outchitels*),* having already flogged two of them to death."

"Heaven help me! And you've decided to accept a position at the house of such a monster?"

"What else can I do, officer? He's offering me a good salary: three thousand roubles a year, plus room and board. Perhaps I'll be luckier than the others. I have an aged mother, for whose keep I shall be sending off half my salary; from the rest I can accumulate in five years sufficient capital to secure my independence; and then, *bonsoir*, I'm going to Paris and will set up a business."

"Does anybody know you at Troyekurov's house?" asked the officer.

"Nobody," the tutor answered. "He had me sent down from Moscow through the good offices of an acquaintance whose cook, a compatriot of mine, recommended me. I should mention that I had intended to become a confectioner, not a tutor, but I was told that in your country the calling of tutor is far more lucrative..."

The officer was lost in deep thought.

"Listen," he interrupted the Frenchman, "what would you say if instead of this prospective position someone offered you ten thousand roubles ready cash on condition that you immediately return to Paris?"

The Frenchman looked at the officer in astonishment, broke into a smile, and shook his head.

"The horses are ready," said the superintendent, entering. The footman came in to confirm the same.

"Presently," said the officer. "Leave the room for a minute." The superintendent and the footman both left. "I'm not joking," he continued in French. "I can pay you ten thousand roubles; all I ask in exchange are your absence and your papers." With these words he opened the travelling box and drew out several bundles of banknotes.

The Frenchman's eyes bulged. He did not know what to think.

"My absence and my papers..." he repeated in amazement. "Here are my papers... But you must be joking. What would you want my papers for?"

"That is my own business. I ask you: do you agree or don't you?"

The Frenchman, still not believing his ears, handed his papers to the young officer, who examined them quickly.

"Your passport... That's good. A letter of recommendation. Let's see. Birth certificate: that's splendid. Well, here's your money; return home. Goodbye."

The Frenchman stood as if rooted to the ground.

The officer returned.

"I almost forgot the most important thing. Give me your word of honour that all this will remain between us. Your word of honour."

"I give you my word of honour," replied the Frenchman, "but what about my papers? How do I get by without them?"

"Report in the first town you come to that you were robbed by Dubrovsky. They will believe you and give you the necessary attestation. Farewell; may God grant you a safe and speedy journey to Paris, and may you find your mother in good health."

Dubrovsky left the room, got into his carriage, and galloped away.

The superintendent looked out of the window, and when the carriage drove away, he turned to his wife with the exclamation, "What do you know, Pakhomovna! That was Dubrovsky!"

The postmistress dashed to the window, but it was already too late: Dubrovsky was far away. She started scolding her husband.

"Don't you fear the Lord, Sidorych? Why didn't you tell me before, so I could've taken a good look at Dubrovsky? Now you can wait until kingdom come, he'll never drop in again. You have no conscience, have you?"

The Frenchman still stood as if rooted to the ground. The agreement with the officer, the money and all the rest still seemed like a dream to him. But the bundles of bank notes were there, in his pocket, eloquently confirming that the amazing incident was real.

He decided to hire horses to the nearest town. The coachman drove him at a snail's pace, and it was night by the time they got there.

Before reaching the town gate, at which a broken sentry box stood instead of a guard, the Frenchman ordered the driver to stop, got out of the carriage, and set out to go the rest of the way on foot, explaining to the coachman by hand signs that he was giving him both the carriage and the suitcase as a tip. The driver was as much astounded by the Frenchman's generosity as the Frenchman had been by Dubrovsky's offer. He came to the conclusion, however, that the foreigner had gone out of his mind; he thanked him with a profound bow and, not thinking it wise to ride into town, proceeded to a house of entertainment he knew, whose landlord was an intimate friend of his. There he spent the night; the next morning he went on his way with his team of horses, without the carriage or the suitcase, but with swollen cheeks and red eyes.

Dubrovsky, having obtained the Frenchman's papers, boldly presented himself, as we have seen, at Troyekurov's house and settled there. Whatever his secret intentions might have been (we shall learn about them later), his conduct was blameless. It is true that he did not pay much attention to little Sasha's education, giving free rein to the boy's pranks and not requiring him to complete exercises that had been set only for appearances' sake. On the other hand, he followed with particular attention his female pupil's progress in music, sitting with her by the piano for hours at a time. Everyone liked the young tutor: Kirila Petrovich for his daring agility in hunting; Maria Kirilovna for his boundless zeal and quiet attentiveness; Sasha for his lenience toward his pranks; and the servants for his good nature and a generosity that seemed incompatible with his station. He himself appeared to have grown attached to the whole family and to regard himself as one of its members.

About a month had passed between the time he had taken up the calling of tutor and the memorable holiday feast; yet no one suspected that the modest young Frenchman was in fact the dreaded robber whose name alone was enough to strike terror in the hearts of all the landowners of the neighbourhood. All through that month Dubrovsky had not left Pokrovskoye, yet rumours about his robberies did not stop circulating, thanks perhaps to the inventive imagination of local people, or perhaps because his band continued its exploits even in the absence of its chief

When, however, he found himself spending the night in the same room with a man whom he had every reason to regard as a personal enemy and one of the chief architects of his misfortune, Dubrovsky could not resist the temptation: he knew about the existence of the pouch and resolved to lay his hands on it. We have seen how he astounded poor Anton Pafnutych by his unexpected metamorphosis from tutor into robber.

At nine o'clock in the morning the guests who had spent the night at Pokrovskoye began to gather in the drawing room, where a samovar was already boiling; seated before it were Maria Kirilovna, in her morning dress, and Kirila Petrovich, in a flannel jacket and slippers, drinking his tea from a cup as wide as a slop basin. The last to appear was Anton Pafnutych; he looked so pale and seemed so downcast that everybody was struck by his appearance, and Kirila Petrovich even inquired after his health. Spitsyn gave an incoherent answer and kept glancing with horror at the tutor, who sat there as if nothing had happened. In a few minutes a servant came in to announce that Spitsyn's carriage was ready; Anton Pafnutych hastened to make his farewell bows and, despite his host's protestations, hurried from the room in order to drive off immediately. Nobody could understand what had happened to him; Kirila Petrovich eventually decided that he must have overeaten. After tea and a farewell breakfast, the other guests began to take their leave, and Pokrovskoye became deserted, everything returning to normal.

12

NOTHING REMARKABLE HAPPENED for several days. Life at Pokrovskoye had its routine. Kirila Petrovich rode out to hunt every day, and Maria Kirilovna was occupied with reading, walks, and above all, music lessons. She was beginning to understand her own heart, confessing to herself with involuntary vexation that she was by no means indifferent to the young Frenchman's good qualities. On his part he never allowed himself to step beyond the limits of respect and strict propriety, which both flattered her pride and reassured her, beset as she was with alarming doubts. She gave herself over to her enjoyable routine with more and more confidence. She felt listless when Desforges was not there, and in his presence gave him her full attention, wishing to know his opinion about everything and always agreeing with him. Maybe she was not yet in love, but her passion was ready to flare up at the first sign of an accidental obstacle or an unexpected twist of fate.

One day, as she entered the room where the tutor waited for her, she was surprised to see signs of confusion on his pale face. She lifted the lid of the piano and sang a few notes, but Dubrovsky, excusing himself with a headache, interrupted the lesson; and as he folded over the sheet of music he surreptitiously slipped a letter into her hand. Maria Kirilovna, given no time to refuse it, took the letter; she immediately regretted it, but by that time Dubrovsky had left the room. She went to her room, opened the letter, and read the following:

Come to the arbour by the brook at seven o'clock this evening. I must speak to you.

Her curiosity was strongly aroused. She had long expected a confession, both wishing for it and fearing it. She would have enjoyed hearing a confirmation of what she had suspected, but she was conscious that it would be improper for her to listen to such a declaration on the part of a man who, due to his station, could never hope to gain her hand. She resolved to go to the rendezvous, but was not sure how to receive the tutor's confession: whether to respond with aristocratic indignation, friendly remonstrances, light banter or silent sympathy. In the meantime she kept looking at the clock every minute. It grew dark, the candles were lit, Kirila Petrovich sat down to play boston with some neighbours who had driven over. The clock on the table struck a quarter to seven. Maria Kirilovna inconspicuously stepped out onto the porch, looked around her in all directions and ran into the garden.

The night was dark, the sky covered with clouds, and one could not see two steps ahead, but Maria Kirilovna could make her way along familiar paths even in the dark. It took her only a minute to reach the arbour. Here she stopped to catch her breath so as to be able to meet Desforges with an indifferent and unhurried air. But Desforges was already standing before her.

"I am grateful to you," he said in a low and sad tone, "for not refusing my request. I would have fallen into despair if you had decided not to come."

Maria Kirilovna answered with the ready phrase, "I hope you will not make me regret my compliance."

He stood in silence, as if to gather his thoughts.

"Circumstances demand... I must leave you," he said at last. "Soon you will probably learn the reason yourself... But before we part I owe you an explanation."

Maria Kirilovna made no answer. She took these words as an introduction to the confession she had expected.

"I am not who you think I am," he confessed, lowering his head. "I am not the Frenchman, Desforges: I am Dubrovsky."

She let out a shriek.

"Don't be afraid, for Heaven's sake: you need not fear my name. Yes, I am the unfortunate person whom your father has deprived of his last piece of bread, driven from his parental home and sent onto the highways to rob. But you need not fear me, either for yourself or for him. The matter is closed. I have forgiven him, and mark you, it was you who saved him. My first bloody act ought to have been directed against him. I prowled around his house, determining where the fire should start, which way to get into his bedroom and how to cut off all his routes of escape, but at that moment you passed by me like a heavenly vision, and forgiveness filled my heart. I understood that the house where you lived was sacred, and that no being related to you by the bond of blood could be subject to my curse. I renounced vengeance as madness. For days I roamed near the Pokrovskoye gardens in the hope of catching sight of your white dress at a distance. I followed you on your incautious walks, stealing from bush to bush and feeling elated at the thought that I was guarding you, that there could be no danger for you where I was secretly present. At last an opportunity presented itself. I came to live in your house. These three weeks have been a period of happiness for me. Recalling them will always be a consolation amid my sad days... News that I have received today makes it impossible for me to stay here any longer. I take leave of you today... at this very moment... But first I had to reveal my thoughts to you, so that you might not curse or despise me. Think of Dubrovsky sometimes; be assured that he was born for a different destiny, that his soul was capable of loving you, that he would never..."

Just then a low whistle was heard, and Dubrovsky fell silent. He seized her hand and pressed it to his burning lips. The whistle was repeated.

"Farewell," said Dubrovsky, "they're calling me, and a minute's delay may bring my downfall."

He walked away, while Maria Kirilovna stood motionless. Then he came back and took her hand again.

"If at any time in the future," he said to her in a gentle, touching voice, "if at any time misfortune befalls you and you cannot expect help or protection from anyone, will you promise me that in such a case you will turn to me and demand all that I am capable of, in order to rescue you? Will you promise not to scorn my devotion?"

Maria Kirilovna wept in silence. The whistle was heard a third time.

"You're bringing my downfall on me!" cried Dubrovsky. "I will not leave until you give me an answer. Will you, or will you not, promise?"

"I promise," whispered the lovely girl in her misery.

Maria Kirilovna, agitated by her meeting with Dubrovsky, walked back towards the house. She realized that the servants were all running about – the whole house was in a commotion, there were a lot of people in the courtyard and a carriage stood by the porch. She could hear Kirila Petrovich's voice at a distance, and she hurried inside, fearing that her absence might be noticed. She was met by Kirila Petrovich in the hall. His guests stood around the local police chief – our acquaintance – and showered him with questions. The police chief, dressed for the road and armed to the teeth, gave his answers with a mysterious and preoccupied air.

"Where have you been, Masha?" asked Kirila Petrovich. "Did you happen to see Monsieur Desforges?"

Masha could just barely utter a negative reply.

"Just imagine," continued Kirila Petrovich, "the police chief's come to capture him, and he's trying to convince me that the man is Dubrovsky himself."

"He fits the description exactly, Your Excellency," said the superintendent respectfully.

"Pooh, friend!" interrupted Kirila Petrovich. "I'll tell you where to go with your descriptions! I'm not going to hand my Frenchman over to you until I've sorted this matter out myself. You can't take on trust what Anton Pafnutych says, for he's a coward and a liar: he must have just dreamt that the tutor wanted to rob him. Why didn't he say a single word about it to me that morning?"

"The Frenchman scared the life out of him, Your Excellency," answered the police officer, "and made him swear to keep mum—"

"A pack of lies," declared Kirila Petrovich. "I'll clear up the matter this minute. Where's that tutor?" he said, turning to a servant who was just entering.

"He can't be found anywhere, sir," answered the servant.

"Then go and search for him," shouted Troyekurov, beginning to entertain some doubts. "Show me your vaunted description," he said to the police chief, who immediately produced the paper.

"Hm, hm. Twenty-three years... Well, that's correct, but it doesn't prove anything by itself. Well, where is the tutor?"

"Can't find him," was the answer once more.

Kirilia Petrovich began to grow anxious. Maria Kirilovna looked more dead than alive.

"You're pale, Masha," remarked her father. "You've been frightened."

"No, Papa," replied Masha, "I just have a headache."

"Go to your room, Masha, and don't be alarmed."

Masha kissed his hand and retired to her room, where she threw herself on the bed and burst into hysterical sobs. The maidservants came running; they undressed her and with difficulty managed to calm her by means of cold water and all kinds of spirits. They put her to bed, and she finally settled into sleep.

The Frenchman had still not been found during all this time. Kirila Petrovich paced up and down the hall, dourly whistling, 'May thou, thunder of victory, rumble'. The guests whispered among themselves, the local police chief looked foolish, and the Frenchman was still not to be found. Evidently he had managed to escape, having been warned. But by whom and how – that remained a mystery.

The clock struck eleven, but nobody even thought of going to bed. At length Kirila Petrovich angrily said to the police chief, "Surely now, you can't stay until morning. My house is not a tavern. It'd take a smarter man than you, lad, to catch Dubrovsky, if he is indeed Dubrovsky. Off with you now, and be a little quicker in future. And it's time for you too to go home," he continued, turning to his guests. "Give orders to have your horses hitched up: I want to go to bed."

Such was the ungracious manner of Troyekurov's parting with his guests.

13

S OME TIME WENT BY without anything remarkable happening. At the beginning of the following summer, however, some great changes occurred in Kirila Petrovich's family life.

At a distance of thirty versts from Pokrovskoye there was a prosperous estate owned by Prince Vereysky. The Prince had spent a long time abroad, leaving the management of his estate to a retired major and thus there had been no commerce between Pokrovskoye and Arbatovo. At the end of May, however, the Prince returned from abroad and came to live on his estate, which he had never seen before. Used to a life full of distractions, he could not bear solitude, and on the third day after his arrival he came over to dine with Troyekurov, whom he had known at one time.

The Prince was about fifty but looked much older. Excesses of all kinds had undermined his health and left on him their indelible mark. His outward appearance was nevertheless pleasant, even remarkable; and having spent his whole life in society, he had acquired a certain charm, especially in his dealings with women. He had a constant need for distractions and was constantly bored. Kirila Petrovich was highly gratified by his visit, taking it as a mark of respect from a man who mingled in high society, and he treated him, as was his habit, to a tour of his various establishments, including his dog kennels. But the Prince almost suffocated in the canine atmosphere and hastened to quit it, holding a scented handkerchief to his nose. The old-fashioned garden with its pruned lime trees, square-shaped pond and symmetrical paths did not please him, since he was fond of English gardens and so-called nature, but he nonetheless handed out compliments and showed enthusiasm. A servant came to announce that the meal was served. They went to dine. Exhausted by his walk, the prince limped along, already regretting his visit.

In the dining hall, however, Maria Kirilovna met them, and the old skirt-chaser was struck by her beauty. Troyekurov seated his guest next to her. Her presence revived the Prince; he was cheerful company and managed to capture her attention several times with interesting anecdotes. After dinner Kirila Petrovich suggested a ride on horseback, but the Prince excused himself, pointing at his velvet boots and half-jokingly complaining of gout; in fact he preferred a jaunt in a carriage, understanding that he would not then be separated from the delightful girl he had been sitting with. The horses were hitched to the carriage. The two old men and the young beauty got in and rode off. The conversation never flagged. Maria Kirilovna was listening with pleasure to the flattering and humorous compliments this man of the world was offering her, when suddenly Vereysky turned to Kirila Petrovich and asked him what that burnt-down building was and to whom it belonged. Kirilia Petrovich frowned: the recollections evoked by the burnt-down homestead were unpleasant to him. He answered that the land was now his, but earlier it used to belong to Dubrovsky.

"To Dubrovsky?" repeated Vereysky. "To the famous robber?"

"To the robber's father," answered Troyekurov, "who was pretty much of a robber himself."

"Incidentally, what's become of our Rinaldo?* Is he alive? Has he been captured?"

"Both alive and at large; and he won't be caught either, whilst we have police who are in collusion with brigands. By the way, Prince, Dubrovsky has paid a visit to your Arbatovo, hasn't he?"

"Yes, last year, if I'm not mistaken, he burnt down something or plundered something. Wouldn't it be interesting, though, Maria Kirilovna, to make the acquaintance of this romantic hero?"

"Wouldn't it indeed!" said Troyekurov. "She *is* acquainted with him: he gave her music lessons for three weeks without, thank God, taking any wages."

Kirila Petrovich launched into his story about the French tutor. Maria Kirilovna sat on tenterhooks. Vereysky listened to it all with great interest, found it all very strange, and changed the topic. On their return to the house, he gave orders to have his carriage made ready and, despite Kirila Petrovich's earnest entreaties to stay the night, left right after tea. Before he did so, however, he asked Kirila Petrovich to pay him a visit with Maria Kirilovna; and the haughty Troyekurov accepted the invitation because, considering the Prince's title, two stars, and ancestral estate with three thousand serfs, he regarded him to some degree as his equal.

Two days after this occasion Kirila Petrovich set out with his daughter to repay the visit. Approaching Arbatovo, he could not help admiring the peasants' clean and cheerful cottages and the landlord's stone house, built in the style of an English castle. Before the house there stretched a rich green meadow on which Swiss cows grazed, tinkling their bells. An extensive park surrounded his house on all sides. The host came out onto the porch to greet his guests and shook hands with the beautiful young girl. They entered the magnificent dining hall, where the table was set for three. The host led his guests up to a window, from which they beheld a charming view. The Volga flowed below; heavily loaded barges under full sail floated on it, and here and there small fishing vessels, so aptly known as "death traps",* could be glimpsed fleetingly. Hills and fields stretched beyond the river, with some villages enlivening the landscape. Then the host and his guests went to look at the gallery of paintings the Prince had bought abroad. The Prince explained to Maria Kirilovna what the different pictures signified, told her the life stories of the painters and pointed out the merits and shortcomings of their canvases. He spoke about the paintings, not in the pedant's abstract language, but with feeling and imagination. Maria Kirilovna listened to him with pleasure. They went in to dine. Troyekurov fully appreciated both the wines of this Amphitryon* and the artistry of his cook; and Maria Kirilovna did not feel the slightest embarrassment or constraint in conversing with a man whom she had seen only once before. After dinner the host proposed that they repair to the garden. They drank coffee in an arbour on the shore of a wide lake, which was strewn with islands. Suddenly the sound of a wind ensemble could be heard, and a six-oared boat drew up to moor right by the arbour. They went boating on the lake, passing by some islands and landing on others. On one they found a marble statue, on another a secluded cave, and on the third a monument with a mysterious inscription that aroused Maria Kirilovna's curiosity, but she was left to wonder by the Prince's polite half-explanations. Time passed imperceptibly; it began to grow dark. The Prince, under the pretext of chill and damp air, hurried them back to the house, where the samovar was waiting for them. He asked Maria Kirilovna to assume the role of hostess in the house of an old bachelor. She poured the tea, listening to the amiable chatterer's endless stories; suddenly a sound like a shot was heard and a rocket illuminated the sky. The Prince handed Maria Kirilovna her shawl, inviting her and her father to come out onto the balcony. In the dark, in front of the house, fireworks of different colours flared up, began to spin, rose upwards in the shape of ears of grain, palm trees, fountains, then scattered like drops of rain or falling stars, now extinguished, now flaring up anew. Maria Kirilovna enjoyed herself like a child. Prince Vereysky was pleased with her delight, and Troyekurov felt no less satisfied, for he took *tous les frais** of the Prince as gestures of respect and homage paid to him.

The quality of the supper was in no way inferior to that of that the dinner. The guests retired to the rooms assigned to them, and in the morning took leave of their amiable host amidst mutual promises to meet again.

14

MARIA KIRILOVNA was sitting over her embroidery by the open window of her room. Unlike Konrad's mistress, who in her amorous distraction embroidered a rose in green,* Maria did not get her silk mixed up. Under her needle, the canvas unerringly reproduced the features of the original, even though her thoughts were far away.

Suddenly a hand was thrust through the window, quietly depositing a letter on her embroidery frame and disappearing again, before Maria Kirilovna realized what was happening. At the same moment a servant entered to call her to Kirila Petrovich. She hid the letter under her kerchief with a trembling hand and hurried to her father's study.

Kirila Petrovich was not by himself. Prince Vereysky sat with him. When Maria Kirilovna appeared, the Prince stood up and silently bowed to her with an air of embarrassment that was unusual for him.

"Come here, Masha," said Kirila Petrovich. "I have some news, which I hope will gladden you. Here is a suitor for you; the Prince is asking for your hand."

Masha stood rooted to the ground; a deathly pallor spread over her face. She kept her silence. The Prince went up to her, took her hand and asked in a touched tone whether she would consent to make him happy. Masha kept her silence.

"Consent? Of course she'll consent," said Kirila Petrovich. "But you know, Prince, how difficult it is for a girl to pronounce that word. Well, children, kiss each other and be happy."

Masha stood motionless, the old Prince kissed her hand, then suddenly tears coursed down her pale cheeks. The Prince frowned slightly.

"Go to your room, go to your room," said Kirila Petrovich. "Wipe your tears and come back to us again a bit more cheerful.

They all cry when they get engaged," he continued, turning to Vereysky. "This is a custom with them. And now, Prince, let's talk business, that is, let's discuss the dowry."

Maria Kirilovna eagerly availed herself of the opportunity to retire. She ran to her room, locked herself in, and let her tears flow freely as she imagined herself as the old Prince's wife: he had suddenly become repugnant and hateful to her... the marriage frightened her like an executioner's block or the grave...

"No, and a thousand times no," she repeated to herself in despair. "I'd sooner die, I'd sooner retire to a convent, I'd sooner marry Dubrovsky."

This reminded her of the letter, and she eagerly started reading it, sensing that it must be from him. It was indeed written by him and consisted only of the following words:

"Ten o'clock this evening at the same place."

15

THE MOON WAS SHINING. It was a still July night. The wind rose now and then, and a light rustle ran across the entire garden.

Like a light shadow, the lovely young girl drew near the appointed meeting place. Nobody was yet in sight. Suddenly Dubrovsky, coming out from behind the arbour, appeared in front of her.

"I know all about it," he said to her in a soft, sad voice. "Do remember your promise."

"You are offering me your protection," answered Masha. "Don't feel offended, but that frightens me. In what way can you help me?"

"I could rid you of that hateful man."

"For Heaven's sake, don't touch him, don't dare touch him if you love me. I don't want to be the cause of some horrible deed…"

"I will not touch him: your wish is sacred to me. He owes his life to you. No evil deed will ever be committed in your name. You must remain blameless, whatever my crimes are. But how can I save you from your cruel father?"

"There is still some hope. Perhaps I can touch him with my tears and despair. He is obstinate, but he loves me so much."

"Do not hope in vain: in your tears he will see only the usual timidity and revulsion common to young girls when they marry not from love but from careful calculation. What if he takes it into his head to make you happy despite yourself? What if they lead you to the altar by force, putting your life forever into the hands of an old husband?"

"Then… there is nothing else we can do: come for me, and I will be your wife."

Dubrovsky trembled. A crimson flush spread across his pale face which, in the next moment, became even paler than before. He remained silent for a long time, with his head bent.

"Summon up all your spiritual strength, beseech your father, throw yourself at his feet, depict for him the full horror of the future, your youth fading by the side of a decrepit and corrupt old man; bring yourself to make a harsh declaration: tell him that if he remains unbending, then... then you will find a terrible deliverance; tell him that riches will not bring you one moment of happiness; that luxury gladdens only the poor, and even then for only a short time while they are still not used to it; don't stop pestering him, don't be afraid of his anger or threats while there is still a faint glimmer of hope, for Heaven's sake, don't stop pestering him. But if there is really no other way..."

Here Dubrovsky covered his face with his hands and seemed to be gasping for air. Masha wept...

"My unhappy, unhappy destiny," he said with a bitter sigh. "I would give my life for you; just to see you from a distance, to touch your hand used to be ecstasy for me. And now, when there might be an opportunity for me to clasp you to my agitated heart and say, 'Angel! Let us die together!' – now I have to beware of happiness, have to avoid it, unlucky creature that I am, by every means possible. I dare not throw myself at your feet and thank Heaven for an inexplicable, undeserved reward. Oh, how I ought to hate the man who... but I feel that at this moment there can be no room for hatred in my heart."

He gently put his arm around her slender waist and gently drew her to his heart. She leant her head trustingly on the young robber's shoulder. Both were silent.

Time flew.

"I must go," said Masha at last.

Dubrovsky seemed to be waking from a trance. He took her hand and slipped a ring on her finger.

"If you decide to resort to my help," he said, "bring this ring here and drop it into the hollow of this oak. Then I shall know what to do."

Dubrovsky kissed her hand and disappeared among the trees.

16

PRINCE VEREYSKY'S MARRIAGE PROPOSAL was no longer a secret in the neighbourhood. Kirila Petrovich received congratulations, and preparations for the wedding were going forward. Day after day Masha postponed making a decisive declaration. In the meanwhile her manner with her old suitor was cold and strained. The Prince did not seem to mind. He made no effort to inspire love: all he wished for was her tacit consent.

But time was passing. At length Masha decided to act, and wrote a letter to Prince Vereysky: she tried to awaken magnanimity in his heart, openly confessing that she had not the least inclination towards him and beseeching him to give her up himself and thereby protect her from the tyranny of her father. She surreptitiously handed the letter to Prince Vereysky. He read it in private and was not in the least touched by his fiancée's frankness. On the contrary, he realized that it was necessary to hold the wedding earlier, and for that reason thought it advisable to show the letter to his future father-in-law.

Kirila Petrovich flew into a rage; the Prince had great difficulty persuading him not to let on to Masha that he had been informed of the letter. Eventually Kirila Petrovich agreed not to speak about it to her, but he resolved not to waste time and fixed the wedding for the next day. The Prince found the idea well-advised. He came to see his fiancée and told her that her letter had greatly saddened him, but that he was hoping to win her affections with time; that the thought of losing her would be too much for him to bear; and that he simply did not have the strength to sign his own death warrant. After this he respectfully kissed her hand and left for home, not saying a word to her about her father's decision.

He was scarcely past the gate, however, when her father entered her room and commanded her without further ado to be ready for the next day. Maria Kirilovna, already agitated by Prince Vereysky's explanation, burst into tears and threw herself at her father's feet.

"Papa," she cried in a plaintive voice, "Papa, don't ruin me; I don't love the Prince and don't want to be his wife."

"What is the meaning of this?" said Kirila Petrovich sternly. "Until now you've kept silent and been in agreement, but now, when everything is decided, you take it into your head to behave capriciously and start refusing him. Don't play the fool: it'll get you nowhere with me."

"Don't ruin me," repeated poor Masha. "Why are you driving me from you, handing me over to a man I don't love? Have you grown so tired of me? I want to remain with you as before. Papa, it'll be sad for you without me, and sadder still when you remember that I'm unhappy, Papa; don't force me, I don't want to get married…"

Kirila Petrovich was touched, but concealed his feelings and pushed her away, saying severely, "All this is nonsense, do you hear? I know better than you what you need for happiness. Your tears won't help: your wedding will be the day after tomorrow."

"The day after tomorrow!" exclaimed Masha. "My dear God! No, no, that's impossible, it cannot be. Papa, listen to me, if you are resolved to ruin me, I will find a protector, one you can't even think of, and you will see, you will be horrified to see, what you have driven me to."

"What? What is this?" said Troyekurov. "Threats? Are you threatening me, insolent wench? Well, let me tell you, I'm going to do something with you that you can't even imagine. You dare try to scare me with a protector? We will see who this protector will be."

"Vladimir Dubrovsky," replied Masha in her despair.

Kirila Petrovich thought she must have lost her mind and stared at her in astonishment.

"Very well," he said to her after a pause. "Wait for whomever you think will deliver you; but in the meanwhile sit in this room, which you're not going to leave until the very moment of your wedding."

With these words Kirila Petrovich left and locked the door behind him.

The poor girl wept for a long time, imagining the fate awaiting her. The tempestuous exchange with her father had, however, lightened her heart; she could now view her situation more calmly and consider what she needed to do. The main thing was to escape the odious wedding: the life of a robber's wife seemed like paradise to her in comparison with the fate they were preparing for her. She glanced at the ring Dubrovsky had left with her. She fervently wished to see him alone and consult with him once more before the decisive moment. A presentiment told her that she could find him in the garden near the arbour that evening, and she resolved to wait for him there as soon as it became dark. It grew dark. Masha got ready to go, but her door was locked. The chambermaid answered from behind it that Kirila Petrovich had given orders not to let her out. She was under arrest. Deeply insulted, she sat down by her window and stayed there late into the night without undressing, with her eyes fixed on the dark sky. At dawn she dozed off, but her light sleep was troubled by melancholy visions, and the rays of the rising sun soon awakened her.

17

MARIA KIRILOVNA'S FIRST waking thought brought back to mind the full horror of her situation. She rang for her maid, who came in and told her in response to her questions that last night Kirila Petrovich had driven over to Arbatovo and returned late; that he had given strict instructions not to let her out of her room and not to let her speak with anyone; and that, incidentally, no particular preparations for the wedding were evident except for an order given to the priest not to leave the village under any circumstances. After communicating these pieces of information, the maid left Maria Kirilovna, once more locking the door on her.

The maid's words embittered the young prisoner. Her brain seething and her blood boiling, she resolved to let Dubrovsky know about everything, and began to look for some means of conveying the ring into the secret hollow of the oak. At that moment a pebble hit her window, clinking against the pane. Looking out into the yard, Maria Kirilovna saw little Sasha making furtive signs at her. Sure of his attachment to her, she was glad to see him and opened the window.

"Hello Sasha," she said. "Why are you calling me?"

"I came to find out, sister, if you need anything. Papa is cross and forbade the whole household to take orders from you, but you just tell me what you want, and I'll do anything."

"Thank you, my dear Sashenka. Listen: do you know the old hollow oak close to the arbour?"

"Yes, sister, I do."

"Well, then, if you love me, run down there and put this ring in the hollow. Take care, though, not to let anybody see you."

With these words she threw the ring to him and closed the window.

The boy picked up the ring, dashed off with all his might, and in three minutes reached the secret tree. Once there, he stopped, caught his breath, looked around on every side, and placed the ring in the hollow. Having safely accomplished his task, he was about to report back to Maria Kirilovna, but suddenly a little red-haired, cross-eyed boy, in tattered clothes, darted out from behind the arbour, dashed to the oak and thrust his hand into the hollow. Sasha, faster than a squirrel, pounced on him and dug his nails into him.

"What are you doing here?" he asked menacingly.

"None of your business," answered the boy, trying to get away from him.

"Leave that ring alone, ginger-head," shouted Sasha, "or else I'll show you who you've picked a fight with."

Instead of answering him, the boy struck him in the face, but Sasha did not let go and started yelling with all his might, "Help, thief! Help, thief!"

The boy struggled to free himself. He was, apparently, a couple of years older and much stronger than Sasha, but Sasha was more agile. They fought for several minutes, until at last the red-haired boy gained the upper hand. He threw Sasha on the ground and seized him by the throat.

At this moment, however, a strong hand grabbed the boy by his frizzy red hair, and the gardener Stepan lifted him almost half a metre off the ground.

"You red-haired devil," said the gardener. "How dare you beat the young master?"

By this time, Sasha had jumped to his feet and recovered himself.

"You got me under my arms," he said, "otherwise you'd never have thrown me down. Give me the ring at once and get out of here."

"Not likely," answered the redhead and, suddenly twisting himself around, he freed his frizzy locks from Stepan's hand. He tried to run away, but Sasha caught up with him and pushed him in the back so that the boy fell flat on his face. The gardener seized him once more and tied him up with his belt.

"Give me the ring!" shouted Sasha.

"Wait, young master," said Stepan. "Let's take him to the steward for him to sort this matter out."

The gardener led the prisoner into the courtyard, accompanied by Sasha, who kept anxiously looking at his trousers, torn and stained by grass. Suddenly all three found themselves face to face with Kirila Petrovich, who was on his way to inspect the stables.

"What's going on?" he asked Stepan.

Stepan described the incident in a few words. Kirila Petrovich listened attentively.

"You scapegrace," he turned to Sasha. "Why did you get into a fight with him?"

"He stole the ring from the hollow of the tree, Papa; tell him to give it back to me."

"What ring, from what hollow?"

"Well, the one Maria Kirilovna... the ring that..."

Sasha became confused, and stammered. Kirila Petrovich frowned and said, shaking his head, "So Maria Kirilovna is mixed up in this. Confess everything, or else I'll give you such a thrashing that you own mother won't recognize you."

"I swear by God, Papa, I, Papa... Maria Kirilovna didn't send me on any errands, Papa."

"Stepan, go and cut me some good fresh birch switches."

"Wait, Papa, I'll tell you everything. As I was running about the yard today, sister Maria Kirilovna opened her window and I ran under it, and she accidentally dropped a ring, and I hid it in the hollow of the tree, and... and... this redhead wanted to steal it..."

"She dropped it accidentally, did she? And you wanted to hide it? Stepan, go and get those switches."

"Wait, Papa, I'll tell you everything. Sister Maria Kirilovna told me to run down to the oak and put the ring in the hollow, and I ran and put it in, but this horrid boy..."

Kirila Petrovich turned to the horrid boy and asked menacingly, "Whose are you?"

"I am a house serf of the master, Dubrovsky," answered the red-haired boy.

A cloud came over Kirila Petrovich's face.

"So you don't acknowledge me as your master. Very well. And what were you doing in my garden?"

"I was stealing raspberries," answered the boy with perfect equanimity.

"Aha, like master, like servant; like priest, like parish. And do you find raspberries growing on oak trees in my garden?"

The boy made no reply.

"Papa, tell him to give me the ring," said Sasha.

"Be quiet, Alexander," answered Kirila Petrovich, "and don't forget I'm still planning to settle accounts with you. Go to your room. And you, squint-eyes, it seems to me you're nobody's fool. Give me the ring and go home."

The boy opened his fist to show that there was nothing in his hand.

"If you confess everything to me, I will not thrash you; I shall even give you a five-copeck piece to buy some nuts with. But if you don't, I'll do something to you that you've never even imagined. Well?"

The boy made no reply – just stood with his head inclined and with the air of a perfect simpleton.

"Very well," said Kirila Petrovich, "lock him up somewhere, but watch out, don't let him run away, or else I'll skin every one of you."

Stepan led the boy off to the pigeon house, locked him up there and posted the old poultry woman, Agafia, to watch over him.

"And now we must send to town for the police chief," said Kirila Petrovich as he followed the boy with his eyes, "and do it as fast as possible."

"There can be no doubt. She has kept in touch with that damned Dubrovsky. But was she really trying to call for his help?" mused Kirila Petrovich, pacing up and down his room and angrily whistling 'May thou, thunder of victory'... "But perhaps I am at last hot on his track, and he won't slip away from us. We'll seize the opportunity. Ha! A bell! Thank God, this must be the police officer – hey, bring that captured boy in here!"

Meanwhile, a cart had driven into the courtyard, and our acquaintance, the police chief, all covered with dust, came into the room.

"Wonderful news," said Kirila Petrovich to him. "I've caught Dubrovsky."

"Praises be to God, Your Excellency," said the policeman, overjoyed. "Where is he?"

"Well, not exactly Dubrovsky, but one of his gang. They'll bring him in presently. He'll help me catch the robber chief himself. Here he is."

The police chief, who had expected a ferocious brigand, was astonished to see a thirteen-year-old boy of rather puny appearance. He turned to Kirila Petrovich in bewilderment, waiting for an explanation. Kirila Petrovich related what had happened in the morning without any mention, however, of Maria Kirilovna.

The police chief listened to him attentively, casting frequent glances at the little miscreant who, pretending to be a simpleton, seemed to be paying no attention to what was going on around him.

"Allow me, Your Excellency, to speak with you in private," said the police chief at last.

Kirila Petrovich led him into an adjacent room and locked the door.

Half an hour later they came back to the hall, where the captive was waiting for his fate to be decided.

"The master wanted you to be put in the city jail, lashed with the whip and then deported," said the police chief, "but I've interceded on your behalf and persuaded him to pardon you. You can untie him."

They untied the boy.

"Well, thank your master, won't you?" asked the officer.

The boy went up to Kirila Petrovich and kissed his hand.

"Very well, go home," said Kirila Petrovich to him, "and in the future don't steal raspberries from hollow trees."

The boy went outside, joyfully jumped off the porch, and without looking back, set out at a gallop across the field toward Kistenevka. When he reached it, he stopped by a little tumbledown hut at the edge of the village and knocked at the window. The window was raised, and an old woman appeared in it.

"Granny, some bread," said the boy. "I haven't eaten since the morning; I'm starving."

"Oh, it's you Mitya. Where did you vanish to, you little devil?"

"I'll tell you later, granny, but give me some bread for God's sake."

"Well, come inside, won't you?"

"I haven't got time, granny; I must still run to another place. Bread, for Christ's sake, bread!"

"Always itching to go," grumbled the old woman. "Here, take this hunk," and she handed him a piece of black bread through the window.

The boy eagerly bit into it and, chewing, immediately set out on his further errand.

It was beginning to grow dark. Mitya made his way to the Kistenevka wood, stealing past barns and vegetable gardens. Reaching two pine trees that stood at the edge of the wood like sentries at an outpost, he stopped, looked about him on every side, let out a brief shrill whistle, and started to listen. A long, soft whistle answered him; someone came out of the wood and approached him.

18

KIRILA PETROVICH PACED up and down the hall, whistling his march more loudly than usual; the whole house was in commotion, the servants dashing to and fro, the maids bustling about, the coachmen getting the carriage ready in the shed. A crowd gathered in the courtyard. In the young mistress's boudoir, a lady surrounded by maids stood before the mirror and dressed the pale, motionless Maria Kirilovna. Masha's head bent languidly under the weight of diamonds; she started slightly each time a careless hand pricked her, but otherwise silently and absently stared at herself in the mirror.

"How much longer?" sounded Kirila Petrovich's voice from behind the door.

"Just one minute," answered the lady. "Maria Kirilovna, stand up and take a look: is everything right?"

Maria Kirilovna rose and made no answer. The door opened.

"The bride is ready," said the lady to Kirila Petrovich. "Please order the carriage."

"With God's grace," answered Kirila Petrovich, and took an icon from the table. "Come here, Masha," he said to her with emotion, "and receive my blessing."

The poor girl collapsed at his feet and burst into sobs.

"Papa... Papa," she repeated in tears, and her voice died away. Kirila Petrovich hastened to bless her; she was lifted up and almost borne to the carriage. Her mother by proxy and a maid sat with her. They drove to the church. The bridegroom was already waiting there. He came out to greet his bride and was struck by her paleness and strange look. They entered the cold, empty church together, and the doors were locked behind them. The priest emerged from the sanctuary and began the ceremony without delay. Maria Kirilovna neither saw nor heard anything. Her mind was fixed on one idea: she had been waiting for Dubrovsky ever since the morning, not giving up hope for one minute. When the priest turned to her with the customary questions, she shuddered and froze with fear, but she still hesitated, still did not give up hope. However, the priest, not waiting for her reply, pronounced the irrevocable words.

The ceremony was over. She felt her unloved husband's cold kiss and heard those present joyfully congratulating her, but she still could not believe that her life was fettered for ever, and that Dubrovsky had not come flying to deliver her. The Prince turned to her with tender words, which she did not comprehend. They came out on the porch, where the peasants of Pokrovskoye were crowding. Her glance quickly ran over them, then she resumed her air of indifference. The newly-weds got into the carriage together and drove off to Arbatovo; Kirila Petrovich had set out ahead of them in order to greet the young couple there. Left alone with his young wife, the Prince did not in the least feel discomfited by her cold look. He did not importune her with unctuous explanations or ludicrous raptures: his words were simple and required no reply. They covered about ten versts this way; the horses ran fast over the bumps of the country lanes, but the carriage hardly rocked on its English springs. Suddenly the shouts of a pursuing party could be heard; the carriage stopped, a band of armed men surrounded it and a man in a half-mask, opening the door on the young Princess's side, said to her, "You are free: alight."

"What does this mean?" shouted the Prince. "Who the Devil are you?"

"It is Dubrovsky," said the Princess.

The Prince did not lose his presence of mind, but drew from his side pocket a travelling pistol and shot at the masked bandit. The Princess screamed and, horror-stricken, covered her face with both hands. Dubrovsky was wounded in the shoulder, and the blood was beginning to show through. The Prince, losing no time, drew another pistol, but he was given no opportunity to fire it: the door on his side opened and several strong hands pulled him out of the carriage and took the pistol from him. Knives flashed above him.

"Don't touch him!" shouted Dubrovsky, and his fearsome companions drew back.

"You are free," resumed Dubrovsky, turning to the pale Princess.

"No," she answered. "It's too late. I am already married. I am the wife of Prince Vereysky."

"What are you saying?" cried Dubrovsky in despair. "No, you are not his wife, you were coerced, you could never give your consent—"

"I did consent. I made my vow," she rejoined resolutely. "The Prince is my husband; please give your orders to let him go, and leave me with him. I did not deceive you. I waited for you till the last moment… But now, I am telling you, it's too late. Let us go free."

Dubrovsky could no longer hear her: the pain of his wound and the violent agitation of his soul had taken away his strength. He collapsed by the wheel; his bandits gathered around him. He managed to say a few words to them and they put him on his horse, two of them supporting him, while a third led the animal by the bridle. They all rode off across the fields, leaving the carriage in the middle of the road, with the men tied up and the horses unharnessed, but without plundering anything or shedding one drop of blood in revenge for the blood of their chief.

19

I N A NARROW CLEARING in the middle of a dense forest there was a small earthwork, consisting of a rampart and a trench, behind which a few huts and earth shelters could be seen.

In the enclosure a large number of people, readily identifiable by their varied dress and uniform weaponry as bandits, were eating their dinner, with their heads bare, seated around a shared cauldron. On the rampart a sentry sat cross-legged at a small cannon. He was sewing a patch on his garment, plying his needle with the skill of an experienced tailor; at the same time he kept glancing around on every side.

Although a ladle had been passed round from hand to hand several times, a strange silence reigned over the crowd; the bandits finished their dinner, rose to their feet, and said their prayers one after the other; some dispersed among the huts, while others straggled into the woods or lay down for a nap according to the Russian custom.

The sentry finished his work and shook his tattered garment, admiring the patch on it, then struck his needle into his sleeve, sat astride the cannon, and burst into a sad old song at the top of his voice:

> *Don't rustle your branches, green mother, dear oak wood;*
> *Brave lad, don't disturb me from thinking my thoughts.*

Immediately the door of one of the huts opened and an old woman in a white cap, dressed neatly and properly, appeared on the threshold.

"Enough of that, Stepka," she said angrily. "The master's asleep, but you must bawl: have you no conscience or pity?"

"I beg pardon, Yegorovna," answered Stepka. "I won't any more. Let the young master sleep and get better."

The old woman withdrew, and Stepka started pacing to and fro on the rampart.

In the hut from which the old woman had emerged, on a camp bed behind a partition, lay the wounded Dubrovsky. His pistols sat on a small table next to him and his sabre hung on the wall at the head of the bed. The mud hut was covered and hung all over with luxurious carpets and in the corner there was a woman's silver washbasin with a cheval glass. Dubrovsky held an open book in his hands, but his eyes were closed. The old woman, who kept peeping at him from behind the partition, could not be sure whether he was asleep or just lost in thought.

Suddenly Dubrovsky started: an alarm was sounded in the fortification, and Stepka poked his head through the window.

"Vladimir Andreyevich, young master," he shouted, "our men have given the signal: a search party is coming."

Dubrovsky jumped off his bed, seized his weapons, and stepped outside the hut. The bandits were noisily gathering in the enclosure; but as soon as he appeared among them deep silence set in.

"Is everyone here?" asked Dubrovsky.

"Everyone except the sentries," was the answer.

"Take up your positions!" shouted Dubrovsky.

Each bandit took up his assigned position. At this moment the three sentries came running to the gates. Dubrovsky went forward to meet them.

"What is it?" he asked them.

"There are soldiers in the woods," they replied. "They're encircling us."

Dubrovsky gave orders to lock the gates and went to check the small cannon. Several voices could be heard in the woods; they came closer; the bandits waited silently. Suddenly three or four soldiers emerged from the woods, but they immediately withdrew, signalling to their comrades with shots.

"Prepare for combat!" said Dubrovsky, and a murmur passed through the bandits' ranks, after which all grew quiet again.

Then the noise of an approaching detachment could be heard. Weapons flashed among the trees; some one hundred and fifty soldiers poured out of the woods and dashed for the rampart with shouts. Dubrovsky held the fuse to the cannon, and fired successfully: one soldier's head was torn off, and two others were wounded. The soldiers were thrown into confusion, but when their officer dashed forward they followed and jumped into the trench. The bandits shot at them with rifles and pistols, and were ready with axes in hand to defend the rampart, which the frenzied soldiers stormed, leaving behind some twenty comrades in the trench, wounded. A hand-to-hand battle ensued. The soldiers were already on the rampart, forcing the bandits to retreat, but Dubrovsky went right up to their officer and shot him point-blank in the chest. The officer fell over backwards. Some soldiers picked him up in their arms, hastening to carry him off into the woods, while the others, deprived of their commander, stopped. The emboldened bandits took advantage of this moment of confusion and crushed the soldiers' ranks, forcing them back into the trench. The besiegers took flight, and the bandits pursued them with shouts. The battle was won. Trusting that the enemy had been thrown into complete disorder, Dubrovsky stopped his men and withdrew behind the locked gates of the fort, giving orders to gather up the wounded, to double the guard, and not to leave the fort.

These last developments drew the government's serious attention to Dubrovsky's bold robberies. Intelligence was gathered concerning his whereabouts. A company of soldiers was dispatched to capture him dead or alive. It was learnt, however, from some of his followers who had been caught, that he was no longer with the band. And indeed, a few days after the last battle he had gathered all his followers, declaring to them that he would leave them for good, and advising them that they, too, should change their way of life.

"You've grown rich under my command, and each of you has a false passport with which you can make your way to some remote province and live for the rest of your life in honest work and prosperity. But you are all ruffians and will probably not want to give up your trade."

After this speech he left them, taking with him only R. Nobody knew where he had disappeared to. The authorities at first doubted the truth of these depositions, for the bandits' attachment to their chief was well known. It was supposed that they were only trying to save him. But subsequent events proved the deposition right. The terrible raids, burnings and robberies ceased. The highways became safe again. From other reports it was learnt that Dubrovsky had escaped abroad.*

A TALE OF ROMAN LIFE*

(1833, 1835)

CAESAR WAS TRAVELLING; a number of us, with Titus Petronius, were following him at a distance. When the sun set, the slaves erected the tent and arranged the couches; we lay down to feast and engaged in cheerful conversation. At dawn we resumed our journey and, fatigued by the heat and the night's amusements, pleasantly dozed off, each on his litter.

We reached Cumae and were about to proceed further when a messenger from Nero arrived. He brought Petronius an order from Caesar to return to Rome and there to await word about his fate – the consequence of an invidious denunciation.

We were horror-stricken. Petronius alone listened to the verdict with equanimity; he dismissed the courier with a gift and announced to us that he intended to remain in Cumae. He sent off his favourite slave to choose and rent a house for him, while he waited in a cypress grove consecrated to the Eumenides.*

We gathered around him anxiously. Flavius Aurelius asked him how long he intended to stay in Cumae and whether he was not afraid of rousing Nero's ire by his disobedience.

"Not only do I not intend to disobey him," answered Petronius with a smile, "but I propose to anticipate his wishes. As for you, my friends, I advise you to return. On a clear day a traveller will rest in the shade of an oak, but in a storm he will be wise to move away from it for fear of thunderbolts."

We all declared our wish to remain with him, and he thanked us warmly. The servant returned and led us to the house he had chosen. It was on the outskirts of the city. An old freedman was looking after it in the absence of its owner, who had left Italy a long time ago. A few slaves, under his supervision, kept the rooms and the gardens tidy. On the wide portico we found images of the Nine Muses, and two centaurs stood at the entrance.

Petronius stopped at the marble threshold and read the greeting carved on it: "Long life and health!" A sad smile came over his face. The old custodian led him to the *bibliotheca*, where we inspected some scrolls; then we proceeded to the master bedroom. It was appointed simply, with only two statues, both of the family. One represented a matron seated in an armchair, the other a little girl playing with a ball. A small lamp stood on the bedside table. Petronius stayed here for a rest, dismissing us and inviting us to gather in his room towards evening.

My heart was so full of sorrow that I could not go to sleep. I regarded Petronius not only as a generous patron, but also as a friend, genuinely attached to me. I respected his capacious mind and loved his exquisite soul. My conversations with him gave me a knowledge of the world and people – subjects I otherwise knew more from the teachings of the divine Plato* than from my own experience. His judgement was usually quick and sure. His unvarying equanimity saved him from bias, and his forthright attitude towards himself made him perspicacious. Life could no longer present anything new to him; he had experienced all its pleasures; his feelings were dormant, lulled by habit, but his mind had preserved an astonishing freshness. He loved the free play of ideas as much as the euphony of words. An avid listener to philosophical discussions, he himself composed poems not inferior to those of Catullus.*

I went out into the garden and spent a long time walking along paths that meandered under ancient trees. I sat down on a bench, in the shade of a tall poplar, next to the statue of a young satyr carving a reed pipe. Wishing somehow to dispel my sad thoughts, I took out my writing tablet and translated one of Anacreon's odes.* Here is my translation, preserved in memory of that sad day:

> *Grey and thin now are the curls,*
> *erstwhile glory of my head;*
> *teeth are loosened in my gums;*
> *dimmed the fires that lit my eyes.*
> *Few the days now left to me –*
> *few to live and to enjoy;*
> *of them Fate keeps strict account.*
> *Tartarus* awaits my ghost –*

fearsome's the chill vault below,
open to whoever comes;
from it, though, there's no way out…
all go down – to oblivion.

The sun was declining towards the west; I went to Petronius. I
found him in the library. He was pacing up and down: his personal
physician, Septimius, was with him. Seeing me, Petronius stopped
and jokingly recited the following lines:

"Mettled steeds you'll recognize
by the brand scorched on their hides;
Parthian lords you'll recognize
by their turbaned heads held high.
I, though, always recognize
happy lovers by their eyes."

"You have guessed correctly," I answered him, handing him my
tablet. He read my verses. A cloud of pensiveness passed over his
features but immediately dispersed.

"When I read poems like these," he said, "I am always curious
to know about the fate of those who had been so struck by the
thought of death: how did they actually die? Anacreon insists that
Tartarus frightened him, but I don't believe him any more than I be-
lieve in Horace's faint-heartedness. Do you know this ode of his?*

"Which god has brought you back to me –
my friend with whom I shared my first
campaigns, first tasted battle's terrors,
the time when desperate Brutus led us
in that vain bid for freedom's phantom;
my friend with whom in camp I'd drown
war's troubles in a bowl of wine,
wreathing my curling locks with ivy
and smearing them with Syrian myrrh?

Do you recall the fearsome conflict,
when I – no soldier now – in terror
threw down my shield and ran away,
extemporizing vows and prayers?
How scared I was! And how I ran!
But Hermes suddenly enwrapped me
in mist* and whisked me far away,
thus saving me from certain death.

"The shrewd versifier wanted to make Augustus and Maecenas laugh at his faint-heartedness only because he did not want to remind them that he had been a comrade-in-arms of Cassius and Brutus. I don't know how you feel, but I find more sincerity in his exclamation: 'Pleasant and honourable it is to die for the fatherland'."*

MARIA SCHONING*

(1834 OR 1835?)

W...

25th April

My dear Maria,

What has happened to you? For more than four months I have not received a single line from you. Are you in good health? If I had not been so busy all the time, I would have come to visit you, but as you know, twelve miles is not a joke. Without me the household would come to a dead stop: Fritz is not good at it; he is just like a child. Have you perhaps married? No, I am sure you would have thought of me and not neglected to delight your friend with the news of your happiness. In your last letter you wrote that your poor father was still sickly; I hope the spring has helped him, and he is better now. About myself I can say that, thanks to God, I am well and happy. My work brings in little, but I am still incapable of bargaining or charging too much. It might be just as well to learn how to. Fritz is also quite well, though lately his wooden leg has been causing him trouble. He gets about very little, and in bad weather wheezes and groans. Otherwise he is just as cheerful as before, still likes his glass of wine, and has still not finished telling me the story of his campaigns. The children are growing and getting more and more beautiful. Frank is turning out a clever little fellow. Just imagine, dear Maria, he is already running after girls, though he is not yet three. What do you think of that? And what a mischief-maker he is! Fritz can't rejoice in him enough and spoils him terribly: instead of checking the child, he goads him on and delights in his every prank. Mina is much calmer; but then of course she is a year older. I have begun teaching her to read. She is very sharp-witted and, it seems, will be pretty. But what is the good of being pretty? If she will grow into a good and sensible girl, she'll be happy too, for sure.

PS: I am sending you a scarf as a little present: wear it for the first time next Sunday, when you go to church. It was a present to me from Fritz, but red goes better with your black tresses than with my blonde hair. Men do not understand such things. Blue and red are all the same to them. Farewell, my dear Maria; I have chattered long enough. Do write as soon as you can. Give my sincere regards to your dear father. Let me know how he is doing. I shall never forget the three years spent under his roof, during which he treated me, a poor orphan, not as a hired servant but as a daughter. The mother of our pastor advises him to drink red camomile instead of tea: it is a very common herb – I have even found out its Latin name – any apothecary can point it out to you.

MARIA SCHONING TO ANNA HARLIN

28th April

I received your letter last Friday but have not read it until today. My poor father died the very day you wrote, at six o'clock in the morning, and yesterday was his funeral.

I never thought his death was so imminent. Lately he had been doing much better, so much so that Herr Költz had hopes for his complete recovery. On Monday he even took a walk in our little garden and got as far as the well without running out of breath. When he returned to his room, however, he felt slightly shivery; I put him to bed and ran off to Herr Költz. He was not at home. When I returned to my father I found him asleep. Sleep, I thought, might relax him and make him feel entirely better. Herr Költz called on us in the evening. He examined the patient and was unhappy with his condition. He prescribed a new medicine for him. Father awoke in the middle of the night and asked for something to eat; I gave him some soup; he swallowed one spoonful, but did not feel like any more. He dozed off again. The next day he had spasms. Herr Költz did not leave his bedside. Towards the evening his pain abated, but he was seized by such restlessness that he could not lie in the same position for more than five minutes at a time. I had to keep turning him from one side to the other... Towards morning he grew calm and slept for a couple of hours. Herr Költz left his room, promising to return in about two hours. Suddenly father sat up and called me. I came and asked what he wanted. He said, "Maria, how come it is so very dark? Open the shutters."

I answered in alarm, "Dear father, can't you see? The shutters are open."

He started searching about him, grasped my hand, and said, "Maria, Maria, I feel very bad – I am dying... Let me give you my blessing while I can."

I threw myself on my knees and placed his hand on my head. He said, "Oh Lord, reward her; oh Lord, I put her in your hands."

He grew quiet; then suddenly his hand felt heavy. Thinking he had fallen asleep again, I did not dare stir for several minutes. Presently Herr Költz entered, took my father's hand off my head, and said, "Leave him alone now, go to your room."

I glanced at father: he lay there pale and motionless. It was all over.

The good-hearted Herr Költz did not leave our house for two full days, and made all the necessary arrangements, for I was not in a state to do so. In the final days I had been looking after the patient by myself, since there was no one to relieve me. I often thought of you and bitterly regretted that your were not with us...

Yesterday I got up and was preparing to follow the coffin, but all of a sudden felt bad. I went down on my knees in order to take leave of my father at least from a distance. Frau Rotberg remarked, "What an actress!" These words, just imagine, my dear Anna, returned my strength to me. I followed the coffin with surprisingly little difficulty. In the church, it seemed to me, everything was exceedingly bright, and everything around me was reeling. I did not weep. I felt suffocated and kept wanting to laugh.

He was carried to the cemetery, the one behind St Jacob's Church, and I was present when they lowered him into the grave.

Suddenly I felt like digging it up again, for I had not quite taken my leave of him. But there were still many people walking about the cemetery, and I was afraid Frau Rotberg might remark again, "What an actress!"

How cruel it is not to let a daughter say goodbye to her dead father the way she wants to...

Returning home, I found several strangers, who told me it was necessary to seal all my father's property and papers. They let me stay in my little room, but they carried everything out of it except for the bed and a chair. Tomorrow is Sunday. I shall not be able to wear the scarf you gave me, but I want to thank you for it very much. Give my regards to your husband and kiss Frank and Mina for me. Farewell.

I am writing standing by the window sill; I have borrowed an inkpot from the neighbours.

MARIA SCHONING TO ANNA HARLIN

My dear Anna,

An official came to me yesterday and declared that all of my late father's property must be sold at auction to the benefit of the city treasury, because he had not been taxed according to his financial status: the inventory showed that he had been much wealthier than they had thought. I cannot understand any of this. Lately we had spent a great deal on medicine. All the ready cash I had left was twenty-three thalers; I showed it to the officials, but they said I could keep it, since the law did not require me to surrender it.

Our house will be auctioned off next week, after which I have no idea where I shall go. I have been to see Herr Bürgermeister. He received me kindly but declared that there was nothing he could do to help me. I do not know where I could take service. Write to me if you need a maidservant: as you know, I can help you around the house and with needlework; moreover, I can look after the children and Fritz in case he should fall ill. I have learnt how to look after the sick. Please let me know whether you need me. And do not feel embarrassed about it. I feel sure that it will not change our relationship in the least: in my eyes you will always remain the same good and kind friend.

*   *   *   *   *   *   *

Old Schoning's house was full of people. They crowded around the table at which the auctioneer presided. He shouted:

"A flannel camisole with brass buttons: X thalers. One – two: anybody with a higher offer? A flannel camisole: X thalers – three."

The camisole passed into the hands of its new owner.

The buyers examined the exhibited items with curiosity and abusive comments. Frau Rotberg scrutinized the dirty linen left unwashed after Schoning's death; she pulled at it and shook it open, repeating, "What trash, what rubbish, what old rags," at the same time raising her bid by one groschen at a time. The inn-keeper, Hürtz, bought two silver spoons, half a dozen napkins and two china cups. The bed in which Schoning had died was brought by Karoline Schmidt, a girl heavily made up but otherwise of a modest and humble appearance.

Maria, pale as a shadow, stood there silently watching the pillage of her poor belongings. She held X thalers in her hand, ready to buy something from the spoils, but she did not have the courage to outbid the other buyers. People were leaving, carrying their purchases.

Two portraits, in frames that had once been gilt-edged but were now flyspecked, were still unsold. One showed Schoning as a young man, in a red coat; the other, his wife Christiana with a lapdog in her arms. Both portraits were painted in sharp, bright outlines. Hürtz wanted to buy these too, in order to hang them in the corner room of his inn, whose walls were too bare. The portraits were valued at X thalers. Hürtz drew out his purse; but this time Maria overcame her timidity and raised the bid in a trembling voice. Hürtz threw a contemptuous glance at her and began to haggle. Little by little the price reached Y thalers. Maria at last bid Z. Hürtz gave up, and the portraits remained in her possession. She handed over the price, put the remainder of her money in her pocket, picked up the two portraits, and left the house, not waiting for the end of the auction.

Having walked out on the street with a portrait under each arm, she stopped in bewilderment: where was she to go?...

A young man with gold-framed glasses came up to her and very politely offered to carry the portraits for her wherever she wished to take them...

"I am much obliged to you... but I truly don't know."

She kept wondering where to take the portraits for the time being until she found a position.

The young man waited a few moments, then went on his way. Maria decided to take the portraits to Költz, the physician.*

A RUSSIAN PELHAM*

(1834 OR 1835)

1

I REMEMBER MY LIFE from very early childhood. Here is a scene that has remained fresh in my memory.

My nurse brings me into a large room, dimly lit by a candle under a shade. In the bed behind green curtains lies a woman dressed all in white; my father takes me by the hand. She kisses me and weeps. My father sobs aloud; I am frightened and begin to cry. Nurse leads me out of the room, saying:

"Mama wants to go beddy-bye."

I also remember a great commotion, a lot of guests, people running from room to room. The sun shines through all the windows and I feel exceedingly cheerful. A monk with a gold cross on his chest blesses me; a long red coffin is borne through the door. That is all the impression my mother's funeral has left in my heart. As I was to gather later from stories of people who had not recognized her true worth, she had been a woman of exceptional intellect and sensitivity.

At this point my recollections become confused. I can give a clear account of myself beginning only with the age of eight. But first I must say a few words about my family.

My father was appointed sergeant when he was still in my grandmother's womb. He was raised at home up to the age of eighteen. His tutor, Monsieur Décor, was a simple and warm-hearted little old man, with an excellent knowledge of French orthography. It is not known whether my father was ever instructed by any other teacher, but it seems that he had no sound knowledge of any subject except French orthography. He married, against his parents' wishes, a girl several years his senior, and retired to live in Moscow that same year. Old Savelich, his valet, told me later that those first years of my father's marriage had been happy. My mother managed to bring about a reconciliation between her husband and his family, who grew very fond of her. But my father's frivolous and inconstant character did not allow her to enjoy tranquillity and happiness. He formed a liaison with a woman well known in society for her beauty and amorous adventures. For his sake she divorced her husband, who was willing to relinquish her to my father for 10,000 roubles and who afterwards came to dine with us quite frequently. My mother was aware of everything but kept quiet. Her mental anguish undermined her health. She took to her bed, never to rise from it again.

My father had 5,000 male serfs. In other words, he was one of those noblemen whom the late Count Sheremetev used to call smallholders, sincerely amazed at how they could make ends meet! The point is that my father lived no worse than Count Sheremetev, though he was quite twenty times poorer. Muscovites still remember his dinners, his domestic theatre and brass ensemble. A couple of years after my mother's death, Anna Petrovna Virlatskaya, the agent of her undoing, came to live in his house. She was what you might call a woman of striking appearance, though no longer in the first bloom of youth. A boy in a red shirt with cuffs was also brought into the house and introduced to me as my little brother. I stared at him wide-eyed. Mishenka shuffled his foot, first to the right, then to the left, and then wanted to play with my toy gun; I snatched it from his hands; he burst into tears; my father made me stand in the corner and gave my gun to my little brother as a present.

Such a beginning did not augur well for the future. And indeed I cannot recall one pleasant impression from my further sojourn under my father's roof. My father did, of course, love me, but he did not trouble himself about me, leaving me to the care of Frenchmen, who were perpetually being hired and dismissed. My first tutor turned out to be a drunkard; the second one, a man not without intelligence and knowledge, had such a violent temper that once he almost clubbed me to death for having spilt some ink on his waistcoat; and the third one, who lived in our house for almost a full year, was a madman, which was discovered only when he went to Anna Petrovna to complain against me and Mishenka for having allegedly incited all the bedbugs in the house to pester him, and for letting a demon build nests in his nightcap. The other Frenchman could not get on with Anna Petrovna, who did not give them wine with dinner or let them have horses on Sundays; besides, their salaries were paid very irregularly. I ended up being blamed: Anna Petrovna declared that not one of my tutors was able to cope with such an impossible little boy. It is true, actually, that there was not one among them whom I had not turned into a domestic clown within two weeks after his arrival. I remember with particular pleasure a certain M. Grauget, a respectable fifty-year-old Genevan, who, thanks to me, believed that Anna Petrovna was in love with him. It was quite something to behold his virtuous horror, mixed with an element of sly coquetry, when Anna Petrovna glanced at him askance at table, muttering under her breath, "What a glutton!"

I was naughty, lazy and quick-tempered, but at the same time sensitive and ambitious; a kind person could have formed me any way he liked. Unfortunately, however, nobody could take me in hand, even though everybody tried to interfere with my education. As for my teachers, I laughed at them and played tricks on them; with Anna Petrovna fought tooth and nail; and with Mishenka constantly quarrelled and exchanged blows. These affairs often led to stormy explanations with my father, which concluded with tears on both sides. At last Anna Petrovna persuaded him to send me off to a German university... I was fifteen years old at the time.

2

O F UNIVERSITY LIFE I have pleasant memories, even though, when you come to think of them, they relate to rather insignificant, and sometimes even unpleasant events. Youth, however, is a great magician: I would pay a lot to be able to sit once more over a tankard of beer, amidst clouds of tobacco smoke, with staff in hand and a soiled velvet cap on my head. I would pay a lot for my room, always full of people – Heaven only knows what kinds of people! – for our Latin songs, schoolboyish duels, and altercations with the Philistines!

A liberal university education did me more good than the domestic lessons had. Yet, all in all, the only subjects I thoroughly learnt in the course of it were fencing and how to make rum punch. I received money from home at irregular intervals, which taught me to run up debts and live carelessly. Three years passed; then I received a command from Petersburg, from my father, to leave the university, return to Russia, and enter some kind of service. Some words of his about ruined affairs, extra expenses and a changed way of life seemed strange to me, but I did not pay too much attention to them. I gave a farewell feast on the eve of my departure, during which I swore eternal fidelity to friendship and mankind, and vowed never to accept the position of a censor; and the next day set out with a headache and a heartburn.

WE WERE SPENDING THE EVENING AT PRINCESS D.'S DACHA...*

(1835?)

W E WERE SPENDING THE evening at Princess D.'s dacha. The name of Madame de Staël* happened to come up in the conversation. Baron Dahlberg, in broken French, recited very badly the well-known anecdote of how she asked Bonaparte whom he considered the most outstanding woman in the world, and his amusing answer, "The one who has borne the most children" ("*Celle qui a fait le plus d'enfants*").

"What a splendid epigram!" remarked a male guest.

"And she deserves it too!" said one of the ladies. "How could she fish for compliments so clumsily?"

"To me it seems," said Sorokhtin, who had been taking a nap in a couple of Hambs' armchairs,* "to me it seems that neither was Madame de Staël asking to have her praises sung, nor did Napoleon have an epigram in mind. She asked her question out of simple curiosity, which was perfectly understandable, and Napoleon expressed literally what he thought. But you don't trust the simple-mindedness of geniuses."

The guests began to argue, and Sorokhtin dozed off again.

"But really," said the hostess, "whom do you consider the most outstanding woman in the world?"

"Watch it: you're fishing for compliments too..."

"No, seriously..."

A discussion ensued: some named Madame de Staël, others the Maid of Orleans, still others Queen Elizabeth of England, Madame de Maintenon, Madame Roland,* and so forth.

A young man standing by the open fireplace (for a fireplace is never superfluous in Petersburg) decided to join the conversation for the first time.

"To my mind," he said, "the most outstanding woman ever was Cleopatra."*

"Cleopatra?" responded the guests. "Well, of course... but why in particular?"

"There is one episode in her biography that has so gripped my imagination I can hardly look at a woman without thinking of Cleopatra."

"What episode is that?" asked the hostess, "Tell us."

"I can't: it's a queer story to tell."

"In what sense? Is it improper?"

"Yes, like almost everything that vividly depicts the dreadful mores of antiquity."

"Oh! Tell us, please tell us!"

"Oh no, don't tell us," interrupted Volskaya, a widow by divorce primly casting down her fiery eyes.

"Come, come!" cried the hostess with impatience. "*Qui est-ce donc que l'on trompe ici?** It was only yesterday that we watched *Antony*, and a copy of *La Physiologie du mariage** is lying right here on the mantelpiece. Improper! Whom are you trying to frighten? Stop playing tricks on us, Alexei Ivanych! You're not a journalist. Tell us simply what you know about Cleopatra; be proper, though, if possible…"

Everyone laughed.

"God be my witness," said the young man, "I quail: I've become as bashful as the censorship. But if you wish… I must mention that among the Latin historians there is a certain Aurelius Victor, of whom you have probably never heard."

"Aurelius Victor?" interrupted Vershnev, who had at one time studied under the Jesuits. "Aurelius Victor was a writer of the fourth century. His works have been ascribed to Cornelius Nepos and even to Suetonius;* he wrote the book *De viris illustribus** – about the noteworthy men of the city of Rome – I'm familiar with it."

"Exactly so," continued Alexei Ivanovich. "His little book is rather insignificant, but it contains the legend about Cleopatra that has so captured my imagination. And what is most remarkable, in this particular passage the dry and boring Aurelius Victor equals Tacitus in force of expression: '*Haec tantæ libidinis fuit ut sæpe prostiterit; tantæ pulchritudinis ut multi noctem illius morte emerint.*'"*

"Splendid!" cried Vershnev. "It reminds me of Sallust – do you recall? '*Tantæ…*'"

"What is this, gentlemen?" asked the hostess. "Now you think fit to converse in Latin! How very amusing for the rest of us! Tell us, what does your Latin phrase mean?"

"The crux of the matter is that Cleopatra offered her beauty for sale, and many bought a night with her at the price of their lives."

"How awful!" said the ladies. "But what did you find so marvellous about it?"

"So marvellous? It seems to me that Cleopatra was not a trivial flirt, and that the price she attached to herself was not low. I suggested to X. that he write a narrative poem about it; he did start one, but gave it up."

"Very wisely so."

"What did he think he could get out of this subject? What was his main idea, do you remember?"

"He begins with a description of a feast in the Egyptian Queen's garden:

Dark, sultry night has invested the African sky; Alexandria has fallen asleep; its squares and streets have become quiet, and its houses have faded into shadows. Only the faraway light of Pharos* burns in solitude in the city's spacious harbour, like a lamp at a sleeping beauty's bedside.

Bright and noisy are the halls of the Ptolemys:* Cleopatra is spreading a feast before her friends; the table is set with ivory spoons; three hundred youths are waiting on the guests; three hundred maidens are bearing amphorae full of Greek wines around the table, under the silent, watchful gaze of three hundred eunuchs.

The colonnade of porphyry, open to south and north, awaits the breath of Eurus;* but the air is motionless, the lanterns' tongues of flame are burning motionlessly; the smoke from the incense-burners is borne aloft in a straight, motionless column; the sea, like a mirror, lies motionless by the steps of the rose-coloured semicircular portico. In it, the gilt claws and granite tails of guardian sphinxes find themselves reflected. Only the strains of cithara and flute ruffle the flames, the air and the sea.

Suddenly the Queen became pensive and hung her exquisite head low; her sadness cast a gloom over the bright feast, as a cloud casts gloom over the sun.

What makes her sad?

> *Why is she so weighed down with sorrow?*
> *What can the Queen of ancient Egypt*
> *desire that's not already hers?*
> *Protected by unnumbered minions,*
> *she reigns untroubled and at peace*
> *in her resplendent capital.*
> *Earth's creative masters do her bidding,*
> *her halls are full of wondrous works.*
> *In heat of Africa by day,*
> *in chill of night – at any hour –*
> *rich art and craftsmanship combine*
> *to afford her slumbering senses pleasure.*
> *Each land, each heaving sea, conveys her*
> *its special gift of finery,*
> *which she, without a thought, keeps changing –*
> *now she's arrayed in gleaming gemstones;*
> *now she selects a veil and gown*
> *dyed purple, Tyrian women's work;*
> *next she'll be floating on the Nile's*
> *grey waters in her golden trireme*
> *beneath a sumptuous canopy –*
> *the image of a youthful Venus.*
> *Delicacies in quick succession*
> *are passed before her listless eyes,*
> *and unimagined mysteries*
> *are hers to indulge in through the night.*

In vain! A dull pain gnaws her heart;
She thirsts for pleasures yet unknown –
the Queen's exhausted, surfeited,
sickened that she no more can feel.

Cleopatra awakens from her pensiveness.

The feasting's ceased, the guests are drowsing;
then once again she lifts her head,
a new fire lights her haughty eyes,
and, smiling now, she starts to speak:
'You men, will my love give you pleasure?
Then listen well to what I say:
I'll disregard our different status –
Yes, you can have your time of bliss.
I challenge you – so who'll come forward?
I offer nights with me for sale.
Which of you, tell me then, will buy
one night with me? The price? Your life.'"

*   *   *   *   *   *   *

"This subject should be brought to the attention of Marquise George Sand,* who is as shameless as your Cleopatra. She would adapt your Egyptian anecdote to contemporary mores."

"That would be impossible. It would completely lack verisimilitude. This is an anecdote exclusively of the ancient world; a bargain of this kind would be as impractical today as the erection of pyramids."

"Why impractical? Couldn't you find one among today's women who would want to test in deed the truth of what men repeat to her every minute – that her love is dearer to them than their lives?"

"That would be interesting to find out, I suppose. But how could you carry out your scientific experiment? Cleopatra had at her disposal all the necessary means to make her debtors pay. But do we? After all, you cannot draw up such agreements on legal paper and have them ratified in civil court."

"In that case it would be possible to rely on the man's *word of honour*."

"How would that be?"

"A woman could accept a man's word of honour that he would shoot himself the following day."

"And the following day he could leave for foreign lands, making a fool of his lady."

"Yes, if he was willing to remain for ever dishonest in the eyes of the woman he loves. When you consider, is the condition itself so hard to accept? Is life such a treasure that one would begrudge sacrificing it for happiness? Just think of it: the first scamp happening by, whom I despise, says something about me that cannot hurt me in any way, yet I expose my forehead to his bullet. I have no right to deny this satisfaction to the first bully coming my way who takes it into his head to test my sangfroid. And yet you think I would act like a coward when my bliss is at stake? What is life worth if it is poisoned by dejection and unfulfilled desires? What remains in it if all its delights have been sapped?"

"Would you really be capable of entering into such a contract?"

At this moment Volskaya, who had been sitting silently with her eyes cast down, quickly glanced at Alexei Ivanovich.

"I am not speaking about myself. But a man truly in love would not hesitate for a moment."

"Is that so? Even for a woman who didn't love you? (If she agreed to such a proposal she would certainly not be in love with you.) The very thought of such bestial cruelty would be enough to destroy the most reckless passion..."

"No: in her agreement I would see only an ardency of imagination. As for requited love... that I do not demand: why should it be anyone's business if I am in love?"

"Oh, stop it – Heaven knows what you're saying. So that's the anecdote you didn't want to tell us."

*   *   *   *   *   *   *

The young Countess K., a plump and ugly little woman, tried to lend an air of importance to her nose, which looked like an onion stuck into a turnip, and said, "There are women even today who value themselves highly."

Her husband, a Polish count who had married her out of (they say mistaken) calculation, cast his eyes down and drank up his tea.

"What do you mean by that, Countess?" asked the young man, hardly able to restrain a smile.

"What I mean is," answered the Countess K., "that a woman who respects herself, who respects…" But she became entangled in her thought. Vershnev came to her rescue.

"You think that a woman who respects herself will not wish death on the sinner, right?"

*　　　*　　　*　　　*　　　*　　　*　　　*

The conversation changed course.

Alexei Ivanych sat down next to Volskaya and, leaning over as if examining her needlework, said in a whisper, "What do you think of Cleopatra's contract?"

Volskaya remained silent. Alexei Ivanych repeated his question.

"What shall I say? Today, too, some women value themselves highly. But the men of the nineteenth century are too cold-blooded and sober-minded to enter into such contracts."

"You think," said Alexei Ivanych in a voice that had suddenly changed, "you really think that in our time, in Petersburg, one can find a woman who has enough pride and spiritual strength to demand Cleopatra's condition of her lover?"

"I think so; I am even convinced."

"You're not deceiving me? Just consider: that would be too cruel, more cruel even than the condition itself."

Volskaya looked at him with her fiery, penetrating eyes and pronounced in a firm voice, "No, I am not."

Alexei Ivanych rose and disappeared on the instant.

EGYPTIAN NIGHTS*

(1835?)

1

C HARSKY WAS A KIND of person indigenous to St Petersburg. He was not quite thirty, not married, and held a position in the civil service that placed no great burden on him. His late uncle, who had been a vice-governor at a propitious time, had left him a handsome estate. He was in a position to lead a very pleasant life, but he was unfortunate enough to be a writer and publisher of verses. In the journals they called him a poet, in the servants' quarters a scribbler.

Despite all the great advantages enjoyed by versifiers (it must be admitted that, apart from the privileges of using the accusative instead of the genitive case and one or two other acts of so-called poetic licence, we do not know of any particular advantages Russian versifiers could be said to enjoy) – however that may be, despite all their imaginable advantages these people are subject to a great deal of trouble and unpleasantness. The most bitter and intolerable bane of the poet is his title, his sobriquet, with which he is branded and of which he can never rid himself. The public look on him as though he were their property: in their opinion, he was born for their "benefit and pleasure". If he has just returned from the country, the first person he runs into will ask him, "Have you brought with you a new little something for us?" If he is sunk in thought about his tangled finances or about the illness of someone close to his heart, this will immediately provoke the inane exclamation, accompanied by an inane smile, "No doubt you are composing something!" And should he fall in love, the lady of his heart will promptly buy an album at the English store and be ready to receive an elegy. If he goes to see a man whom he hardly knows about an important business matter, the man will inevitably call in his young son, ordering him to recite some poetry; and the lad will treat the poet to the latter's own verses, with distortions. And these are only the laurels of his profession! What must its pains be like? The salutations, enquiries, albums and little boys irritated him so much, Charsky confessed, that he constantly had to be on his guard lest he make some rude response.

Charsky did everything in his power to rid himself of the insufferable sobriquet. He avoided the company of his fellow men of letters, preferring to them people of high society, even the shallowest. His conversation was of the most commonplace character, and he never touched on questions of literature. In his dress he always followed the latest fashion with the exaggerated respect and awe of a young Muscovite visiting Petersburg for the first time in his life. In his study, furnished like a lady's bedroom, nothing betrayed the habits of a writer: there were no books scattered about, on or under the tables; the sofa was not stained with ink; there was no sign of the sort of disorder that reveals the presence of the muse and the absence of broom and brush. He was thrown into despair if any of his society friends caught him with pen in hand. It was hard to believe to what pettiness he could stoop, even though, as a matter of fact, he was a gifted man, endowed with ready wit and feeling. He always pretended to be something else: now a passionate lover of horses, now a desperate gambler, now the most discriminating gastronome, though he could in no way tell a mountain pony from an Arabian steed, could never remember the trump cards, and secretly preferred baked potatoes to all the inventions of French cuisine. He led the most distracted existence: he hung about all the balls, overindulged himself at all the diplomatic dinners, and was just as unavoidable at every reception as Rezanov's* ice cream.

He was a poet nevertheless, and his passion for poetry was indomitable: when he felt this "nonsense" coming on (that was what he called inspiration), he locked himself in his study and wrote from morning till late night. He confessed to his genuine friends that he knew true happiness only at such times. The rest of the time he led his dissipated life, put on airs, dissembled, and perpetually heard the famous question, "Have you written a new little something?"

One morning Charsky felt he was in that exuberant state of mind when fantasies arise before you in clear outline, when you find vivid, unexpected words in which to incarnate your visions, when verses readily flow from your pen, and when resonant rhymes run up to meet well-ordered thoughts. His spirit was immersed in sweet oblivion... Society, the opinions of society and his own conceits were all banished from his mind. He was writing a poem.

Suddenly the door of his study creaked and an unfamiliar face appeared in it. Charsky started and frowned.

"Who is it?" he asked with irritation, mentally cursing his servants who never stayed in post in the entrance hall.

A stranger entered.

He was tall and thin and looked about thirty. The features of his swarthy face were distinctive: his pale high forehead, framed in black locks, his sparkling black eyes, his aquiline nose and his thick beard, which encircled his sunken, tawny cheeks, all revealed the foreigner in him. He wore a black frock coat, already greying along the seams, and a pair of summer trousers (though the season was well into the autumn); a fake diamond glittered on the yellowing shirt front under his worn black tie; his fraying hat appeared to have seen both rain and sunshine in its day. If you had met this man in the woods, you would have taken him for a robber; in society, for a political conspirator; and in an entrance hall, for a charlatan peddling elixirs and arsenic.

"What do you want?" Charsky asked him in French.

"*Signor*," answered the foreigner with low bows, "*Lei voglia perdonarmi se...*"*

Charsky did not offer him a chair but stood up himself; the exchange continued in Italian.

"I am a performing artist from Naples," said the stranger. "Circumstances forced me to leave my country. I have come to Russia hoping to make use of my talent here."

Charsky thought that the Neapolitan intended to give some cello concerts and was selling tickets door to door. He was about to hand the man his twenty-five roubles, hoping to get rid of him fast, but the stranger added:

"I hope, *signor*, that you will do a brotherly favour for a fellow artist and will introduce me to the houses to which you yourself have access."

It would have been impossible to deliver a sharper blow to Charsky's vanity. He cast a haughty glance at the man who called himself his fellow artist.

"Allow me to ask who you are and what you take me for," he said, making a great effort to keep his indignation under control.

The Neapolitan noticed his irritation.

"*Signor*," he answered falteringly, "*ho creduto… ho sentito… la Vostra Eccellenza mi perdonerà…*"*

"What do you want?" Charsky repeated drily.

"I have heard a great deal about your marvellous talent, and I am convinced that men of quality in this country consider it an honour to offer their patronage in every way to such an excellent poet," answered the Italian, "and therefore I have taken the liberty of presenting myself to you…"

"You are mistaken, *signor*," Charsky interrupted him. "The calling of poet does not exist in our country. Our poets do not make use of the patronage of men of quality: our poets are men of quality themselves, and if any Maecenas* here (Devil take him!) should fail to realize this, so much the worse for him. With us there are no tattered *abbés* whom a composer might pick up on a street corner to write a libretto. With us, poets do not walk door to door soliciting donations. As for my being a great poet, somebody must have been pulling your leg. It is true that I wrote a few bad epigrams at one time, but, thank Heavens, I have nothing to do, nor wish to have anything to do, with *messieurs les poètes*."

The poor Italian became confused. He gazed around him. The pictures, marble statuettes, bronze busts and expensive gewgaws, arranged inside a Gothic display cabinet, amazed him. He understood that the arrogant dandy who stood before him wearing a tufted brocade skullcap and a gold-embroidered Chinese dressing gown, girded by a Turkish sash, could have nothing in common with him, a poor itinerant artist, in a frayed cravat and worn frock coat. He uttered some incoherent apologies, bowed, and made as if to leave. His pathetic figure moved Charsky who, despite the petty vanities of his character, had a warm and noble heart. He felt ashamed of his irritable sense of self-pride.

"Where are you going?" he said to the Italian. "Wait a minute… I had to disclaim the title undeservedly conferred on me and had to declare to you that I was no poet. But let us now speak about your affairs. I am willing to be at your service in whatever way I can. Are you a musician?"

"No, *Eccellenza*!" answered the Italian. "I am a penniless *improvvisatore*."

"*Improvvisatore!*" exclaimed Charsky, fully realizing the cruelty of his conduct. Why didn't you tell me sooner that you were an *improvvisatore*?" And Charsky pressed his hand with a feeling of sincere regret.

His friendly air reassured the Italian. He launched trustingly into details of what he contemplated doing. His outward appearance was not misleading: he did need money, and he was hoping in some way to improve his affairs in Russia. Charsky listened to him attentively.

"I hope," he said to the poor artist, "that you will have success: our society here has never heard an *improvvisatore*. People's curiosity will be aroused; it is true that Italian is not in use among us, and therefore you will not be understood, but that doesn't matter: the main thing is that you should be in vogue."

"But if nobody among you understands Italian," said the *improvvisatore*, pondering the matter, "who will come to listen to me?"

"They will come, don't worry: some out of curiosity, others just to kill the evening somehow, still others to make a show of understanding Italian; the only important thing, I repeat, is that you should be in vogue, and you will be, I give you my word."

Charsky parted with the *improvvisatore* amiably, taking down his address, and he set about making arrangements for him that same evening.

2

"I'm king, I'm slave, I'm worm, I'm god."
— Derzhavin*

THE NEXT DAY CHARSKY sought out room No. 35 along the dark and dirty corridor of a tavern. He stopped at the door and knocked. The Italian opened it.

"Victory!" said Charsky to him. "It's all arranged. The Princess X will let you have her reception room; I already had occasion at last night's soirée to recruit half St Petersburg; you must have your tickets and announcements printed. I can guarantee you, if not triumph, at least some profit..."

"And that is the main thing!" cried the Italian, demonstrating his joy by lively gestures, characteristic of his southern race. "I knew you would help me. *Corpo di Bacco!* You are a poet, just as I am; and say what you like, poets are splendid fellows! How can I express my gratitude? Wait a second... Would you like to hear an improvisation?"

"An improvisation?... Surely, you can't do without an audience, music and the thunder of applause, can you?"

"All that's nonsense. Where could I find a better audience? You are a poet, you will understand me better than any of them, and your quiet encouragement will be dearer to me than a whole storm of applause... Sit down somewhere and give me a theme."

Charsky sat down on a trunk. (Of the two chairs in the cramped cubicle, one was broken, the other one laden with a heap of papers and linen.) The *improvvisatore* picked up a guitar from the table and stationed himself before Charsky, strumming on the strings with his bony fingers and waiting for his request.

"Here is a theme for you," said Charsky, "*a poet chooses the subjects of his songs himself: the crowd has no right to command his inspiration.*"

The Italian's eyes flashed; he played a few chords, proudly raised his head, and impassioned stanzas, the expression of his momentary feeling, rose harmoniously from his lips… Here they follow – a free transcription by one of our friends of what Charsky could recall:

> There was a poet on his way –
> with open eyes, but seeing no one.
> Another man, though, passing by
> seized him by his lapel and asked him:
> "You're wandering aimlessly – why so?
> You've hardly made it to the top,
> when – there! – you're looking down already
> and hastening to descend again.
> This handsome world you view but poorly;
> the fire within you burns in vain;
> themes that attract and exercise you
> are always insignificant.
> True genius should aim for heaven;
> for poetry to be inspired
> a real poet needs to choose
> themes that are lofty and sublime."
>
> Why does the wind whirl in the gully
> whipping up leaves and clouds of dust,
> when ships becalmed upon the ocean
> impatiently await its breath?
> Why does an eagle, mighty, fearsome,
> fly from the crags past lofty towers
> to a rotten tree stump? Ask him, then!
> Why does the youthful Desdemona
> bestow her love on black Othello,
> just as the moon, too, loves black night?
> The reason is that wind and eagle
> and a girl's heart obey no rule.
> So too a poet: like a gale
> he gathers anything he wants;
> he flies, like the eagle, where he will;
> and, asking no one for permission,

like Desdemona, he insists
on choosing the object of his love."

The Italian fell silent... Charsky sat without a word, astonished and moved.

"Well?" asked the *improvvisatore*.

Charsky grasped his hand and pressed it firmly.

"Well?" asked the *improvvisatore*. "How was it?"

"Astonishing," answered the poet. "How can it be that someone else's idea, which had only just reached your ear, immediately became your own property, as if you had carried, fostered and nurtured it for a long time? Does this mean that you never encounter either difficulty, or a dampening of spirit, or the restlessness that precedes inspiration?... Astonishing, astonishing!..."

The *improvvisatore*'s reply was:

"Every talent is inexplicable. How can a sculptor see a Jupiter hidden in a slab of Carrara marble and bring it to light, chipping off its shell with a chisel and hammer? Why is it that a thought emerging from a poet's head is already equipped with four rhymes and measured in concordant, uniform feet? Similarly, no one except the *improvvisatore* himself can comprehend this alacrity of impressions, this close tie between one's own inspiration and another's external will: it would be in vain even if I tried to explain it to you. However... it's time to think about my first evening. What do you think? What should be the price of a ticket that would neither burden the public too much nor leave me out of pocket? *La signora Catalani*,* they say, charged twenty-five roubles. That's not a bad price..."

It was unpleasant for Charsky to fall so suddenly from the height of poetry down into the cashier's office, but he understood the demands of everyday life very well, and plunged into mercantile calculations with the Italian. The occasion revealed so much unbridled greed in the Italian, such unabashed love of profit, that Charsky became disgusted with him and hastened to leave him, in order not to lose altogether the feeling of elation that the brilliant improvisation had aroused in him. The preoccupied Italian did not notice this change, and accompanied his guest along the corridor and down the staircase with deep bows and assurances of his everlasting gratitude.

3

The tickets are 10 roubles each; the performance begins at 7 p.m.

– from a poster

Pᴿᴵɴᴄᴇꜱꜱ ɴ.'ꜱ ʀᴇᴄᴇᴘᴛᴵᴏɴ ʀᴏᴏᴍ had been put at the *improvvisatore*'s disposal. A platform had been erected, and the chairs had been arranged in twelve rows. On the appointed day, at seven in the evening, the room was illuminated, and an old lady with a long nose, wearing a grey hat with drooping feathers and a ring on every finger, sat by the door behind a little table, charged with the sale and collection of tickets. Gendarmes stood by the main entrance. The audience was beginning to gather. Charsky was one of the first to arrive. Very much concerned with the success of the performance, he wanted to see the *improvvisatore* in order to find out if he was satisfied with everything. He found the Italian in a little side room, impatiently glancing at his watch. He was dressed in a theatrical fashion: he wore black from head to foot; the collar of his shirt was thrown open; the unusual whiteness of his neck contrasted sharply with his thick black beard; and loosely hanging locks framed his forehead and brows. Charsky found it very disagreeable to see a poet dressed as an itinerant mountebank. After a brief exchange of words, he returned to the reception room, which was filling up with more and more people.

Soon all the rows of armchairs were occupied by resplendent ladies; the men, as though forming a tight frame around them, stood by the platform, along the walls, and behind the last row of chairs. The musicians with their stands took up the space on either side of the platform. On the table in the centre stood a porcelain vase. The audience was sizeable. Everybody waited impatiently for the beginning of the performance; at last the musicians began to stir at half-past seven, getting their bows ready, and then started playing the overture to *Tancredi*.* Everybody settled down and grew quiet; the overture's last thunderous notes resounded… And then the *improvvisatore*, greeted with deafening applause on all sides, advanced to the very edge of the platform with deep bows.

Charsky anxiously waited to see what impression the first minute would create, but he noticed that the costume, which had appeared so inappropriate to him, was not having the same effect on the audience. He himself found nothing ludicrous in the man when he saw him on the platform, his pale face brightly illuminated by a multitude of lamps and candles. The applause died away; all conversation ceased… The Italian, speaking in broken French, asked the ladies and gentlemen present to set a few themes for him, writing them down on pieces of paper. At this unexpected invitation, the guests all looked at one another in silence, not one person making any response. The Italian, after waiting a little, repeated his request in a timid and humble voice. Charsky stood right below the platform; he grew anxious; he could see that the affair could not be carried through without him, and that he would be compelled to write down a theme. Indeed several ladies turned their heads towards him and began calling out to him, at first in a low tone, then more and more loudly. Hearing Charsky's name, the *improvvisatore* looked for him and, seeing him at his feet, gave him a pencil and piece of paper with a friendly smile. Charsky found it very unpleasant to have to play a role in this comedy, but there was no getting round it: he took the pencil and paper from the Italian's hand and wrote down a few words; the Italian picked up the vase from the table, came down from the platform, and held the vase out to Charsky, who dropped his theme into it. His example had its effect: two journalists, in their capacity as men of letters, felt duty-bound to write a theme each; the secretary of the Neapolitan Embassy and a young man* who had just returned from a journey and was still raving about Florence both placed their rolled-up slips of paper in the urn. Finally, at her mother's insistence, a plain-looking girl with tears in her eyes wrote a few lines in Italian and, blushing to her ears, handed them to the *improvvisatore*, while other ladies watched her in silence with a barely perceptible smile of contempt. Returning to his platform, the Italian placed the urn on the table and started drawing the pieces of paper out, one after the other, reading each aloud:

The Cenci family (*La famiglia dei Cenci*)
L'ultimo giorno di Pompei
Cleopatra e i suoi amanti
La primavera veduta da una prigione
*Il trionfo di Tasso**

"What is the pleasure of the honourable company?" asked the humble Italian. "Do you wish to select one of the suggested themes, or let the matter be decided by lot?"

"By lot!" said a voice from the crowd.

"By lot, by lot!" was repeated throughout the audience.

The *improvvisatore* came down from the platform once more, holding the urn in his hands, and asked, "Who will be so good as to draw a theme?"

He searched the front rows with an imploring glance. Not one of the brilliant ladies seated there would move a finger. The *improvvisatore*, unaccustomed to northern reserve, seemed distressed... but suddenly he noticed that on one side of the room a small hand in a tight-fitting white glove was raised: he swiftly turned and walked up to a majestic young beauty seated at the end of the second row. She rose without the slightest embarrassment, put her small aristocratic hand into the urn with the most natural gesture, and drew out a rolled-up piece of paper.

"Would you be kind enough to unroll it and read it?" the *improvvisatore* asked her.

The beautiful girl unrolled the paper and read out the words: "*Cleopatra e i suoi amanti*."

She read these words in a soft tone, but the silence reigning over the room was so complete that everybody could hear her. The *improvvisatore* bowed deeply, with a look of profound gratitude, to the beautiful lady, and returned to his platform.

"Ladies and gentlemen," he said turning to the audience, "the lot bids me to improvise on the theme of Cleopatra* and her lovers. I humbly ask the person who suggested this theme to elucidate the idea: which lovers are in question, *perché la grande regina ne aveva molti?*...*

Several men burst into loud laughter at these words. The *improvvisatore* appeared somewhat confused.

"I would like to know," he continued, "what historical episode the person suggesting the theme was alluding to... I should be most grateful if that person would kindly explain."

Nobody hastened to answer. Some ladies directed their glance towards the plain girl who had written down a theme at her mother's command. The poor girl noticed this malevolent attention and became so embarrassed that tears welled up in her eyes...

Charsky could not bear this any longer. Turning to the *improvvisatore*, he said in Italian: "I was the one who suggested the theme. I had in mind the testimony of Victor Aurelius, who claims that Cleopatra named death as the price of her love, and that some admirers were found to whom such a condition was neither frightening nor repellent...* But maybe the subject is somewhat embarrassing... Would you rather choose another one?'

But the *improvvisatore* already sensed the divine presence... He signalled to the musicians to play... His face grew alarmingly pale; he trembled as if in fever; his eyes sparkled with wondrous fire; he smoothed his black hair back with his hand, wiped the beads of sweat off his high forehead with a handkerchief... and suddenly stepped forward, folding his arms across his chest... The music stopped... The improvisation began:

> *The hall was glistening. Choirs sang out*
> *to accompaniment of flutes and lyres.*
> *The Queen's bright voice and sparkling eyes*
> *lent animation to the banquet*
> *and won the hearts of all the guests.*
> *Then all at once, her golden goblet*
> *half-raised, she paused in contemplation,*
> *bowing the head that all admired.*
>
> *It seemed a trance fell on the feast;*
> *the guests, the singers all fell quiet.*
> *Then once again she raised her brow,*
> *and with unfaltering gaze she spoke:*

"You men, will my love give you pleasure?
Then pleasure now is yours to buy...
So listen to me: I am ready
to place us all on equal terms.
Who'll come to passion's trading floor?
I offer you my love for sale.
Which of you, tell me then, will buy
one night with me? The price? Your life.

"I vow – oh Mother of Delights,
I'll serve you in a way unheard of:
a common prostitute, I'll mount
my bed and there I'll test their passion.
Hearken to me, then, mighty Venus,
and you too, Lords of the Underworld,
you deities of dreaded Hades,
I vow – until the break of day
I'll satisfy voluptuously
the lusts of those who've purchased me
and slake their appetite for pleasure
with love play known to me alone.
But once divine Aurora's beam
has lit the world with morning purple,
I vow – each lucky suitor's head
shall fall beneath the deadly axe."

She spoke. The guests sat horror-struck,
and hearts began to race with passion...
The company's excited murmur
she heard with air of cold defiance
and scanned with a contemptuous glance
the circle of her devotees...
Then suddenly one man strode forth
from out the throng, then two men more.
Their step was firm; their eyes were fearless;
the Queen rose from her throne to greet them.
The deal was done: three nights were purchased –
such was the fatal bed's appeal.

The banqueters looked on transfixed:
under the blessing of the priests
the lots were now drawn one by one
from out the urn of destiny.
Flavius was first, a doughty warrior,
grown grey in bearing arms for Rome;
he'd been unable to endure
a woman's arrogant disdain,
and so he'd answered to the summons
of pleasure, as in war he'd answered
the summons of a battle cry.
Next Crito, young philosopher,
reared in the groves of Epicurus,*
a worshipper and celebrant
of Venus, Cupid and the Graces.
Last, winsome both to heart and eyes,
like a spring flower scarcely opened,
came one who's left posterity
no name. A first soft down still shaded
the youngster's cheeks and chin but lightly;
his eyes, though, gleamed with ecstasy.
The force, still newly felt, of passion
was seething in his youthful heart.
On him Queen Cleopatra rested
a gaze of special tenderness.

And now the light of day is gone,
the golden-hornèd moon is rising;
a soft and lovely shade enfolds
the halls of Alexandria.
Fountains are playing, lanterns burning,
a haze of incense drifts aloft,
and breaths of cooler air will soon
refresh the mighty lords of Egypt.
Within a dimly sumptuous chamber,
amidst entrancing masterworks,
canopied round with purple hangings,
there stands the glistening couch of gold.

IN 179– I WAS RETURNING...*

(c.1835)

IN 179– I WAS returning to Livonia with the happy thought of embracing my old mother after a separation of four years. The closer I got to our country house, the more impatient I felt. I prodded my coachman, a phlegmatic compatriot of mine, and sincerely missed Russian drivers and reckless Russian rides. To make matters worse, my carriage broke down. I was forced to stop. Fortunately, there was a station not too far off.

I walked to the village to fetch some people for my feeble carriage. It was the end of the summer. The sun was setting. Ploughed fields stretched out along one side of the road; meadows, overgrown with low shrubs, along the other. A young Estonian woman's melancholy song could be heard from a distance. Suddenly, in the midst of general stillness, a cannon shot boomed distinctly... and died away without an echo. I was surprised. There was not one fort in the neighbourhood: how could a cannon shot be heard in this peaceful region? I came to the conclusion that there must be a camp nearby, and my imagination carried me back for a moment to the preoccupations of military life, which I had only just left behind.

Approaching the village, I saw a small manor house on one side. Two ladies were sitting on the balcony. I bowed to them as I passed by, and went on to the post station.

I had scarcely settled things with the lazy blacksmiths when a little old man, a retired Russian soldier, came up to me and invited me in the name of his lady for a cup of tea. I accepted with pleasure and went back to the manor house.

On the way there I learnt from the soldier that the old lady was called Karolina Ivanovna, that she was a widow, that her daughter, Yekaterina Ivanovna, was of a marriageable age, that they were both such good-hearted ladies, and so forth...

In 179– I was twenty-three years old, and the very thought of *a young lady* was enough to arouse my keen interest.

The old lady received me kindly and in a hospitable spirit. On hearing my name, she discovered we were related: I learnt that she was the widow of von W., a distant relative and a valiant general, killed in 1772.

While to all appearances I was attentively listening to the good-hearted Karolina Ivanovna's genealogical explorations, I was also casting some surreptitious glances at her charming daughter, who was pouring the tea and spreading fresh amber-coloured butter on small slices of home-baked bread. Her eighteen years, round, rosy cheeks, dark, narrow eyebrows, small, fresh mouth and blue eyes fully lived up to my expectations. We soon made friends, and by the third cup of tea I was treating her like a cousin. In the meanwhile my carriage had been fetched, and Ivan came to report that it would not be ready before next morning at the earliest. This news did not distress me at all, and, accepting Karolina Ivanovna's invitation, I stayed for the night.

THE LAST OF THE LINEAGE
OF JOAN OF ARC*

(1837)

(Translated by Michael Basker)

L AST YEAR, 1836, SAW the death in London of a certain Mr
Dulys (Jean-François-Philippe Dulys), a descendant of the
brother of Joan of Arc, the famous Maid of Orleans. Mr Dulys
settled in Britain at the beginning of the French Revolution; his
wife was British, and there were no surviving children. His last
testament nominated as his heir one of his wife's relatives, James
Bailey, an Edinburgh bookseller. Among his papers were original
deeds of title from Kings Charles VII, Henri III and Louis XIII,*
attesting the nobility of the family of d'Arc Dulys. All these deeds
of title were sold at public auction for a very considerable sum, as
too was a curious manuscript: a letter from Voltaire to the father
of the late Mr Dulys.

Dulys *père* was evidently a good nobleman with scant interest in
literature. Around 1767 it nevertheless came to his attention that a
certain Mr de Voltaire had published a work of some description
on the heroine of Orleans. The book was very expensive. Mr Dulys
nevertheless resolved to purchase it, expecting to find a true his-
tory of his illustrious forebear. He experienced a most unpleasant
surprise when he received the small booklet, printed in Holland
and embellished with some astonishing pictures. In the first flush
of indignation, he wrote to Voltaire the following letter, a copy of
which was found in the papers of the deceased. (The letter, along
with Voltaire's reply, was published in the *Morning Chronicle*.)

Sir,
*I recently had occasion to acquire, for six louis d'or, your his-
tory of the siege of Orleans in 1429. This work is overladen
not merely with crude errors, unforgivable in a person know-
ing anything of French history, but also with inept slander
concerning King Charles VII, Joan of Arc, known as the Maid
of Orleans, Agnès Sorel, Seigneurs La Trimouille, Laguire,
Baudricourt* and other noble and aristocratic personages. From*

the enclosed copies of reliable letters of title, retained by me in my chateau (Tournebu, Bailliage du Chaumont en Touraine), you will clearly perceive that Joan of Arc was the sister of Lucas d'Arc, seigneur du Feron, from whom I am descended by direct lineage. And hence I not only consider it my right, but regard it as my indispensable duty to demand from you satisfaction for the impertinent, malicious and mendacious testimony which you have permitted yourself to publish concerning the above-mentioned Maiden. I therefore ask you, sir, to inform me of the time and place, and also of the weapon of your choice, to bring this affair to a speedy conclusion.

I have the honour and so forth.

Notwithstanding the comic aspect of this affair, Voltaire took it seriously. He took fright at the scandal which it might have pro-voked, perhaps also at the sword of the ticklish nobleman, and at once dispatched the following reply.

22nd May 1767

Sir,

The letter with which you honoured me found me in my bed, which I have not left for the past eight months or more. You would appear to be unaware that I am a poor old man, burdened by sickness and woes, and not one of those brave knights from whom you are descended. I can assure you that in no wise did I participate in the compilation of the crude rhymed chronicle (l'impertinente chronique rimée) *of which you saw fit to write to me. Europe is inundated with printed idiocies which the public magnanimously ascribes to me. Some forty years ago I happened to publish an epic poem entitled* La Henriade. *Enu-merating therein the heroes who have glorified France, I made so bold as to address your famous relative* (votre illustre cousine) *in the following words:*

...Et toi, brave Amazone,
La honte des Anglais et le soutien du trône.

That is the only mention in my works of the immortal heroine who saved France. I regret that I did not dedicate my feeble talent to the glorification of divine miracles instead of labouring for the satisfaction of a thoughtless and ungrateful public. I have the honour, sir, to be
  Your humble servant
      Voltaire (gentilhomme de la chambre du roi)

An English journalist made the following remarks in connection with the publication of this correspondence:

The fate of Joan of Arc in regard to her own country is worthy of amazement. We must of course share with the French the shame of her trial and execution. But the barbarity of the English might be excused by the prejudices of the age and the bitterness of an injured national pride which sincerely ascribed the feats of the young herdswoman to the workings of an unclean spirit. The question remains: how to excuse the pusillanimous ingratitude of the French? Not of course through fear of the Devil, of whom they had long been unafraid. We have done something at least for the memory of the illustrious Maid; our poet laureate dedicated to her the first virginal stirrings of his (still uncorrupted) inspiration. Britain gave refuge to the last of her relations. But how did France seek to redress the mark of blood staining the most melancholy page of her chronicle? True, nobility was granted to the relatives of Joan of Arc; but their descendants eked out their lives in obscurity. Not a single d'Arc or Dulys was to be seen at the court of the Kings of France, from Charles VII to Charles X* himself. Modern history presents no more touching subject, no life and death more poetic, than those of the Maid of Orleans; but what did Voltaire, that worthy representative of his people, make of this? Once in his life it befell him to be a true poet, and this is the use to which his inspiration is put! With satanic breath he fans the sparks that glow in the ash of the martyr's bonfire, and dances like a drunken savage around the flames of his own amusement. Like a Roman executioner he joins profanity to the mortal torments of the Maid. Our laureate's poem of course falls short of Voltaire's in force of conception, but Southey's* creation is the heroic work of an honest man, and the fruit of noble rapture. Let us note that Voltaire, who in France was surrounded by enemies and beset by envy, subjected at his every step to the most poisonous reproof, found barely an accuser when his criminal poem appeared. His most desperate enemies were disarmed. All rapturously acclaimed a book in which contempt for everything that is considered sacred to a man and citizen is reduced to the utmost degree of cynicism. It occurred to none to defend his country's honour; and had the good, honest Dulys's challenge become public, it would have aroused inexhaustible laughter not only in the philosophical salons of Baron d'Holbach and Mme Geoffrin,* but in the ancient halls of the heirs of Laguire and La Trimouille. Paltry age! Paltry nation!

Note on the Text

Professor Debreczeny translated the works in this volume from the Russian texts as given in the Soviet Academy's ten-volume collected edition of Pushkin (B.V. Tomashevsky, ed., *Polnoye sobraniye sochineniy*, Moscow: *Akademiya Nauk SSSR*, 1962–66) collated with the large, seventeen-volume edition (V.D. Bonch-Bruyevich al., eds., *Polnoye sobraniye sochineniy*, Moscow: *Akademiya Nauk SSSR*, 1937–59).

Notes

p. 5, *The Queen of Spades*: This short story was written in the autumn of 1833 at Pushkin's country estate at Boldino and published the following year. A revealing error in the earliest editions is that three times in Chapter I the old lady is referred to as Princess rather than Countess. This error gives credence to what Pushkin's friend P. V. Nashchokin was later to mention: that the old lady was at least partially modelled on Princess Natalya Petrovna Golitsyna (*née* Chernyshova – 1741–1837), who was present, like an indispensable ornament, at every Petersburg Court function in the early 1830s. According to Nashchokin, Golitsyna's grandson told Pushkin that once, having lost a large sum of money at cards, he had asked his grandmother for help; the old lady did not give him any money but named three secret cards, of which she had been told in Paris by Count Saint-Germain. With the aid of these cards, according to the story, the grandson did indeed recoup his losses. Princess Golitsyna had visited Paris twice – once with her father in 1761, before her marriage; and a second time with her husband and children in 1786–90 – but the details of Pushkin's account of her stay in Paris are fictional. Although many of the features of Pushkin's Countess were taken by Pushkin's contemporaries to recall Princess Golitsyna, some aspects of her appearance and character also reflected those of another St Petersburg old lady, Natalya Kirillovna Zagryazhskaya, a great-aunt of Pushkin's wife.

p. 7, *But on days when it rained... on business*: Pushkin's own verses, untitled and written in 1828.

p. 7, *a card party*: The card game here is faro, which was imported to Russia from the Court of Louis XIV. It was strictly a gambling game, allowing very little, if any, latitude for skill and strategy. Each player (punter) picked a card of his own choice from his deck and put it on the table face down, placing his bet on it. The dealer (banker) shuffled the cards of another deck (an unused one if the stakes were high) and flipped up cards, placing them alternately on his right and on his left. If the card falling to the banker's right matched the punter's card in rank (the various suits making no difference), the banker won; if the card falling to his left matched the punter's card, the punter received a win equivalent to what he had put on his card. The punter, though he knew what he had picked, did not turn his card face up until he saw a matching one placed on the table by the banker.

p. 7, *a mirandole game*: The term *mirandole* denotes a cautious tactic in faro, consisting in small bets, with gains withdrawn rather than staked in a new round. *Routé* meant that the punter wanted to double his bet and play the same card he had just won on. *Paroli* meant that the punter, after a win, wanted to include his winning in his new bet, thereby doubling the original stake. To indicate this, he bent down a corner of the new card he had just picked.

p. 8, *Richelieu*: For the Duc de Richelieu see note to 'The Negro of Peter the Great', p. 52.

p. 9, *Count Saint-Germain*: A famous adventurer of obscure origins, who appeared in Paris around 1750 and became a close friend of Louis XV. He was a man of vast knowledge, a linguist, musician and painter, and was especially well versed in chemistry and alchemy. He attracted attention by his enormous wealth and rumoured preternatural longevity. He himself told stories of events many centuries back, of which he claimed to have been an eyewitness. As a result of court intrigues he was compelled to leave France in 1760, after which he travelled through Europe and even visited Russia. He probably died in 1784.

p. 9, *Wandering Jew*: According to medieval legend a Jewish shoemaker had refused to let Christ rest at his house on the way to Calvary and had been condemned to wander the world until the Second Coming.

p. 9, *Casanova... Memoirs*: The *Memoirs of Giovanni Giacomo Casanova de Seingalt*, another famous eighteenth-century adventurer, were being published posthumously in Pushkin's own time. Pushkin derives his characterization of Saint-Germain largely from Casanova.

p. 9, *au jeu de la Reine*: "At the Queen's card party." (French)

p. 9, *sonica*: Winning *sonica* meant that the player won on the very first turn of the cards in a new deal.

p. 10, *powdered cards*: Playing cards treated by dishonest players with a special powder that could be used to hide or reveal symbols according to the requirements of the game.

p. 10, *Zorich*: S.G. Zorich (1745–99), a distinguished soldier, was Catherine II's favourite in 1777–78, but incurred her displeasure through excessive gambling at cards.

p. 10, *paroli-paix*: Chaplitsky doubled his bet, a *paroli*, on his second card, and won. He then let all his gains ride on a third card – a *paroli-paix*, indicated by bending the card in the middle as if to make a bridge out of it.

p. 11, *Il paraît que monsieur... plus fraîches*: "It appears that monsieur has a strong preference for ladies' maids." "What do you expect, madame? They are fresher." (French)

p. 14, *Bitter is the bread... staircase*: A quote from Dante's *Paradiso*, XVII, 58.

p. 18, *Vous m'écrivez... puis les lire*: "You write me four-page letters faster, my angel, than I can read them" (French).

p. 21, *Mme Lebrun*: Elisabeth Vigée-Lebrun (1755–1842) was a Parisian portrait painter. Having fled from France at the time of the Revolution, she toured Europe, spending several years in St Petersburg around 1800, during which time she painted a portrait of the Countess N.P. Golitsyna's daughter.

p. 21, *the famous Leroy*: Both Julien Le Roy (1686–1759) and his son Pierre (1717–85) were famous French makers of timepieces; son succeeded father as watchmaker to King Louis XV.

p. 21, *Montgolfiers' balloon and Mesmer's magnetism*: The brothers Joseph-Michel Montgolfier (1740–1810) and Jacques-Étienne Montgolfier (1745–99), of Annonay, France, launched the first hot-air balloon in 1783. The German physician Franz-Anton Mesmer (1734–1815) (whose name gave us the word "mesmerize") developed a theory of "animal magnetism", according to which patients' disorders could be treated by the inducing of trances. Although Mesmer's theory of "magnetism" was soon discredited, his techniques of trance inducement led to the modern practice of hypnotism.

p. 22, *a Voltaire-style armchair*: An easy chair with a padded seat, arms and back. Voltaires had high and reclining backs and were used especially by the sick and elderly.

p. 25, *7 mai 18—, Homme sans mœurs et sans religion*: "7th May 18—, A man with no morals and no religion!" (French).

p. 26, *oubli ou regret*: "Oblivion or regret" (French). This was an invitation to dance. The man so approached had to choose one of the words without knowing which lady it stood for. The third lady mentioned was probably a chaperone.

p. 28, *hair combed à l'oiseau royal*: I.e combed like the showy crest of a species of crane.

p. 29, *That night... Swedenborg*: This quotation has not been found in the works of the Swedish mystic Emanuel Swedenborg (Svedberg;

1688–1772) and is taken to be Pushkin's own playful invention in the spirit of anecdotes circulating about the adventures of the clairvoyant theologian.

p. 29, *waiting for the midnight bridegroom*: The preacher had in mind Christ's parable of the wise and foolish virgins in Matthew 25:1–13.

p. 32, *"Attendez"... sir*: Punters used the peremptory French term *attendez* ("wait") to indicate to the banker that they wished to make or change a bet between actions. When pronounced with excited emphasis, this exclamation could sound like a rather rude command, offensive to the banker if he was a man of mature years and high rank. P.A. Vyazemsky records in his Old Notebook that a certain Count Gudovich, having attained the rank of colonel, stopped taking the role of banker in faro games, explaining that "it is undignified to subject yourself to the demands of some greenhorn of a sub-lieutenant who, punting against you, almost peremptorily yells out: *attendez*!" It was probably this anecdote, current in St Petersburg at the beginning of the 1830s, that inspired Pushkin's epigraph to the chapter.

p. 33, *writing the amount above his card in chalk*: That is, chalking the amount on the green felt of the table.

p. 35, *Obukhov Hospital*: The Obukhov Hospital had a dismal reputation as a place for the care of the impoverished.

p. 37, *Kirdzhali*: This story was written in the autumn of 1834 and published the same year. It is set at the time of the Greek uprising against the Turks in 1821 and its aftermath. Between 1820 and 1823 Pushkin was serving in Kishinyov – chief town of Bessarabia, the northern district of Moldavia recently annexed by Russia from Turkey – and had therefore a personal knowledge of some of the events and personalities mentioned.

Kirdzhali is the name of a town and district in southern Bulgaria, which was then part of the Turkish Empire. In the late seventeenth and early eighteenth centuries it gave its name to a species of bandit that plagued that area of the Balkans. Pushkin's "kirdzhali", whose given name was Georg, was a robber chiefly active in Turkish Moldavia, who joined Alexander Ypsilantis's uprising with his band in 1821, escaped to Russia after the Hetairists' defeat later that year, was arrested by the Russian authorities in 1823, and was handed over to the Turks. He escaped from prison that year, but was recaptured and hanged in Jassy in 1824. Pushkin, who took some notes about leading Hetairists while living in Kishinyov between 1820 and 1823, was aware of Kirdzhali's extradition to Turkey at the time it happened (see his lyrical fragment of 1823, 'The Civil Servant and the Poet').

Although this story is based largely on historical facts, its account of the hero's escape from prison after his extradition and of subsequent events is fiction – either knowingly invented by Pushkin, or recounted to him by an informant who had been beguiled by a tradition owing more to folklore than to fact and perhaps also to a confusion between Kirdzhali the person and kirdzhali the generic name for bandits in that part of the Balkans.

The non-Russian – Greek, Bulgarian, Albanian, Romanian, Turkish – personal and place names in this story often exist in several different forms and spellings. Unless a standard English version of a name is available, the present edition, for consistency, simply transliterates Pushkin's Russian version of the names, giving any important variants in the notes.

p. 39, *kirdzhali in Turkish means warrior, daredevil*: The Balkan Turkish word *kircali* means "marauder", "irregular soldier". It is derived from the name of a provincial centre in southern Bulgaria, Kurdzhali, so called after its founder Kırca Ali.

p. 39, *Alexander Ypsilantis proclaimed his uprising*: Alexander Ypsilantis (1792–1828), whose father had been Hospodar ("Governor") of autonomous Wallachia-Moldavia (modern Romania) under the Turks before he fled to Russia with his family in 1805, came of a princely family of the Greek Balkan diaspora. He himself had fought in the Napoleonic Wars for Russia, rising to major general in the Russian army in 1817. In April 1820 he became head of the so-called *Philikí Hetaireía* ("Society of Friends"), a secret society of those committed to fight for Greek independence from the Turkish Empire. In February 1821 Ypsilantis crossed the River Prut into Turkish Moldavia with a detachment of Hetairists and published in the capital Jassy (modern-day Iaşi) a proclamation calling for an uprising against the Turks.

p. 39, *ill-fated battle... took his place*: A reference to the Hetairists' defeat at Drăgăşani in Turkish Wallachia, on 7th June 1821. Many of the young Greek soldiers had been recruited from the Greek colony in Odessa. Olimbioti (b.1772) (aka Georgios Olympios, and various other spellings) was a Greek who had been prominent in the anti-Turkish struggle in the Balkans and who perished the same year at Seku.

p. 39, *Most of these cowards... ten to one*: The references are to the battles of Seku and Skulyany (Sculeni) on the Prut River, the latter of which took place on 16th–17th June 1821. Olympios and the remains of his unit had taken refuge from their Turkish pursuers in the monastery of Seku, where they had reportedly blown themselves up. In fact, after a lengthy resistance, they had surrendered to the Turks, who treacherously killed them.

p. 39, *Georgy Kantakuzin*: Prince G.M. Kantakuzin (d.1857) was a colonel in the Russian cavalry, who had fought in the Napoleonic wars. He was a member of the *Philikí Hetaireía* and had been appointed by Ypsilantis commander of the insurrectionary forces in Turkish Moldavia, but on the eve of the battle of Skulyany he had deserted his troops and taken refuge on Russian territory. He was married to the sister of one of Pushkin's school friends.

p. 40, *The commander of the border station*: S.G. Navrotsky, who had entered service in 1767.

p. 40, *Nekrasa's descendants*: At the beginning of the 18th century, a group of Cossack Old Believers under the leadership of Ataman Ignat Nekrasa had fled to Turkey from religious persecution in Russia and settled in what is now Romania.

p. 41, *beşliks*: Small Turkish silver coins.

p. 42, *an important official*: This was M.I. Leks (1793–1856), whom Pushkin knew in Kishinyov and Odessa in the early 1820s and met again in St Petersburg in the 1830s. By that time Leks has risen to the post of director of the chancery at the Ministry of Internal Affairs.

p. 42, *căruţă*: A Romanian word for cart or wagon (cf. Italian *carrozza*).

p. 42, *end of September 1821*: This is an error on Pushkin's part; Kirdzhali was extradited in 1823.

p. 42, *dolman*: A long-skirted Turkish garment with buttons on the chest and narrow sleeves, tied with a broad sash.

p. 44, *galbens*: Moldavian word for gold coins.

p. 44, *from one burial mound to the next*: The Russian term is *kurgan*; ancient burial mounds were scattered all across the Ukrainian and Moldavian steppes.

p. 49, *The Negro of Peter the Great*: The first six chapters of this unfinished historical novel were written in the summer of 1827 in Mikhaylovskoye, and one more page – which is all that remains of Chapter 7 – was added in the spring of 1828. Two fragments – from Chapters 4 and 3, respectively – were published in literary journals in 1829 and 1830. The assembled text of all the extant parts was published, with a few omissions, after Pushkin's death in 1837 by the editors of the journal *Sovremennik*, who also gave it its title and distributed the epigraphs, all written together on the first page of the manuscript, among the various chapters.

p. 49, *Russia transformed... Yazykov*: From the poem 'Ala' (1824) by Pushkin's friend N. Yazykov (1803–46).

p. 51, *I am in Paris... Diary of a Traveller*: From lines 1 and 2 of Part I of the poem 'NN.'s Journey to Paris and London' (1803) by I.I. Dmitriev (1760–1837).

p. 51, *Ibrahim, a godson of the Emperor*: The prototype for Ibrahim was Pushkin's maternal great-grandfather, Abram Hannibal (spelt "Gannibal" in Russian), a black African, who had been brought to Russia as a child during the reign of Peter I (b. 1672; r. 1682–1725) and did indeed become Peter's godson. Pushkin's chief historical source on his ancestor, apart from oral family tradition, was a handwritten biography of Abram Hannibal in German, which Pushkin received from a great-uncle. This source was not entirely reliable, but it served as an inspiration for several scenes of the projected novel. In this fictional account of his great-grandfather's life, Pushkin himself was not aiming at complete historical accuracy: for example, he makes Peter propose to the Rzhevskys on Ibrahim's behalf, though the real Hannibal did not marry until well after Peter's death; and he makes Ibrahim's betrothed a member of the ancient Russian nobility, though the real Hannibal's wife was the daughter of a Greek sailor.

p. 51, *Spanish War*: The Anglo-French campaign of 1719–20 against Spain for alleged violations of the Peace of Utrecht (1713).

p. 51, *Duke of Orleans*: Philippe II, Duc d'Orléans (1674–1723) became Regent of France in 1715, on the death of Louis XIV.

p. 51, *Law made his appearance on the scene*: John Law (1671–1729), Scottish financier and speculator, founded in 1716 the Banque Générale, the first bank in France, which by issuing prodigious quantities of banknotes, brought the French economy to the brink of ruin by 1720.

p. 52, *Duc de Richelieu... Alcibiades*: Armand de Vignerot du Plessis, Duc de Richelieu (1696–1788), a great-nephew of Cardinal Richelieu, bore the title of *Maréchal de France* and later played a prominent role in French public life under Louis XV. As a young man he was known as *l'Alcibiade français*, after the Athenian statesman Alcibiades (*c.*450–404 BC), both being notorious for their dissolute and extravagant lifestyles.

p. 52, *Temps fortuné... pénitence*: From Voltaire's *La Pucelle* (1755), XIII. In Ernest Dowson's English translation it reads:

> *The pleasant reign of License had its prime,*
> *As Folly, tinkling loud her bells in hand,*

With lightsome step tripped over Gallia's land,
Where to devotion not a soul was prone,
And every act save penitence was known.

p. 52, *Arouet... Chaulieu... Montesquieu... Fontenelle*: Arouet was Voltaire's original name, which he dropped in 1718. At the time described by Pushkin, the early 1720s, Voltaire (1694–1778), thinker, man of letters and satirist, was in his twenties. Guillaume Amfrye, Abbé de Chaulieu (1639–1720), was a lyric poet. Charles de Secondat, Baron de Montesquieu (1689–1755), social commentator and political thinker, was just at the time publishing his *Lettres persanes* (1721), in which two imaginary Persian visitors to Paris record their outsiders' impressions of French society and culture. Bernard le Boviet de Fontenelle (1657–1757), French rational philosopher and man of letters, was the permanent secretary of the Académie Française.

p. 57, *No more does beauty... Derzhavin*: From the ode 'On the Death of Prince Meshchersky' (1779) by Gavrila A. Derzhavin (1743–1816), the greatest Russian poet of the eighteenth century.

p. 59, *twenty-eight versts*: A verst is a Russian measure of length equivalent to just over one kilometre.

p. 60, *Yekaterina... Two beautiful young girls*: Peter's second wife Yekaterina, born a commoner, outlived him to reign briefly as the Empress Catherine I (1725–27). They had two daughters who were teenagers at this time. The younger of these, Yelizaveta ("Liza"), later reigned as the Empress Elizabeth (1741–61) and remained a patroness of the historical Abram Hannibal, presenting him with the lands in western Russia that included Mikhaylovskoye, subsequently Pushkin's mother's inheritance and often visited by Pushkin.

p. 61, *Menshikov... Dolgoruky... Bruce... Raguzinsky*: Prince Alexander Danilovich Menshikov (1673–1729), son of a corporal or a groom, and once reportedly a pie vendor, began his career as the boy Peter's orderly in the Preobrazhensky Regiment, but later became Peter's favourite, was loaded with honours and remained his close associate for the whole of his reign. He was several times investigated for corruption and suffered punishment at Peter's own hands, yet managed to maintain his position. Y.F. Dolgoruky (1659–1720) was a senator and president of the Auditing Collegium. If, as other details indicate, Ibrahim returned to Russia in the early or mid 1720s, he could not have met Dolgoruky. Jacob Bruce (1670–1735), of Scottish background, was an outstanding military engineer. He had been born in Russia and belonged to the second generation of foreign settlers in Muscovy.

The Raguzinsky famous for his role as a diplomat and close adviser to Peter was Count Savva Lukych (1670–1738), but he was already in his fifties at the time described by Pushkin and the reference here is probably to a younger member of his family.

p. 63, *Just like the clouds... Kyukhelbeker*: Words from Act 3 of a tragedy *Argivyane* (1822–25) by Pushkin's friend V.K. Kyukhelbeker (1799–1846).

p. 63, *Sheremetev... Golovin invited Ibrahim to dinner*: Field Marshal Count Boris Sheremetev (1652–1719) commanded the Russian army in several important campaigns during Peter's reign. As noted above, if indeed Ibrahim returned to Russia in the 1720s, he could not have met Sheremetev. I.M. Golovin (1680–1738), an ancestor of Pushkin's on his father's side, served Peter in senior positions in the army and navy.

p. 63, *Buturlin... Feofan, Gavriil Buzhinsky and Kopievich*: I.I. Buturlin (1661–1738), a senator, was a senior military figure under Peter and a close associate of his. Feofan Prokopovich (1681–1736), at this time bishop of Pskov and Narva but resident in Petersburg, was an outstanding polymath, writer and ardent supporter of Peter's reforms. Gavriil Buzhinsky (1680–1731) was another senior church-man who supported Peter's reforms. I.F. Kopievich (1651–1714) was a printer and translator who had been employed by Peter to purchase books for him abroad. He is not known to have spent much time in Petersburg and cannot have been there in the early 1720s; so possibly Pushkin had another Kopievich in mind.

p. 64, *young Korsakov*: This character, Ivan Yevgrafovich Korsakov, is also based on a historical figure, V.Y. Rimsky-Korsakov (1702–57), who had been sent to France in 1716 to study naval science and returned to Russia in 1724.

p. 67, *Tsaritsa Natalya Kirilovna's sable hat*: Natalya Kirilovna Nary-shkina (1651–94) was second wife of Tsar Alexei Mikhaylovich and Peter I's mother. Here she symbolizes the old pre-Petrine regime of Muscovite isolationism and suspicion of everything foreign. Peter ordered the aristocracy to abandon Muscovite clothes and other fashions and to dress in a western manner.

p. 67, *Que diable est-ce que tout cela*: "What the Devil is all this?" (French).

p. 70, *Our forebears... Ruslan and Lyudmila*: From Pushkin's early narrative poem *Ruslan and Lyudmila*, I, 10–13 (1820), where he is describing a traditional banquet given by Grand Prince Vladimir I of Kiev for the wedding of his daughter Lyudmila to Prince Ruslan.

After the feast the sorcerer Chernomor snatches away Ruslan's bride before their marriage is consummated.

p. 70, *shot through at Narva*: Although the Russians were defeated in the Battle of Narva (1700), they scored several victories over Sweden in Livonia and Estonia the following year, taking numerous prisoners. The reference later in the chapter to "the campaign of 1701" indicates that that was the time when the officer in question was taken prisoner.

p. 71, *order of precedence*: The Russian term is *mestnichestvo*, meaning order of precedence both in appointments to public office and in seating at table on festive occasions. The precedence was based on ancient lineage and offices held by ancestors.

p. 73, *the wife see that she reverence her husband*: From St Paul's letter to the Ephesians, 5:33.

p. 76, *I shall find a wife... The Miller*: Quotation, in somewhat altered form, from A. Ablesimov's comic opera *The Miller, the Wizard, the Cheat and the Matchmaker* (1779), Act I, Sc. 4.

p. 78, *Bova the King's Son and Yeruslan Lazarevich*: Popular Russian fairy tales.

p. 79, *the rebellion*: Gavrila Afanasyevich seems to be referring to the rebellion of the *streltsy* ("musketeers" – the permanent garrison of infantrymen who guarded the Kremlin and policed Moscow). In 1698 several regiments of *streltsy* mutinied against Peter's government and tried to replace him with his disgraced half-sister Sofya. Peter had the rebellion crushed and thousands of the *streltsy* executed in punishment.

p. 80, *fifteenth parallel*: The figure was left blank in Pushkin's manuscript. It has been filled in by editors on the basis of the tradition that Abram Hannibal's original home was in Ethiopia.

p. 83, *j'aurais planté là*: "I'd have dumped" (French).

p. 83, *une petite santé*: "A delicate little thing" (French).

p. 83, *mijaurée*: "Affected woman", "little madam" (French).

p. 87, *Charles XII*: King Charles XII of Sweden had fought against Russia in the Great Northern War from 1700 until his death in 1718. Successful at first, his fortunes had suffered a series of reversals, notably a crushing defeat by Peter at Poltava in 1709.

p. 87, *so shall ve speak*: No outline in Pushkin's own hand has survived to show how he intended to continue the novel. There is, however, an entry for 16th September 1827, in the diary of his friend, A. Vulf, reporting how Pushkin had said he would continue the plot. The relevant sentence in Vulf's diary reads: "The central intrigue in this novel, as Pushkin says, will be the infidelity of the Negro's wife, who will give birth to a white baby and will be banished to a convent for it."

p. 89, *The Guests Were Arriving at the Dacha*: These fragments of a projected psychological novel were not prepared for publication by Pushkin and bore no title; they are known by the opening words of the first fragment. Fragments 1 and 2 were written in 1828, Fragment 3 in 1830. Although Fragment 3 was not juxtaposed to the first two fragments in Pushkin's manuscripts, it appears to be clearly connected with them, since the same Spaniard and Russian here seem to be resuming their conversation interrupted in Fragment 1. The three fragments have been assembled as a continuum only in Russian editions.

p. 91, *compared it with a tow-haired Russian beauty*: A reference to the idyll "Fishermen" (1821) by N.I. Gnedich (1784–1833). Pushkin's character, however, in keeping with his flippant tone, avoids Gnedich's expression *rusye lokon volny* ("blond waves of locks"), using instead the much less poetic *belobrysaya* ("tow-haired").

p. 92, *se mit à bouder*: "Set about sulking" (French).

p. 92, *Il n'en fera rien, trop heureux de pouvoir la compromettre*: "He'll do nothing of the kind: he'll be all too glad to have the chance to compromise her" (French).

p. 93, *Hussein Pasha*: Bey of Algiers from 1818 to 1830, when he was deposed by France.

p. 94, *Les Liaisons dangereuses*: A novel by Pierre Choderlos de Laclos (1782) about cynicism, seduction and malice in French aristocratic society.

p. 94, *Jomini*: Henri Jomini (1779–1869) was a French general and military theorist who served in Napoleon's army during the Russian campaign, but switched sides in 1813 and became a high-ranking general and military adviser in the Russian army under both Alexander I and Nicholas I.

p. 95, *Quand j'étais à Florence*: "When I was in Florence…" (French).

p. 95, *Et puis c'est un homme à grands sentiments*: "And besides, he's a man of grand passions" (French).

p. 97, *considers Ryurik and Monomakh its forefathers*: Ryurik was a Scandinavian adventurer of the ninth century whom legend credited with founding the Russian state and ruling dynasty. Vladimir II Monomakh, one of his most distinguished descendants, reigned as Grand Prince of Kiev from 1113 to 1125. Those Russians in later centuries who could trace their ancestry back to the Kievan grand princes and to Ryurik were entitled to call themselves *knyaz* ("prince"). Throughout this passage Pushkin is speaking tongue-in-cheek through the Russian interlocutor in drawing a distinction between the "old nobility" descended from the princely and other boyar families of pre-Petrine times, and the "new nobility" created by Peter and his successors on the basis of supposed merit without regard to national or social origins. Pushkin himself took pride in being descended on his father's side from an ancient noble family which, though in his own time of little account, had been prominent in Muscovite affairs in the sixteenth and seventeenth centuries.

p. 97, *Duke of Montmorency... Clermont-Tonnerre*: The Montmorencys, one of whose titles was "premier baron chrétien", were one of France's oldest aristocratic families, dating back to the eleventh century. The Clermont-Tonnerres were another noble French family going back to the eleventh century.

p. 97, *Karamzin*: Nikolai Mikhaylovich Karamzin (1766–1826) was a Russian poet, littérateur and historian, whose greatest work was a monumental *History of the Russian State* in eleven volumes published between 1818 and 1824 (a twelfth was published posthumously in 1829).

p. 97, *barbarity and immorality*: This is where the text breaks off. The following outlines for the projected novel have been preserved among Pushkin's papers (the original is partly in French, partly in Russian):

A man of high society courts a fashionable lady and seduces her, but marries another one out of calculation. His wife creates scenes. The other woman confesses everything to her husband; she comforts the wife, visits her. The man of high society is unhappy, ambitious.

A young woman is brought out in society.

Zélie loves a vain egotist; she is surrounded by the cold malevolence of high society, a complaisant husband, a lover who makes fun of her, a lady friend who forsakes her. She becomes frivolous, has a scandalous affair with a man she doesn't love. Her husband repudiates her; she is utterly miserable. Her lover, her husband...

A scene from the life of high society, at the dacha of Count I. The room is full, around the tea table. Zélie's arrival. She sought out with her eyes the man of high society and spends the whole evening with him.

A historical account of the seduction. The liaison. Her lover's indiscreet behaviour.

A young provincial girl's arrival in high society. A scene of jealousy. High society's disapproval.

Rumours of marriage – Zélie's despair. She confesses everything to her husband. Her husband is complaisant. A visit during the wedding night. Zélie falls sick. She reappears in high society; men flirt with her, etc. etc.

p. 99, *A Novel in Letters*: This fragment, written in the autumn of 1829, was first published, in part, in 1857. The title *A Novel in Letters* was given to it by subsequent editors.

p. 101, *Pavlovskoye village*: This was the name of an actual village, owned by P.I. Vulf, in Tver Province. Pushkin was a guest on Vulf's estate in late October and early November 1829, and it is evidently here that he worked on his epistolary novel. In the manuscript the first letter is dated 21st October, and the third one, 1st November. Editors have generally assumed, from the context, that these dates do not belong to the fictional letters but indicate the time of their writing.

p. 102, *your Lamartine*: Alphonse de Lamartine's (1790–1869) *Méditations poétiques* (1820) brought him great fame in both Western Europe and Russia. Translated into Russian in many different versions, his poetry was in vogue among Petersburg ladies, which is reflected in Liza's somewhat contemptuous "*your* Lamartine".

p. 102, *Krestovsky Island*: One of the Neva River islands in suburban St Petersburg.

p. 103, *Clarissa Harlowe*: The heroine of Samuel Richardson's (1689–1761) epistolary novel *Clarissa* (1747–48).

p. 104, *the translator's preface… task*: The reference is to the Abbé Prévost's French translation of Richardson's *Clarissa*, under the title of *Lettres angloises, ou Histoire de Miss Clarisse Harlowe*. Pushkin had the 1777 edition of this work.

p. 104, *Lovelace and Adolphe*: Lovelace is the depraved antihero of Richardson's *Clarissa*; Adolphe, the introspective and melancholy protagonist and narrator of the novel of that name (1816) by the French writer and politician Benjamin Constant (1767–1830).

p. 106, *you know what aristocracy means with us*: For the attitudes of Pushkin and his contemporaries to aristocracy, ancient and modern, see Fragment 3 (and relevant note) of 'The Guests Were Arriving at the Dacha' on p. 96.

p. 106, *Bellecour stammers and Charlotte stutters*: Charlotte is a common enough name for heroines. Bellecour does not occur in any commonly known French novel of the eighteenth century; Liza may be referring to the famous actor Jean-Claude-Gilles Colson (1725–78), known as Bellecour, the idea of whom "stammering" is suitably absurd.

p. 107, *Vyazemsky and Pushkin*: Prince P.A. Vyazemsky (1792–1878) was, like his close friend Pushkin, a poet and literary critic.

p. 107, *accused of immorality and indecency by a former seminary student*: The former seminary student was N. I. Nadezhdin (1804–56), literary critic of the *European Herald*, who in reviewing Pushkin's *Count Nulin* in 1829 had accused him of impropriety.

p. 109, *Fornarina*: La Fornarina ("bakeress" in Italian) is the title of a famous portrait by Raphael of a semi-nude young woman painted between 1518 and 1520. She is traditionally identified with Margherita Luti, Raphael's mistress and a baker's daughter.

p. 111, *Citizen Minin and Prince Pozharsky*: Kozma Minich Zakharyev Sukhoruky (d.1616) (usually known as Kuzma Minin), a Nizhni Novgorod butcher, and Prince D.M. Pozharsky (1578–1642) commanded the Russian army that defeated the Polish King Sigismund III's forces and recaptured Moscow in 1612. A monument in memory of their victory was erected in 1818 in Red Square, where it still stands.

p. 111, *Severin, grandson of a tailor and a cook*: The reference is to D.P. Severin (1792–1865), an official of the Ministry of Foreign Affairs (subsequently Russian ambassador to Sweden), who had been a member of the Arzamas literary society with Pushkin but later snubbed the exiled poet in Odessa. He was the target of Pushkin's 1823 epigram 'A Complaint'.

p. 111, *Affecter le mépris… le gentilhomme*: "To affect scorn for one's birth is ridiculous in an upstart and cowardly in a gentleman" (French). Jean de la Bruyère (1645–96) was a French writer and moralist. Scholars have not been able to find the quotation in La Bruyère, so it may have been invented by Pushkin.

p. 111, *Prostakovs and Skotinins*: Characters from the comedy *Nedorosl* ('The Minor' – 1782) by D.I. Fonvizin (1745–92); they became symbols of brutal Russian feudalism.

p. 112, *because they're patriots*: In Act II, Sc. 5, of A. S. Griboyedov's comedy *Woe from Wit* (1824) Famusov says that in Moscow young ladies run after officers "because the girls are patriots".

p. 112, *fatuité indolente*: "Indolent self-satisfaction" (French).

p. 112, *Servitor di tutti quanti*: "Servant of the lot [of you]" (Italian), a phrase quoted perhaps from Act III of Rossini's opera *The Barber of Seville* (1816).

p. 112, *Un homme sans peur… ni comte aussi*: "A fearless and flawless man, / Who's neither king nor duke, nor even count." (French). These lines are adapted from the mottos of ancient French families.

p. 112, *unless you have rank*: At this point there is a gap in Pushkin's manuscript.

p. 112, *Monsieur Faublas*: The reference is to the main character in *Les Amours du Chevalier de Faublas* (1787–89), a novel by Jean Baptiste Louvet de Couvrai (1760–97), about a serial seducer of young women.

p. 113, *cum servo servorum dei*: "With the servant of the servants of God", i.e. the Pope (Latin).

p. 113, *Adam Smith*: The reference is to the Scottish philosopher and economist Adam Smith (1723–90). The change in social attitudes described was brought about by the death in 1825 of the serious-minded, reclusive and pietistic Alexander I and the accession of his more gregarious and pleasure-loving younger brother Nicholas I.

p. 115, *Notes of a Young Man*: The description of the wayside station, especially of the pictures on the wall, anticipates Pushkin's *The Stationmaster*, and the last paragraph, detailing the hero's attempt to find some reading matter, anticipates the introductory part of *A History of the Village of Goryukhino*. This fragment was first published, in part, in 1855. The title has been given to the fragment by editors on the basis of a draft version of *The Stationmaster*, where Pushkin indicated that the description of the pictures should be copied from *Notes of a Young Man*. On the margin of the manuscript containing the fragment, the following partial outline is written:

The stationmaster, a walk, the courier.
A shower, a carriage, a *gentleman* [in English in the original], love. Homeland.

p. 117, *a regiment in the small town of Vasilkov*: The original version of the manuscript, subsequently crossed out by Pushkin, read: "to join the Ch. Regiment in Kiev *Guberniya*" – a clear allusion to the Chernigov Regiment, stationed in Vasilkov, which mutinied in December 1825, under the leadership of S.I. Muravev-Apostol, in sympathy with the Decembrist uprising in St Petersburg.

p. 118, *parable of the Prodigal Son*: See Luke 15:11–32.

p. 118, *how many hired servants, etc.*: See Luke 15:7: "How many hired servants of my father's have bread enough and to spare, and I perish with hunger!"

p. 119, *verst posts*: See note to p. 59.

p. 121, *My Fate Is Sealed: I Am Getting Married*: This strongly autobiographical fragment was written on 12th and 13th May 1830, less than a week after Pushkin's engagement to Natalya Goncharova. It was first published in 1857.

p. 121, *Translated from the French*: This note is just a mystification on Pushkin's part, who more than once disguised sensitive autobiographical material as a piece of fictitious literary translation.

p. 123, *an ailing uncle*: Pushkin's uncle Vassily L. Pushkin was indeed ill in 1830 and died in August of that year.

p. 124, *Cooper*: James Fenimore Cooper (1789–1851), American writer of historico-romantic novels, sometimes known as "the American Scott", whose work became very popular in Europe as well as America.

p. 124, *My native land, adieu*: The quotation, given in English in the original, is a combination of the first and last lines of Childe Harold's song from Canto One of Byron's *Childe Harold's Pilgrimage* (1810–18).

p. 125, *Mlle Sontag*: Henrietta Sontag (1806–54) was a German opera singer who visited Russia in 1830.

p. 127, *A Fragment*: The manuscript itself bears the title 'A Fragment' and the date 26th October 1830. In the form of a preface to a non-existent story, it amounts to a character sketch of a poet with strongly autobiographical features. Pushkin later used it, in a shortened and less personal form, for the characterization of Charsky in Chapter I of 'Egyptian Nights'. The piece was first published posthumously in 1837.

p. 129, *If he visits the army… too long*: An allusion to Pushkin's own journey to Arzrum to visit friends in the Russian army in 1829. A similar complaint against the journalists' treatment of his visit occurs in a draft version of his Preface to 'A Journey to Arzrum'. What happened was that Pushkin was still on the road when the military correspondent I. Radozhitsky expressed a hope that the poet would derive inspiration from his visit; and Pushkin's enemy, the critic Faddei Bulgarin (1789–1859), subsequently censured Pushkin for his failure to do so.

p. 131, *dangerous in their double line of business*: An allusion to Faddei Bulgarin, who was both a writer and a police agent.

p. 133, *In the Corner of a Small Square*: This fragment, dating from between 1829 and 1831, represents a new attempt on Pushkin's part to treat the same social and psychological theme as that of 'The Guests Were Arriving at the Dacha'. Chapter I was first published posthumously in 1841, and the second, fragmentary chapter first appeared in 1884.

p. 135, *Votre cœur… inédite*: "Your heart is a sponge soaked with bile and vinegar. – an unpublished letter" (French).

p. 138, *Vous écrivez… puis les lire*: "You write your 4-page letters faster than I can read them" (French).

p. 138, *from the English Embankment to Kolomna*: I.e. from an elegant central location to an unglamorous district.

p. 138, *monthly accounts:* We know that Leo Tolstoy was reading some of Pushkin's fragmentary fiction immediately before he began writing *Anna Karenina* in 1873, and it seems certain that these three paragraphs suggested to him the outline of the novel's plot.

p. 139, *Roslavlev*: A fragment of this apparently unfinished novel, written in 1831, was published by Pushkin in his journal *Sovremennik* in 1836; the remainder first appeared in print in V.A. Zhukovsky's posthumous edition of Pushkin's works published in 1841.

"Roslavlev" is the name of a novel *Roslavlev, or The Russians in 1812* (1831) by M.N. Zagoskin (1789–1852). Working on this fragment in June 1831, right after the publication of Zagoskin's novel, Pushkin told a friend that he found Zagoskin's heroine, Polina Lidinaya, flat (from Zagoskin she emerges as little more than a victim of her passion for Sénicour, unconcerned for Russia's troubles) and wished to show how to draw a richer character.

Zagoskin claimed to have modelled his heroine on a real-life prototype, and indeed there were some unfavourable references in the Russian press, right after the Napoleonic invasion, to Russian women who had married French prisoners-of-war and subsequently deserted to the French side. Zagoskin's Polina does just that. In Paris before the war she had fallen in love with a Frenchman, Count Sénicour, but since he was already married she was without hope of ever being united with him. After her return to Russia she half-heartedly agrees to be engaged to the Russian officer, Roslavlev, but keeps postponing the wedding. During the French invasion of Russia, Sénicour, by this time widowed, is taken prisoner-of-war and is sent to live with Polina's family. She marries him, defects to the French side, joining Napoleon's retreating armies, and is eventually killed by a Russian grenade during the siege of Danzig (Gdansk).

Pushkin takes up Zagoskin's claim that he is basing his story on actual events (though he assumes that Zagoskin gave his real-life characters fictitious names). Pushkin accordingly reimagines "Polina" as a real-life Princess N. and retells part of the story from the standpoint of Princess N's friend (who is also "Roslavlev's" sister), in the process redrawing "Polina's" character and motivation as that of a much more interesting woman of patriotic feeling and independent spirit.

How, and even whether, Pushkin intended to continue the story is unclear. Arguably, by the time the narration breaks off his purpose has been achieved and he has fully demonstrated how a richer character for "Polina" can be drawn. Nor is it certain that Pushkin intended his work to be entitled "Roslavlev": Princess N's Russian fiancé Alexei plays only a small part in Pushkin's narrative and is never given a surname, nor does the word "Roslavlev" ever appear, except in the first sentence as the title of Zagoskin's novel. One theory is that the pencilled word "Roslavlev" in Pushkin's manuscript was intended not as a title, but just as an indication of the source of the story.

The "fragment" is a fascinating and highly original product of Pushkin's preoccupation with blurring the boundaries between fiction and real life.

p. 141, *As I was reading Roslavlev*: The grammar of this first sentence in the Russian makes it clear from the start that the narrator is a woman.

p. 142, *decorated with a key and a star*: A golden key signified the rank of chamberlain, and an eight-pointed star was the highest decoration of the state.

p. 142, *Montesquieu... Crébillon... Rousseau*: Montesquieu (see note to p. 52) is important to Polina's characterization, for knowing his works, especially *L'Esprit des lois* (1748), implied a high level of political awareness. The novelist Claude Crébillon (1707–77) also adds an interesting touch to Polina's characterization, for he was famous for his depictions of corruption in high society. The reference to Jean-Jacques Rousseau (1712–78), too, is significant: familiarity with his *Le Contrat social* (1762) would similarly imply high political awareness on Polina's part; a fondness for his novel *La Nouvelle Héloïse* (1761), on the other hand, might dispose her to view favourably a romance between a high-class heroine and a man of lower station (in her case, a prisoner-of-war).

p. 142, *Sumarokov*: A.P. Sumarokov (1717–77) was a Russian poet and playwright whose poetry was much admired in the eighteenth century, less so by the early nineteenth.

p. 142, *brief digression*: In *Eugene Onegin* iii, 26–28 Pushkin himself had complained light-heartedly of Russian girls' disinclination to read and express themselves in Russian: here, tongue-in-cheek, he allows one of them to speak in their defence.

p. 142, *author of Yury Miloslavsky... French translation*: Yury Miloslavsky, or The Russians in 1612 (1829) was another of Zagoskin's novels, a French translation of which by "Mme S.C." was published in Paris in 1831.

p. 142, *Lomonosov*: M.V. Lomonosov (1711–65), both an outstanding scientist and the founder of modern Russian literature, was famous for his patriotic odes, and for fixing the standards of the Russian literary language as well as those of prosody.

p. 142, *Karamzin's History*: The highly acclaimed *History of the Russian State* (1815–24) by Nikolai M. Karamzin (1766–1826).

p. 143, *Sichler's... Kostroma*: A fashionable shop versus the milliners of a provincial town.

p. 143, *Madame de Staël*: Anne Louise Germaine de Staël-Holstein (1766–1817) was an influential novelist, writer, literary critic and celebrity of French-Swiss origin, whose father Jacques Necker served as a Minister of Finance under Louis XVI of France. At the age of twenty she married a Swedish diplomat. Exiled from France under Napoleon, she travelled widely in Europe and visited Russia in 1812. Pushkin not only introduced Mme de Staël as a character in his unfinished novel, but evidently also took some of his description of Moscow society life from her *Dix années d'exil* (1821). Her novel, *Corinne*, to which reference is made in the same paragraph, was published in 1807.

p. 144, *defend their beards*: A hundred years previously Peter I, as part of his modernization programme, had ordered the Russian nobility to shave off their beards, but some had resisted this.

p. 144, *her persecutor*: Napoleon, who was shortly to invade Russia.

p. 145, *Ma chère enfant... de S.*: "My dear child, I am quite ill. It would be very kind of you if you would drop in to cheer me up. Try to obtain your mother's permission to do so, and please give her my best regards, Your friend, de S." (French).

p. 145, *Kuznetsky Bridge*: *Kuznetsky most* in Russian, a street in the centre of Moscow where many French fashion shops were situated.

p. 146, *Confederation of the Rhine*: The formation of the Confederation of the Rhine (1806) put an end to the Holy Roman Empire and brought most of Germany under Napoleon's protection and control.

p. 146, *Count Rastopchin's folksy posters*: In August 1812, F.V. Rastopchin (1763–1828), military governor of Moscow, had many posters displayed on the streets of Moscow with news (mostly falsified and written in a folksy style) about Russian resistance to the advancing French army.

p. 146, *Pozharsky and Minin*: Liberators of Moscow from Polish occupation two hundred years earlier – see note to p. 111, Letter 8 of the 'Novel in Letters'.

p. 146, *Saratov Province*: Saratov was a city and province on the lower Volga, a comfortable distance of some 800 kilometers to the southeast of Moscow.

p. 146, *Presnya Ponds*: An area of Moscow, not yet built up at the time, where people liked to walk; today it is the site of the Moscow Zoo.

p. 147, *Palais Royal*: The gardens of the Palais Royal were a popular place for Parisians to take a stroll.

p. 147, *Charlotte Corday... Mayoress Marfa... Princess Dashkova*: All redoubtable women of history: Charlotte Corday (1768–93) in 1793 assassinated Marat, one of the instigators of the Reign of Terror during the French Revolution; Marfa Boretskaya, widow of the mayor of Novgorod I.A. Boretsky, took a leading part in the city's fight against Muscovite domination in the 1470s; Princess Yekaterina Dashkova (1743–1810) was active in the coup d'état that brought Catherine II to the imperial throne in 1762 and continued to play an independent and influential political role in the years that followed.

p. 147, *Il n'est de bonheur que dans les voies communes*: "There is no happiness except on paths we share" (French). From the novel *René* (1802) by François-René de Chateaubriand (1768–1848).

p. 147, *Young Count Mamonov's*: Matvei A. Dmitriev-Mamonov (1790–1863), an extremely wealthy man who had already entered state service by the time Napoleon's army invaded Russia, joined the Russian army to fight for his country. He also had a separate regiment organized and equipped at his own expense, and in April 1813 he was appointed its major-general.

p. 148, *strategy of that period... liberate Europe*: The strategy referred to was that of abandoning Moscow and retreating into the interior of Russia, thereby stretching thin the French army's supply lines.

p. 149, *théâtre de société*: A domestic theatre with performances for the entertainment of guests (French).

p. 150, *news of his death*: False news, if Pushkin was intending to follow Zagoskin's plot.

p. 153, *A Novel at a Caucasian Spa*: This fragment was written on 30th September 1831, and was untitled. It was first published in 1881. Pushkin prepared various scenarios for the novel during 1831. He clearly intended to draw on his own impressions of the Caucasus, which he had visited for a few weeks in the summer of 1820 and again for two months in the autumn of 1829. He also had real-life prototypes in mind for the principal characters of the novel. Among Pushin's acquaintance was an aristocratic Muscovite family the Rimsky-Korsakovs. In the spring of 1827 Maria Rimskaya-Korsakova (1764–1832), her son

Grigory and daughter Alexandra ("Alina") took a trip to the Caucasus and were waylaid and robbed by mountain tribesmen on their way from one spa to another; there was even an attempt to kidnap Alina. It is clear from the draft scenarios that Pushkin intended to include a similar adventure in the novel.

p. 159, *Dubrovsky*: This is an unfinished novel based on some genuine court cases. The first inspiration for it originated with Pushkin's friend P.V. Nashchokin, who told him in September 1832 about the fate of an impoverished Belorussian nobleman by the name of Ostrovsky: having lost his land to a neighbour in a lawsuit, Ostrovsky became a robber, but was eventually arrested and imprisoned. In search of further information about dispossessed landowners, Pushkin managed to acquire the record of a similar court case, tried in Kozlov District Court in October 1832, bearing the title "On the adverse possession by Lieutenant Ivan Yakovlevich Muratov of the village Novopanskoye in the Kozlov District of Tambov Province, which properly belongs to Colonel of the Guards Semyon Petrovich Kryukov". As the novel began to take shape, Pushkin inserted this court case, without even copying it over, into Chapter II; all he changed were names and dates, but even some of those were left as they stood in the original.

The name of Dubrovsky probably originated with an earlier historical incident. A serf of a certain Aprelev in Pskov Province had escaped to Poland in 1737, allegedly with the aid of two serfs belonging to a neighbour called Dubrovsky. Acting on Aprelev's complaint, the local authorities made several attempts to arrest Dubrovsky's two serfs, but their fellow villagers hid the culprits and put up strong resistance to the authorities, apparently with Dubrovsky's encouragement. Pushkin may also have known of the case of another Dubrovsky, of Nizhny Novgorod Province, whose supposedly legitimate inheritance had been taken away through litigation by the wife of the provincial prosecutor Yudin in 1802.

Inspired by all these real-life cases, Pushkin quickly wrote the first eight chapters (Vol. I) in late October and early November 1832. (Each chapter bears a date in the manuscript.) After 11th November work on the novel stopped, to be taken up again on 14th December. From that date until 22nd January 1833, Pushkin persevered with the project; on 6th February he added one more paragraph to the last chapter; but with that he abandoned his novel, never to show any further interest in it. The existing chapters were published posthumously under the title *Dubrovsky* (provided by the editors) in the collection of Pushkin's works published in 1841.

p. 169, *desyatinas of land*: A *desyatina* was a Russian measure of area, equivalent to 2.7 acres.

p. 176, *Spanish flies*: A species of beetle, parts of which were once used in folk-medicine.

p. 182, *Where was a table spread with food now stands a coffin*: From G.R. Derzhavin's poem 'On the Death of Prince Meshchersky' (1779) – see also epigraph to Chapter II of 'The Negro of Peter the Great'.

p. 183, *May thou, thunder of victory, rumble*: Derzhavin's lyrics celebrating the taking of Izmail in 1791 were set to a tune by O.A. Kozlovsky, which became something of a patriotic anthem.

p. 186, *Vanity of vanities*: Quoted from Ecclesiastes 1:2.

p. 187, *Depart from evil, and do good*: Quoted from Psalms 34:14.

p. 191, *during the Turkish campaign*: The reference is to the Russo-Turkish War of 1787–91. This is one of the incongruities of the unfinished manuscript. Elsewhere it is indicated that the action took place in the 1820s, and that Vladimir was in his twenty-third year; yet his mother's letter refer to him as a child during the Turkish War.

p. 203, *guesses based on Lavater's system*: Johann Kaspar Lavater's so-called science of physiognomy is set out in his four-volume *Physiognomische Fragmente zur Beförderung der Menschenkenntnis und Menschenliebe* (1775–78).

p. 206, *portrait of Kulnev*: Major-General Yakov P. Kulnev (1763–1812), killed in the war against Napoleon, was a popular hero; prints of his portrait were distributed widely.

p. 207, *Radcliffe's mysterious horrors*: The tales of the British novelist Ann Radcliffe (born Ann Ward, 1764–1823) were characterized by mystery plots, an atmosphere of terror and poetically intense landscapes. They helped establish the vogue of the Gothic romance. Her most famous works in this genre include *The Romance of the Forest* (1791), *The Mysteries of Udolpho* (1794), and *The Italian* (1797).

p. 208, *Tsimlyanskoye*: A sparkling red wine from the lower Don region.

p. 211, *Que désire monsieur?*: "What do you wish, sir?" (French).

p. 211, *Jer ver, mua, chey voo cooshey*: I.e. *Je veux, moi, chez vous coucher* – Spitsyn's bad French for "I want to sleep in your room".

p. 211, *Monsieur, tres volontiers... Veuillez donner des ordres en consequence*: "With pleasure, monsieur. By all means give instructions accordingly" (French).

p. 212, *Poorkua voo tooshey*: I.e. *Pourquoi vous touchez?* – "Why are you ***ing?" The question makes no sense in French.

p. 212, *dormir*: "Sleep" (French).

p. 212, *jer ver avek voo parley*: I.e. *je veux avec vous parler* – "I want to talk to you" (French).

p. 212, *Kes ker sey*: I.e. *Qu'est-ce que c'est?* – "What's this?" (French).

p. 213, *a member of the third estate or a foreigner*: In Russia at that time post horses were allocated to travellers in order of rank.

p. 214, *Ma foi, mon officier*: "Upon my word, officer" (French).

p. 214, *outchitels*: "*Outchitel*" is a French transliteration of the Russian word for teacher or tutor.

p. 225, *Rinaldo*: The hero of the novel *Rinaldo Rinaldini, the Robber Chieftain* (1798) by Goethe's brother-in-law Christian August Vulpius (1762–1827).

p. 226, *death traps*: The Russian word for a narrow fishing boat is *dushegubka*, which is also the feminine form of *dushegub*, meaning "murderer".

p. 226, *this Amphitryon*: Amphitryon, a mythological Greek prince whose shape Zeus assumed in order to seduce his wife Alcmene, is shown in Molière's comedy by the same name (1668) as a generous host.

p. 227, *tous les frais*: "All the expenditure" (French).

p. 228, *Konrad's mistress... a rose in green*: The reference is to Canto 5 of the Polish poet Adam Mickiewicz's narrative poem *Konrad Wallenrod* (1828).

p. 247, *Dubrovsky had escaped abroad*: At various stages during his work on the novel, Pushkin made manuscript jottings of possible ways in which the plot might develop. These jottings are so brief as to be hard to interpret, and none of them is entirely consistent with the actual ending of this chapter, to which he has given an impression of semi-finality. The common thread in all cases, however, seems to be an intention on Pushkin's part to bring out the tragic effect of banditry on Dubrovsky's life and the impossibility of happiness for one who has placed himself outside society.

p. 249, *A Tale of Roman Life*: This fragment was first begun by Pushkin in 1833; he added the poems to the prose text in 1835. The extant autograph bears no title. It was first published in part in 1855.

The basis of the tale is the Roman historian Tacitus's account in his *Annals* XVI, 18–20 of the suicide during the reign of the Emperor Nero (r. 54–68 AD) of the Roman writer, aesthete and courtier Gaius (or Titus – ancient writers differ over his *prænomen*) Petronius Arbiter (d. 66 AD), believed to be the author of the satirical novel *Satyricon*, which exposes the excesses and vulgarities of Italian life under Nero. Tacitus describes Petronius as follows: "He spent his days asleep, and his nights at work and enjoyment. Others are famed for their achievements, he for his indolence. But he was not regarded, like most wastrels, as dissipated or extravagant, but as a refined voluptuary. People liked what he said and what he did as much for its straightforwardness as for its lack of inhibition and self-interest… [Accused of treason and knowing Nero meant to have him executed] he did not vacillate between fear and hope. He did not part with life immediately, however, but kept giving instructions for his veins to be opened, then bandaged up again, while he carried on talking with his friends…" Much of the detail of the story, however, is Pushkin's.

p. 251, *the Eumenides*: In Greek mythology the Erinyes or Furies, grim goddesses of vengeance; they were named the Eumenides – "well-disposed ones" – in the hope of propitiating them.

p. 252, *the divine Plato*: The Greek philosopher (427–347 BC), much-respected in the ancient world.

p. 252, *Catullus*: Caius Valerius Catullus (*c.*84–54 BC) was a Roman lyric and erotic poet, admired by Pushkin.

p. 252, *Anacreon's odes*: Anacreon was a Greek lyric poet, who flourished in the late sixth century BC and whose work was very popular in the ancient world and much imitated. The first of the verses here translated by Pushkin is probably authentically Anacreon's; the second fragment probably by a later imitator. The English translations here reproduce Pushkin's metre but (lest the sense be distorted) not his rhymes.

p. 252, *Tartarus*: In Greek mythology, that part of the Underworld where guilty souls were punished.

p. 253, *this ode of his*: Quintus Horatius Flaccus ("Horace") (65–8 BC) was a prolific writer of Latin odes and other lyric, satiric and occasional poetry. As a young Roman studying in Greece, he had joined the republicans under Brutus and Cassius in the civil war that followed the murder of Julius Caesar. At the battle of Philippi (42 BC), however, at which Octavian and Antony crushed the republicans, he had on his own testimony deserted the field in a funk. Subsequently he returned to Italy, where after a few years in obscurity he secured the patronage of Maecenas, a rich and cultivated partisan of Octavian, whose protection he continued to enjoy after the victorious Octavian became the Emperor Augustus. A friend of Horace's, Pompeius Varus, continued to support the republican cause, and it was thirteen years before Pompeius was pardoned by Augustus and allowed to return to Rome. The ode (II, 7), the first half of which is here freely translated by Pushkin, was composed by Horace to recall the events of their youth and to celebrate his friend's return.

p. 254, *Hermes suddenly enwrapped me / in mist*: Horace is here referring ironically to passages in Homer's heroic war epic where gods save warriors from their enemies by enveloping them in clouds and spiriting them from the battlefield (e.g. Aphrodite's rescue of Paris in *Iliad* III, 380 *ff.*).

p. 254, *Pleasant and honourable it is... fatherland*: Dulce et decorum est / pro patria mori (Latin), two famous lines from Horace's *Odes* III, 2, 4, often quoted on military memorials.

The manuscript breaks off here, but an outline preserved in Pushkin's hand suggests what seems to have been the main idea of this tale. Petronius, rather than awaiting a cruel fate at Nero's hands, decided to bleed himself to death; he lies in a warm bath, now opening his vein to let the blood flow, now bandaging it up to prolong his life a little more, while his friends entertain him with pleasant conversation. The outline reads:

"The first evening, such-and-such from among us were there; the Greek philosopher has disappeared – Petronius smiles – and recites an ode (an excerpt). (We find Petronius with his physician. He continues his discussion of kinds of death, chooses a warm bath and blood), a description of the preparations. He bandages the wound, and the telling of anecdotes commences – 1. about Cleopatra; our discussions of the matter; 2 evening, Petronius gives orders to break a precious goblet, dictates *Satyricon*, discussions about the fall of man, the fall of god, the general lack of faith, and Nero's prejudices. A Christian slave..."

The mention of Cleopatra seems to indicate that Pushkin might have planned to introduce here the theme of Cleopatra's nights – a theme that was to be placed in the centre of both 'We Were Spending the Evening at Princess D.'s Dacha' and 'Egyptian Nights'. The reference to a Christian slave suggests that Pushkin may have intended to lead the conversation into a comparison of the pagan and Christian attitudes to religion and death.

p. 255, *Maria Schoning*: This fragmentary opening of a novel is based on a supposedly genuine court case, 'Enfanticide: Procès de Maria Schoning et d'Anna Harlin', recorded in *Causes célèbres étrangères, publiées en France pour la première fois et traduites de l'italien, de l'allemand etc. par une société de jurisconsultes et de gens de lettres*, vol. 2 (Paris: C. L. F. Panckoucke, 1827). Pushkin probably worked on the project in 1834 or 1835.

p. 262, *the young man... the physician*: It is impossible to tell how closely Pushkin was planning to follow the court case, but a précis he made of it (in French) gives at least an approximate idea of the projected plot development:

Maria Schoning and Anna Harlin tried in Nuremberg in 1787

Maria Schoning, the daughter to a Nuremberg artisan, lost her father when she was seventeen years old. She had been looking after him by herself because poverty had forced them to dismiss their only maidservant, Anna Harlin.

When she returned from her father's funeral she found at her house two officials of the tax office, who demanded to see her late father's papers in order to ascertain whether he had been paying his taxes according to the size of his property. They concluded from their investigation that he had not been taxed in proportion to his worth, and they sealed his belongings. The young girl retired to a room stripped of its furnishings until such time as the directors of the Treasury should decide the matter.

The tax officials returned with their superiors' decision and with an order for Maria Eleonora Schoning to vacate the house, which had passed into the possession of the Treasury.

Schoning had been poor but economical. His illness of three years duration exhausted all his savings. Maria went to see the commissioners. She wept, but the officials remained inflexible.

In the evening she went to the St Jacob's Cemetery... In the morning she left the cemetery, but later, faint with hunger, she once more found herself there.

The Nuremburg police pay an award of half a crown to night watchmen for the arrest of a woman after 10 p.m. Maria Schoning was taken to the guardhouse. Next morning they led her before a judge, who set her free but threatened to confine her to a correctional institution if she was caught a second time.

Maria wanted to throw herself into the Pegnitz... she heard someone call her name. She beheld Anna Harlin, her father's former maidservant, who had married a disabled soldier. Anna comforted her. "Life is short, my child," said she, "but heaven is eternal."

For a year Maria found shelter at the Harlins'. Her life with them was quite wretched. At the end of the year Anna fell sick. Winter set in; there was no work available; the price of food rose. They sold all their furniture piece by piece, except for the bed of the veteran, who died towards spring.

An indigent doctor had been giving free treatment to both husband and wife. He would sometimes bring them a bottle of wine, but he himself had no money. Anna recovered from her illness but became apathetic: there was absolutely no work available.

One evening early in March, Maria suddenly went out...

She was arrested by a patrol. The corporal left her with the guards, saying she would be whipped in the morning. She cried out that she was guilty of infanticide... When led before the judge, she declared that she had given birth to a child with the assistance of a certain woman called Harlin, who had subsequently buried the child in the woods, in a place that she no longer remembered. Anna Harlin was immediately arrested and, after pleading innocent, was confronted with Maria – she denied everything.

Tools of torture were brought in. Terrified, Maria seized her alleged accomplice's tied-up hands and said to her: "Anna confess what they are demanding of you. My dear Anna, everything will be over for us, and Frank and Nany will be placed in an orphanage."

Anna understood her, embraced her, and declared that the infant had been thrown into the Pegnitz.

The case was swiftly concluded. Both women were condemned to die. On the morning of the appointed day they were led to a church, where they prayed in preparation for death. In the cart Anna was calm, Maria agitated. Harlin mounted the scaffold and said to her: "In an instant we shall be there (in heaven). Take courage, one more minute, and we shall be before God."

Maria cried out: "She is innocent, I gave false testimony!" She threw herself at the feet of the executioner and the priest... She told them everything. The executioner stops in astonishment. Shouts are heard in the crowd... Questioned by the priest and the executioner, Anna Harlin says with distaste (simplicity): "She has, of course, told the truth. I am guilty of lying and of having no faith in Providence."

A report is sent to the judges. The messenger returns in an hour with the order to proceed with the execution... The executioner fainted after decapitating Anna Harlin. Maria was already dead.

p. 263, *A Russian Pelham*: The title of this fragment, derived from the name Pushkin gave the hero in some of his notes and bestowed by posthumous editors, refers to Edward Bulwer Lytton's *Pelham* or *Adventures of a Gentlemen* (1828), a novel about a young aristocrat Pelham, who sets his sights on a great political career; though capable of rational and sober behaviour, however, he starts out in society as an apparently frivolous and shallow character. The novel presents a broad panorama of British society, introducing real personalities from contemporary life. The novel attracted Pushkin from soon after its publication, and it seems to have been his intention to create a similar novel about Russian social and artistic life in the 1810s and early 1820s in both its wilder and more serious aspects, a period of which he had been a witness and active participant, particularly after his graduation in 1817. As for *A Novel at a Caucasian Spa*, Pushkin left several sets of notes containing outlines for the project. And, as there, they involve real-life personages, among them V.A. Vsevolozhsky (1769–1836), who had conducted an affair with a certain Princess E.M. Khovanskaya and brought her, with her children, into his household after his wife's death, and whose son N.V. Vsevolozhsky (1799–1862) was a friend of Pushkin's. Pushkin's fragment was first published in 1841.

p. 269, *We Were Spending the Evening at Princess D.'s Dacha*: This fragment – or series of fragments – was probably written in 1835, prior to Pushkin's work on 'Egyptian Nights'. The theme of Cleopatra's nights – central to both to this projected work and to 'Egyptian Nights' – was first treated by Pushkin in his 1824 elegy 'Cleopatra'. The elegy was rewritten in 1828 with significant changes, and the incomplete version given in this fragment, half in prose, half in verse, represents the third major version of the poem. The extant manuscripts of *We Were Spending the Evening* consist of several fragments, some in first draft, some in clean copy. The text, as translated, represents a piecing-together of these various segments. The work was first published in part in 1857.

p. 271, *Madame de Staël*: See second note to p. 143.

p. 271, *Hambs' armchairs*: The brothers Hamb were furniture dealers in St Petersburg.

p. 271, *Madame de Maintenon, Madame Roland*: I.e. Françoise d'Aubigné, Marquise de Maintenon (1635–1719), mistress and eventually wife of Louis XIV of France; Mme Marie-Jeanne Roland (b.1754 as Manon Phlipon), celebrated for her salon in revolutionary France, a republican and leading figure in the Girondist faction, beheaded by the Jacobins in 1794.

p. 271, *Cleopatra*: Cleopatra VII (68–30 BC) was the last queen of an independent Egypt, whose capital was Alexandria. Beautiful, sensual and ambitious, she was famous for her liaisons, both passionate and political, first with Julius Caesar and later with Mark Antony. It was her and Mark Antony's defeat by Octavian at the Battle of Actium in 31 BC that led to her suicide and to the incorporation of Egypt into the Roman Empire.

p. 272, *Qui est-ce donc que l'on trompe ici?*: "Who is being fooled here?" (French) – a paraphrase of Don Bazile's words from Act 3, Scene 11, of *Le Barbier de Séville* (1775) by P.-A. Caron de Beaumarchais (1732–99).

p. 272, *Antony... La Physiologie du mariage*: *Antony*, a melodrama (unconnected with Mark Antony) by Alexandre Dumas *père*, was written in 1831 and performed in St Petersburg in 1832. Honoré de Balzac's *La Physiologie du mariage* was published in 1829.

p. 272, *Cornelius Nepos... Suetonius*: Cornelius Nepos (*c*.99–*c*.24 BC) and Suetonius (*c*.70–*c*.140 AD) were noted Roman historical biographers, both of whom wrote sets of biographies of famous Romans known as *De viris illustribus*; Tacitus (*c*. 55–*c*.120 AD) and Sallust (86–35 BC) were also eminent Roman historians and biographers.

p. 272, *he wrote the book De viris illustribus*: Many sets of lives of eminent personages were composed in the Greco-Roman world. Two of them are mentioned in the preceding note. Another – *Liber de viris illustribus urbis Romæ* (*Book about Illustrious Men of the City of Rome*) – is an anonymous work that was at one time ascribed to the late Roman historian Sextus Aurelius Victor (active in the later fourth century AD). The story about Cleopatra that is referred to below (and in 'Egyptian Nights') is almost certainly apocryphal.

p. 272, *Hæc tantæ libidinis fuit... emerint*: "She was so lustful that she often prostituted herself and so beautiful that many men paid with their lives for a night with her" (Latin).

p. 273, *Pharos*: The famous lighthouse, one of the wonders of the ancient world, built on an island of the same name at the mouth of Alexandria's harbour.

p. 273, *Ptolemys*: The Greco-Egyptian dynasty of which Cleopatra was the last representative.

p. 273, *Euros*: An ancient Greek name for the warm south-east wind.

p. 275, *Marquise George Sand*: Pseudonym of the French writer Amantine Aurore Lucile Dupin, later Baroness Dudevant (1804–76), like Cleopatra, another emancipated and much-partnered woman, one of whose intimates was the pianist and composer Chopin.

p. 279, *Egyptian Nights*: This unfinished story (entitled 'Cleopatra' in a draft version) represents a new attempt at treating the Cleopatra theme, which had earlier been the subject of a lyric of 1824 (reworked in 1828) and of the conversation in the fragmentary 'We Were Spending the Evening at Princess D.'s Dacha' (there is also evidence in Pushkin's notes that he intended to introduce it into the discussion with the dying Petronius in 'A Tale from Roman Life'). 'Egyptian

Nights' was first published in 1837, not long after Pushkin's death. Pushkin's manuscript of the story does not include the verse passages. The first improvisation (in Chapter II) originates from some lines of Pushkin's unfinished narrative poem 'Yezersky' (1832–33), which he redrafted and amplified in 1835, clearly intending them for inclusion in this story; and the second improvisation, in Chapter III, by editorial tradition uses the 1828 version of the 'Cleopatra' poem, though it is likely that in the completed story Pushkin would have further reworked this. In the present edition, as in Professor Debreczeny's, a final stanza, apparently intended for 'Egyptian Nights', has been added from a separate Pushkin manuscript, bringing the work to a heightened climax. Thus, as John Bayley remarks in his Foreword, 'Egyptian Nights' has the air of a piece that breaks off at the right moment. "Unlike the novel fragments it does not seem to have been put aside undeveloped, as well as unfinished."

p. 281, *Quel est cet homme?... une culotte*: "What kind of person is this man?"; "Oh, he possesses a great talent; he can make of his voice whatever he wants"; "Madam, he should make himself a pair of trousers from it" (French). From *Almanach des calembours* (1771) by Georges Mareschal Bièvre (1747–89).

p. 282, *Rezanov's*: Rezanov's was a fashionable confectionery shop in St Petersburg.

p. 283, *Signor... perdonarmi se*: "Sir, please excuse me if..." (Italian).

p. 284, *Signor... mi perdonerà*: "Sir, I thought... I believed... forgive me, Your Excellency" (Italian).

p. 284, *Maecenas*: Maecenas was a prodigiously rich patron of the arts, and especially poetry, in ancient Rome under the Emperor Augustus.

p. 284, *tattered abbés*: A reference to Lorenzo da Ponte, the lapsed Italian priest and talented versifier, who at one period of his life composed libretti for operas, including three of Mozart's most famous.

p. 286, *I'm king... Derzhavin*: From G.R. Derzhavin's ode 'God' (1784).

p. 288, *La signora Catalani*: Angelica Catalani (1779–1849) was an Italian singer who performed in St Petersburg several times in the 1820s.

p. 289, *Tancredi*: An opera by Gioachino Rossini (1792–1868), written in 1813 and performed in St Petersburg during the 1834–35 season.

p. 290, *a young man*: The manuscript shows that Pushkin originally intended to mention only one person – "a young diplomat who had just returned from Naples" – instead of a diplomat and an additional young man. This may be the reason for the discrepancy between the number of people suggesting themes (six) and the number of themes read aloud by the *improvvisatore* (five).

p. 291, *The Cenci family... Il trionfo di Tasso*: *La famiglia dei Cenci* refers to the murder, in 1598 by his own wife and children, of the wealthy but cruel Roman, Francesco Cenci, which served as a basis for tragedies by Shelley, *Cenci* (1819), and Adolphe Custine, *Beatrix Cenci* (1833). *L'ultimo giorno di Pompei* (*The last day of Pompeii*) was the subject of a celebrated painting by K.P. Bryulov exhibited in St Petersburg in 1834. *Cleopatra e i suoi amanti* is Italian for "Cleopatra and her lovers". *La primavera veduta da una prigione* ("Spring seen from a prison") refers to the memoir *Le mie prigioni* (1832) by Silvio Pellico (1789–1854). *Il trionfo di Tasso* was a topical theme because of N.V. Kukolnik's play *Torquato Tasso*, performed in St Petersburg in 1833.

p. 291, *Cleopatra*: See note to p. 271.

p. 291, *perché la grande regina ne aveva molti*: "Since the great Queen had a good many of them" (Italian).

p. 292, *the testimony of Victor Aurelius... nor repellent*: See fourth note to p. 272.

p. 294, *Epicurus*: Epicurus (*c*.342–*c*.271 BC) founded a school of philosophy in his garden in Athens; he taught a materialist doctrine, denying any afterlife and advocating a life in this world of tranquillity and pleasure.

p. 295, *In 179– I Was Returning*: This fragment was first published posthumously in 1837.

p. 299, *The Last of the Lineage of Joan of Arc*: This is almost certainly Pushkin's final work. It was written in January 1837, in the same month as his death. It is a complete fiction, notionally about a correspondence between Mr Dulys, a descendant of Joan of Arc, and Voltaire (1694–1778), who wrote, among much else, *La Pucelle d'Orléans* (first published 1762), a satirical epic mocking Joan of Arc and her contemporaries. Pushkin's work springs from the torment and misery of his own private life in his last weeks: Georges d'Anthès, a young Frenchman living in Russia, the adopted son of the Dutch Ambassador Baron Heeckeren, had become an increasingly open admirer of Pushkin's wife. Early the previous November, Pushkin had been humiliated by receipt through the post of a scurrilous and anonymous notice, widely circulated to others, which he believed to have originated with Heeckeren, saying he had been elected "an assistant to the Grand Master of the Order of Cuckolds". As a result Pushkin challenged d'Anthès to a duel, but friends managed by mid-November to persuade him to call it off.

Following this, d'Anthès continued his humiliatingly public affair with Pushkin's wife, and Pushkin became once more increasingly exasperated. It was in this state of anger and frustration that he penned 'The Last of the Lineage of Joan of Arc'. Less than three weeks later Pushkin's rage reached the point where he this time provoked d'Anthès to challenge him to a duel. The duel was fought on 27th January. Pushkin was mortally wounded. He died two days later.

What, though, are the connections between the tragedy of Pushkin's death and the fictional correspondence between Mr Dulys, Pushkin's imaginary descendant of Joan of Arc, and Voltaire? First, two months previously, at the time of Pushkin's first challenge to d'Anthès, Baron Heeckeren had tried to disown the offensive letter and avert the duel in a manner similarly feeble, grovelling and evasive, to that in which Voltaire is fictionally made by Pushkin to write to Dulys. Second, in the fictional correspondence, a challenge to a duel was issued to avenge a family insult. And third, the overt content of 'The Last of the Lineage of Joan of Arc' was suggested to Pushkin by the fact that d'Anthès's adopted father, Baron Heeckeren, was said to look extraordinarily like Voltaire. The English journalist's lament over the long obscurity of Dulys' noble line and over the derisive insouciance of contemporary society towards both the slander and the injured party's challenge also reflect Pushkin's own feelings.

p. 301, *Kings Charles VII, Henri III and Louis XIII*: Kings of France: Charles VII, *r.* 1422–61; Henri III, *r.* 1575–89; Louis XIII, *r.* 1610–43. It was in the early part of Charles VII's reign that Joan of Arc fought for France; she was put to death by the English in 1431.

p. 301, *Agnès Sorel, Seigneurs La Trimouille... Baudricourt*: Historical characters of the period. Agnès Sorel (1421–50) became Charles VII's mistress; Robert de Baudricourt (*c.*1400–54) helped Joan of Arc by giving her an introduction to the French court in 1429. The de la Trimouilles were a noble French family, one of whom figures prominently in Voltaire's poem, as does Sorel and, to a lesser extent, a (possibly fictional) Roger de Baudricour.

p. 303, *Charles X*: King of France from 1824 to 1830.

p. 304, *Our laureate's poem... Southey's*: Robert Southey (1774–1843), British poet laureate from 1813 till his death, wrote an epic poem commemorating Joan of Arc (first published in 1796).

p. 304, *Baron d'Holbach and Mme Geoffrin*: Baron d'Holbach (1723–89) and Madame Geoffrin (1699–1777) were leading members of the French Enlightenment, hosting popular salons in Paris. D'Holbach was noted for his atheistic views.

Extra Material

on

Alexander Pushkin's

*The Queen of Spades
and Other Stories*

Alexander Pushkin's Life

Alexander Sergeyevich Pushkin was born in Moscow in 1799. He came of an ancient, but largely undistinguished, aristocratic line. Some members of his father's family took a part in the events of the reign of Boris Godunov (r. 1598–1605) and appear in Pushkin's historical drama about that Tsar. Perhaps his most famous ancestor – and the one of whom Pushkin was most proud – was his mother's grandfather, Abram Petrovich Gannibal (or Annibal) (c.1693–1781), who was an African, most probably from Ethiopia or Cameroon. According to family tradition he was abducted from home at the age of seven by slave traders and taken to Istanbul. There in 1704 he was purchased by order of the Russian foreign minister and sent to Moscow, where the minister made a gift of him to Tsar Peter the Great. Peter took a liking to the boy and in 1707 stood godfather to him at his christening (hence his patronymic Petrovich, "son of Peter"). Later he adopted the surname "Gannibal", a Russian transliteration of Hannibal, the famous African general of Roman times. Peter sent him abroad as a young man to study fortification and military mining. After seven years in France he was recalled to Russia, where he followed a career as a military engineer. Peter's daughter, the Empress Elizabeth, made him a general, and he eventually died in retirement well into his eighties on one of the estates granted him by the crown.

Family, Birth and Childhood

Pushkin had an older sister, Olga, and a younger brother, Lev. His parents did not show him much affection as a child, and he was left to the care of his grandmother and servants, including a nurse of whom he became very fond. As was usual in those days, his early schooling was received at home, mostly from French tutors and in the French language.

School   In 1811 at the age of twelve Pushkin was sent by his parents to St Petersburg to be educated at the new Lyceum (Lycée, or high school) that the Emperor Alexander I had just established in a wing of his summer palace at Tsarskoye Selo to prepare the sons of noblemen for careers in the government service. Pushkin spent six happy years there, studying (his curriculum included Russian, French, Latin, German, state economy and finance, scripture, logic, moral philosophy, law, history, geography, statistics and mathematics), socializing with teachers and fellow students, and relaxing in the palace park. To the end of his life he remained deeply attached to his memories and friends from those years. In 1817 he graduated with the rank of collegial secretary, the tenth rank in the civil service, and was attached to the Ministry of Foreign Affairs, with duties that he was allowed to interpret as minimal. While still at the Lyceum Pushkin had already started writing poetry, some of which had attracted the admiration of leading Russian literary figures of the time.

St Petersburg 1817–20   Pushkin spent the next three years in St Petersburg living a life of pleasure and dissipation. He loved the company of friends, drinking parties, cards, the theatre and particularly women. He took an interest in radical politics. And he continued to write poetry – mostly lyric verses and epigrams on personal, amatory or political subjects – often light and ribald, but always crisply, lucidly and euphoniously expressed. Some of these verses, even unpublished, gained wide currency in St Petersburg and attracted the unfavourable notice of the Emperor Alexander I.

Pushkin's major work of this period was *Ruslan and Lyudmila,* a mock epic in six cantos, completed in 1820 and enthusiastically received by the public. Before it could be published, however, the Emperor finally lost patience with the subversiveness of some of Pushkin's shorter verses and determined to remove him from the capital. He first considered exiling Pushkin to Siberia or the White Sea, but at the intercession of high-placed friends of Pushkin's the proposed sentence was commuted to a posting to the south of Russia. Even so, some supposed friends hurt and infuriated Pushkin by spreading exaggerated rumours about his disgrace.

Travels in the South   Pushkin was detailed to report to Lieutenant General Ivan Inzov (1768–1845), who was at the time Commissioner for the Protection for Foreign Colonists in Southern Russia based at Yekaterinoslav (now Dnepropetrovsk) on the lower Dnieper.

Inzov gave him a friendly welcome, but little work to do, and before long Pushkin caught a fever from bathing in the river and was confined to bed in his poor lodgings. He was rescued by General Nikolai Rayevsky, a soldier who had distinguished himself in the war of 1812 against Napoleon. Rayevsky, who from 1817 to 1824 commanded the Fourth Infantry Corps in Kiev, was travelling through Yekaterinoslav with his younger son (also called Nikolai), his two youngest daughters Maria and Sofya, a personal physician and other attendants; they were on their way to join the elder son Alexander, who was taking a cure at the mineral springs in the Caucasus. General Rayevsky generously invited Pushkin to join them, and Inzov gave his leave.

The party arrived in Pyatigorsk, in the northern foothills of the Caucasus, in June. Pushkin, along with his hosts, benefited from the waters and was soon well again. He accompanied the Rayevskys on long trips into the surrounding country, where he enjoyed the mountain scenery and observed the way of life of the local Circassian and Chechen tribes. In early August they set off westwards to join the rest of the Rayevsky family (the General's wife and two older daughters) in the Crimea. On the way they passed through the Cossack-patrolled lands on the northern bank of the Kuban river and learnt more about the warlike Circassians of the mountains to the south.

General Rayevsky and his party including Pushkin met up with the rest of the family at Gurzúf on the Crimean coast, where they had the use of a villa near the shore. Pushkin enjoyed his time in the Crimea, particularly the majestic coastal scenery, the southern climate, and the new experience of living in the midst of a harmonious, hospitable and intelligent family. He also fell in love with Yekaterina, the General's oldest daughter, a love that was not reciprocated. Before leaving the Crimea Pushkin travelled with the Rayevskys through the coastal mountains and inland to Bakhchisaray, an oriental town which had till forty years before been the capital of the Tatar khans of the Crimea and where the khans' palace still stood (and stands).

After a month in the Crimea it was time for the party to return to the mainland. During the summer General Inzov had been transferred from Yekaterinoslav to be governor of Bessarabia (the northern slice of Moldavia, which Russia had annexed from Turkey only eight years previously). His new headquarters was in Kishinyov (modern Chişinău, capital of

Moldova), the chief town of Bessarabia. So it was to Kishinyov that Pushkin went back to duty in September 1820. Pushkin remained there (with spells of local leave) till 1823.

Bessarabia 1820–23

Kishinyov was still, apart from recently arrived Russian officials and soldiers, a raw Near-Eastern town, with few buildings of stone or brick, populated by Moldavians and other Balkan nationalities. Despite the contrast with St Petersburg, Pushkin still passed a lot of his time in a similar lifestyle of camaraderie, drinking, gambling, womanizing and quarrelling, with little official work. But he wrote too. And he also, as in the Caucasus and Crimea, took a close interest in the indigenous cultures, visiting local fairs and living for a few days with a band of Moldavian gypsies, an experience on which he later drew in his narrative poem *Gypsies*.

In the winter of 1820–21 Pushkin finished the first of his "southern" narrative poems, *A Prisoner in the Caucasus*, which he had already begun in the Crimea. (The epilogue he added in May 1821.) This poem reflects the experiences of his Caucasus visit. The work was published in August 1822. It had considerable public success, not so much for the plot and characterization, which were criticized even by Pushkin himself, but rather, as he himself acknowledged, for its "truthful, though only lightly sketched, descriptions of the Caucasus and the customs of its mountain peoples".

Having completed *A Prisoner in the Caucasus*, Pushkin went on to write a narrative poem reflecting his impressions of the Crimea, *The Fountain of Bakhchisaray*. This was started in 1821, finished in 1823 and published in March 1824. It was also a great popular success, though again Pushkin dismissed it as "rubbish". Both poems, as Pushkin admitted, show the influence of Lord Byron, a poet whom, particularly at this period, Pushkin admired.

Just before his departure from Kishinyov in 1823, Pushkin composed the first few stanzas of Chapter One of his greatest works, the novel in verse *Eugene Onegin*. It took him eight years to complete. Each chapter was published separately (except Chapters Four and Five, which came out together) between the years 1825 and 1832; the work was first published as a whole in 1833.

Odessa 1823–24

In the summer of 1823, through the influence of his friends in St Petersburg, Pushkin was posted to work for Count Mikhail Vorontsov, who had just been appointed Governor General of the newly-Russianized region south of the Ukraine. Vorontsov's headquarters were to be in Odessa, the port city on the Black Sea founded by Catherine the Great thirty years previously. Despite its newness Odessa was a far more lively, cosmopolitan and cultured place than Kishinyov, and Pushkin was pleased with the change. But he only remained there a year.

Pushkin did not get on well with his new chief, partly because of temperamental differences, partly because he objected to the work Count Vorontsov expected him to do, and partly because he had an affair with the Countess. Vorontsov tried hard to get Pushkin transferred elsewhere, and Pushkin for his part became so unhappy with his position on the Count's staff that he tried to resign and even contemplated escaping overseas. But before matters came to a head the police intercepted a letter from Pushkin to a friend in which he spoke approvingly of the atheistic views of an Englishman he had met in the city. The authorities in St Petersburg now finally lost patience with Pushkin: he was dismissed from the service and sent into indefinite banishment on his mother's country estate of Mikhaylovskoye in the west of Russia. He left Odessa for Mikhaylovskoye on 1st August 1824; he had by now written two and a half chapters of *Eugene Onegin*, and had begun *Gypsies*.

Pushkin spent more than two years under police surveillance at Mikhaylovskoye. The enforced leisure gave him a lot of time for writing. Within a couple of months he had completed *Gypsies*, which was first published in full in 1827. *Gypsies* is a terser, starker, more thoughtful and more dramatic work than *A Prisoner in the Caucasus* or *The Fountain of Bakhchisaray*; along with *Eugene Onegin* it marks a transition from the discursive romanticism of Pushkin's earliest years to the compressed realism of his mature style. At Mikhaylovskoye Pushkin progressively completed Chapters Three to Six of *Eugene Onegin*, many passages of which reflect Pushkin's observation of country life and love of the countryside. He also wrote his historical drama *Boris Godunov* at this period and his entertaining verse tale *Count Nulin*. *Exile at Mikháylovskoye*

In November 1825 Alexander I died. He left no children, and there was initially confusion over the succession. In December some liberal-minded members of the army and the intelligentsia (subsequently known as the "Decembrists") seized the opportunity to attempt a *coup d'état*. This was put down by the new Emperor, Nicholas I, a younger brother of Alexander's. *The Decembrist Revolt 1825*

345

Among the conspirators were several old friends of Pushkin, and he might well have joined them had he been at liberty. As it was, the leading conspirators were executed, and many of the rest were sent to Siberia for long spells of hard labour and exile. Pushkin feared that he too might be punished.

Rehabilitation 1826–31 The following autumn Pushkin was summoned unexpectedly to Moscow to see the new Emperor. Nicholas surprised Pushkin by offering him his freedom, and Pushkin assured Nicholas of his future good conduct. Pushkin complained that he had difficulty in making money from his writing because of the censorship, and Nicholas undertook to oversee Pushkin's work personally. In practice, however, the Emperor delegated the task to the Chief of the Secret Police, and, despite occasional interventions from Nicholas, Pushkin continued to have difficulty with the censors.

After a few months in Moscow Pushkin returned to St Petersburg, where he spent most of his time in the coming years, though he continued periodically to visit Moscow, call at the family's estates and stay with friends in the country. In 1829 he made his only visit abroad, following the Russian army on a campaign into north-eastern Turkey. During the late 1820s he made several attempts to find a wife, with a view to settling down. In 1829 he met Natalya Goncharova, whom he married early in 1831.

It was during the four years between his return from exile and his marriage that he wrote Chapter Seven (1827–28) and most of Chapter Eight (1829–31) of *Eugene Onegin*. In 1828 he also wrote *Poltava* (published in 1829), a kind of historical "novella in verse". This seems to have been the first attempt in Russian at a work of this kind based on the study of historical material. In its application of the imagination to real events, it prefigured Pushkin's later novel in prose *The Captain's Daughter* and helped to set a pattern for subsequent historical novels in Russia. It is also notable for the terse realism of its descriptions and for the pace and drama of its narratives and dialogues. It was during this period, too, that Pushkin began to write fiction in prose, though it was not till late in 1830 that he succeeded in bringing any prose stories to completion.

In the autumn of 1830 a cholera epidemic caused Pushkin to be marooned for a couple of months on another family estate, Boldino, some 600 kilometres east of Moscow. He took advantage of the enforced leisure to write. This was when he virtually completed Chapter Eight of *Eugene Onegin*. He also composed at this time his collection of short stories in prose *The Tales of Belkin*, another verse tale, *The Little House in Kolomna*, and his set of four one-act dramas known together as *The Little Tragedies*.

The 1830s were not on the whole happy years for Pushkin. His marriage, it is true, was more successful than might have been expected. Natalya was thirteen years his junior; her remarkable beauty and susceptibility to admiration constantly exposed her to the attentions of other men; she showed more liking for society and its entertainments than for intellectual or artistic pursuits or for household management; her fashionable tastes and social aspirations incurred outlays that the pair could ill afford; and she took little interest in her husband's writing. Nonetheless, despite all this they seem to have remained a loyal and loving couple; Natalya bore him four children in their less than six years of marriage, and she showed real anguish at his untimely death.

The Final Years 1831–37

But there were other difficulties. Pushkin, though short of money himself and with a costly family of his own to maintain, was often called upon to help out his parents, his brother and sister and his in-laws, and so fell ever deeper into debt. Both his wife and the Emperor demanded his presence in the capital so that he would be available to attend social and court functions, while he would much have preferred to be in the country, writing. Though Nicholas gave him intermittent support socially and financially, many at court and in the government, wounded by his jibes or shocked by his supposed political and sexual liberalism, disliked or despised him. And a new generation of writers and readers were beginning to look on him as a man of the past.

In 1831 Pushkin at length completed *Eugene Onegin*. The final chapter was published at the beginning of 1832, the first complete edition of the work coming out in 1833. But overall in these years Pushkin wrote less, and when he did write he turned increasingly to prose. In 1833 he spent another productive autumn at the Boldino estate, producing his most famous prose novella, *The Queen of Spades*, and one of his finest narrative poems, *The Bronze Horseman*. He also developed in these years his interest in history, already evident in *Boris Godunov* and *Poltava*: Nicholas I commissioned him to write a history of Peter the Great, but alas he left only copious notes for this at his death. He did, however, complete in 1833 a history of the eighteenth-century peasant uprising known as the Pugachov rebellion, and he built on his research into this episode to write his longest work of prose fiction, *The Captain's Daughter* (1836). Over these years too he produced his five metrical fairy stories; these are mostly based on Russian folk tales, but one, *The Golden Cockerel* (1834), is an adaptation of one of Washington Irving's *Tales of the Alhambra*.

Writings　　From his schooldays till his death Pushkin also composed well over 600 shorter verses, comprising many lyrics of love and friendship, brief narratives, protests, invectives, epigrams, epitaphs, dedications and others. He left numerous letters from his adult years that give us an invaluable insight into his thoughts and activities and those of his contemporaries. And, as a man of keen intelligence and interest in literature, he produced throughout his career many articles and shorter notes – some published in his lifetime, others not – containing a wide variety of literary criticism and comment.

It is indeed hard to name a literary genre that Pushkin did not use in his lifetime, or it would be truer to say that he wrote across the genres, ignoring traditional categories with his characteristic independence and originality. All his writing is marked by an extraordinary polish, succinctness and clarity, an extraordinary sense for the beauty of sounds and rhythms, an extraordinary human sympathy and insight, an extraordinary feel for what is appropriate to the occasion and an extraordinary directness and naturalness of diction that is never pompous, insincere or carelessly obscure.

Death　　Early in 1837 Pushkin's career was cut tragically short. Following a series of improper advances to his wife and insults to himself, he felt obliged to fight a duel with a young Frenchman who was serving as an officer in the Imperial Horse Guards in St Petersburg. Pushkin was fatally wounded in the stomach and died at his home in St Petersburg two days later. The authorities denied him a public funeral in the capital for fear of demonstrations, and he was buried privately at the Svyatye Gory monastery near Mikháylovskoye, where his memorial has remained a place of popular pilgrimage.

– Roger Clarke, 2011

Select Bibliography

Standard Edition:

Sobraniye Sochineniy Pushkina (Moscow: Gosudarstvennoye Izdatelstvo Khudozhestvennoy Literatury, 1959–62). Volume V contains all the works in this volume, except for 'The Last of the Lineage of Joan of Arc', which can be found in Volume VI.

This ten-volume collection of Pushkin's works is also available online through the Russkaya virtualnaya biblioteka at www.rvb.ru/pushkin/toc.htm.

Biographies of Pushkin:

Binyon, T.J., *Pushkin: A Biography* (London: HarperCollins, 2002)

Lotman, Yury Mikhaylovich, *Alexandr Sergeyevich Pushkin: Biografiya Pisatelya* (St Petersburg: Iskusstvo-SPB, 1995)

Additional Background Material:

Tomashevsky, B., *Pushkin* (Moscow-Leningrad: Izdatelstvo Akademii Nauk USSR, 1956)

Bayley, John: *Pushkin: a Comparative Commentary* (Cambridge University Press, 1971)

Briggs, A.D.P., *Alexander Pushkin: A Critical Study* (Croom Helm, 1983)

Tertz, Abram, *Strolls with Pushkin* (New Haven and London: Yale University Press, 1993)

Wolff, Tatiana, ed., *Pushkin on Literature* (London: The Athlone Press, 1986)

www.oneworldclassics.com